THE PUNISHED SELF

THE PUNISHED SELF

Surviving Slavery in the Colonial South

ALEX BONTEMPS

CORNELL UNIVERSITY PRESS

ITHACA AND LONDON

First published 2001 by Cornell University Press

Printed in the United States of America

Library of Congress Cataloging-in-Publication Data

Bontemps, Alex, 1945-
    The punished self : surviving slavery in the colonial South / Alex Bontemps.
    p. cm.
    Includes bibliographical references and index.
    ISBN 0-8014-3521-8 (alk. paper)
    1. Slaves—Southern States—Psychology.   2. Slaves—Southern States—Social conditions—18th century.   3. Slaves—Southern States—Social conditions—18th century—Sources.   4. Slavery—Southern States—Psychological aspects.   5. Identity (Psychology)—Southern States—History—18th century.   6. Self-preservation—Southern States—History—18th century.   7. African Americans—Southern States—Social conditions—18th century.   8. Southern States— Race relations—Psychological aspects.   9. Southern States—Race relations—Sources. 10. Southern States—History—Colonial period, ca. 1600-1775.   I. Title.
    E443 .B66 2001
    975'.00496—dc21

                                                        00-012623

Cornell University Press strives to use environmentally responsible suppliers and materials to the fullest extent possible in the publishing of its books. Such materials include vegetable-based, low-VOC inks and acid-free papers that are recycled, totally chlorine-free, or partly composed of nonwood fibers. Books that bear the logo of the FSC (Forest Stewardship Council) use paper taken from forests that have been inspected and certified as meeting the highest standards for environmental and social responsibility. For further information, visit our website at www.cornellpress.cornell.edu.

Cloth printing   10   9   8   7   6   5   4   3   2   1

FSC   FSC Trademark © 1996 Forest Stewardship Council A.C.
         SW-COC-098

The icy evil that struck his father down
and ravished his mother into madness
trapped him in violence of a punished self
struggling to break free.

Robert Hayden, "El-Hajj Malik El-Shabazz (Malcolm X)
O masks and metamorphoses of Ahab, Native Son"

CONTENTS

PREFACE

For captive Africans in the colonial South, survival represented a truly savage paradox. To endure their enslavement with a sense of self, they had to think of themselves as being other-than-Negro, yet they could not survive, much less resist, their subordination without accommodating the Negro identity forced on them. Thus the dilemma: How to be a Negro, and convincingly so, without actually becoming one?[1]

The Punished Self describes the enslavement of captive Africans and their Creole descendants as a systematic assault on their sense of self.[2] The book examines how enslavement implicated survivors in the initiation and perpetuation of their own oppression by structuring the possibility of survival around a dilemma of self-awareness.

First I explore enslavement as a process of objectification, focusing on patterns of representation and reference. Then I look at how the cultural assault of enslavement was initiated, specifically, the ways in which captive Africans were forced to accept a new identity, Negro, and the expectations and behavior involved. Although I necessarily pay some attention to the harsh physical violence used to maintain submissiveness, the point of my discussion is that slavery's true brutality was the psychic condition it imposed on survivors. Finally, I illustrate the dilemma faced by survivors through a series of atypical or extreme individual cases and through the dilemma's manifestation as a reality for survivors in general.[3]

The unwavering support and encouragement that I have received from Shane White, David Sloane, and Roberta Stewart are impossible to acknowledge adequately or ever repay. The friendship of many others, expressed most often in quietly supportive ways, has also been of inestimable value. I can only hope that I have been able to return some small measure of their friendship while struggling to complete this project. To each of them—Mary Kelley, Bruce Nelson, and Annelise Orleck—thank you. In very different ways, and perhaps unbeknownst to them, Syd Nathans, Michael Ermarth, and Graham White have also provided me with vital assistance at critical junctures.

My family has been more than patient. Of course I owe everything to my mother, Alberta Bontemps; and to my wife, Jackie, and to our children, Arna and Fanon. To each of them, to my sister, Connie, and to my sister-in-law, Sonia, thank you for not only tolerating but encouraging my commitment to the completion of the book. Unfortunately, many of the people whose lives helped shape and nurture me died during the course of this project. The book is dedicated to them: Arna Bontemps, my father; Paul Bontemps, my brother; Camille, Poppy, and Joan Bontemps, my sisters; and Avon N. Williams, my brother-in-law.

ALEX BONTEMPS

Hanover, New Hampshire

PART I

SPOTLIGHTS
& SHADOWS

INTRODUCTION:
SEEING THE SUBJECT

"**A** VIRGINIA Planter had a stout healthy Slave, for whom he gave a high price." As the story in the *Virginia Gazette* goes, that slave, an African-born man referred to only as Jack, "*studied* to please his Master; but falling into bad Company, he was persuaded to believe that his Master was a capricious Fellow, and that by doing as he pleased he would soon *level* his Master with himself."[1] Understandably alarmed and apparently frightened by this change in behavior, Jack's master tried to convince his slave to curb his belligerent ways. Then, frustrated in his effort to "gain Access to [Jack's] Quarters," the slave owner, who is never named in the story, petitioned Jack in writing. In "the 'most humble, dutiful, and respectful Manner,' the petition beseeched Jack to behave better, and to do his Work agreeable to a Stipulation which was made by his former Owner." Jack responded by tearing up "two or three Hundred of these Petitions in Pieces," after which he "set a large Bull Dog at his Master, with strict Orders to tear him and his whole Family to Pieces, if they took one more step to make him work."

The slave owner turned to "a Person who had lived with Jack in his own Country, and who knew his Temper perfectly" for advice. The informant advised Jack's owner to "deprive [Jack] for a Year or two of Clothes and spending Money" and "threaten him, if he did not begin to work after that Time." That is, he should make Jack understand that unless he changed his ways he would be tied up and whipped "within an Inch of his Life." To emphasize the latter, Jack's countryman advised the planter to tell Jack "the old Story" about how his—that is, the slave owner's—grandfather had "whipped Caesar to Death, and of his Father's having obliged Black Jem to fly off from his Plantation in a Boat to avoid the same Fate." The story concludes by implying that the informant's advice was followed ("with the most desirable Success"): "Jack broke off his Connections with bad Company, did his Work faithfully, found his Master to be a good Man, and in a little While became the best Servant in the Province."

This story is not what it seems, a story about slavery and Jack and his master. Instead, it is a "rather blatant and contrived loyalist allegory for the relations of the colonies to England" published on the eve of the American Revolution.[2] Yet of course it *is* about slavery both literally and metaphorically. What is most intriguing about "A Short Story," as it was entitled, is that it allegorizes a subject that was rarely if ever discussed in public. Although the process of subjugation it describes was a central reality in all slave societies, the effort of slave owners to establish dominance over their slaves is rarely mentioned in the records that have survived from the period.[3]

Using slavery as a metaphor for their own colonial grievances, slave-owning patriots and their loyalist adversaries have unwittingly pointed us toward one of the principal ways in which enslavement functioned as a continuous and systematic assault on those who survived it: the double silence that exists in the sources on the colonial South. Like Jack, the people of African origin in the surviving records are usually seen rather than heard, and we must infer their perspective from actions they are rarely allowed to describe.[4] Not only are black voices virtually absent from extant records, a corollary silence is the silence of those who view blacks as thinking, seeing, and feeling subjects. So deafening has the silence (and silencing) of black voices been to historians of slavery in America that it has virtually drowned out the silence in extant sources regarding the subjectivity of blacks and blacks as subjects in their own right. The absence becomes discernible only in contrast to the relatively large chorus of voices that speak about blacks as objects to be monitored, accounted for, and controlled.

A noise of objectification suffuses the records, and it is especially loud in documents about slavery which became such an important element of the Enlightenment. Key to the discourse, whether discussed by politician or philosopher, deist or evangelist, patriot or loyalist, was the character of black people and their capacity to be beautiful and to create beauty. This wide-ranging discussion flourished in many parts of the Atlantic world. But it was less audible in the slave societies that had formed in the New World long before the Age of Revolution dawned. In the American South the debate about slavery, both as a moral and as an economic issue, received a very brief and highly circumscribed public hearing only in the most northerly portion of the region, and only for a relatively short period of time.[5] Little was divulged about slavery and slave life by those who publicly participated in the dialogue.[6]

Writing about slavery in the West Indies, though more consistently proslavery, is much richer. This is especially true of Edward Long's *History of Jamaica* (1774), Bryan Edwards's *The History, civil and commercial, of the British colonies in the West Indies* (1793), and Moreau de Saint-Méry's *Description . . . de l'isle Saint-Domingue* (1797–98). Compared with these works, the ethnographic value of Thomas Jefferson's relatively brief published musings about slavery and blacks in America is minimal.[7] Indeed, it is hard to imagine the nation's third president, or any other prominent public official from the South, offering a defense or critique of slavery ethnographically as rich as the proslavery tract composed by a certain Mr. Shirley, a Jamaican planter, in the late 1780s.[8]

Jefferson discussed the intellectual and moral capacity of blacks in his only original full-length book, *Notes on the State of Virginia*. The discussion is largely abstract.[9] On one occasion he mentions a specific black person, Phillis Wheatley, but it is in the context of her poetry. She was of less interest to him than what her poetry represented, for if her poetry had merit, she would have served as a powerful living refutation of arguments that blacks were innately inferior to others. By contrast, Shirley often describes the experiences of blacks in detail and occasionally even allows them to speak for themselves. Indeed, one of the most effective rhetorical strategies Shirley uses is to proclaim, after a lengthy critique of antislavery literature, that "I derive my information not only from the European traders upon the coast [of Africa], but from a much better authority—from my own slaves."[10]

Subsequent generations of proslavery advocates in the American South would perfect the notion that slaves were not unhappy being slaves, but their version of this argument generally relied on the relativizing qualification that blacks in the South were better off than poor whites in the North or in Europe.[11] Shirley does not try in the same way to make us believe that slaves enjoyed being slaves, either in Jamaica or elsewhere. Instead he claims that he lives securely among his slaves because "I trust I have their confidence." He implies that such confidence derives from two sources. First, he says, he recognizes the great diversity among them— coming, as they did, from all parts of "Guinea," some being "very sensible," having been traders, sons of princes, and priests. Of equal if not greater importance, according to Shirley, is that he pays attention to what his slaves have to say about themselves and their experiences.[12] So he explains that he can best prove "that an intercourse in trade between the Africans and Christians [was] not to the prejudice of the first" by relying on the testimony of his own slaves—Coromanties, Fantees, and Eboes. Judged not by his standards but by those of slaves themselves, slavery was rational and predictable.

Of course all of this was self-serving in the extreme, but it allows us to listen to black voices and observe black behavior in ways that Jefferson and most of his Southern contemporaries almost never did. Nor, except on rare occasions, did slave owners agonize in public about slavery's negative effects on their own lives and on those of their families and friends. This, above all else, is what Jefferson's *Notes on the State of Virginia* reveals in a compelling and unprecedented way.

Jefferson can be understood as having betrayed an important Southern tradition of masking (and thereby countering) whatever fear and self-doubt the presence of a large population of enslaved and despised people may have caused.[13] He maintained the tradition of avoiding recognition of black subjectivity, but he betrayed an important corollary tradition denying the relevance of that avoidance to the psychic well-being of white Southerners, especially those like Jefferson who owned large numbers of black slaves. Given how little they tell us about slaves and black life in general, references to such topics by Southerners demonstrate that the public effacement of black subjectivity was vital to the establishment and maintenance of a slave society in the colonial South.

Nowhere is this history of avoidance, and the benefits derived therefrom, more striking than in the pictorial record that survives from the colonial South. Only one painting, referred to by historians as *The Old Plantation*, illustrates blacks by themselves and concerned exclusively with one another. We can neither precisely date the painting, nor locate it geographically, nor make an educated guess who might have painted it. The other black images that have survived are almost always illustrative or decorative. Black faces rarely stand out, and there are no formal portraits at all. Given the nature of the society and the general history of portraiture in colonial America, this of course is not surprising. At the same time, the absence of black faces is striking and profoundly revealing, especially when we consider the presence of blacks elsewhere.[14]

Albert Boime has argued that prior to the nineteenth century "a sign system had been put into place to supplement written texts rationalizing slavery and was inseparable from them. The dissolution of that system and the appearance of variant models coincided with the dissolution of the slave system in Western experience." A landmark in the dissolution of that sign system was John Singleton Copley's painting *Watson and the Shark*, depicting "an incident that occurred in 1749, when young Brook Watson [a wealthy merchant and Tory leader, who was a patron of Copley] was attacked by a shark while swimming in Havana Harbour." It has been suggested that the black man who is such an important part of the painting's composition is also the subject of Copley's portrait *Head of a Negro* (also at one time labeled as *Head of a Favorite Negro*), completed around the same time (1777–78). This "ingenious portrait," according to Guy McElroy, "ranks with [Joshua] Reynolds's *Study of a Black Man* (1770) in the way its completely self-assured execution meshes with the portrayal of a black individual."[15] The importance of these works lies in their humanizing character and how that quality highlights the general absence of portraits of blacks in the colonial South, where the visual sign system sought to efface the black presence rather than to rationalize it.

A portrait by Marie-Guilhelmine Benoist during the last year of the eighteenth century is emblematic of the transition in Western art from a pattern of effacing to a pattern of recognizing the black presence—as well as the transition from Enlightenment to romanticism that the Age of Revolution witnessed and encouraged.[16] According to Hugh Honour, *Portrait d'une négresse* is "perhaps the most beautiful portrait of a black woman ever painted." Honour notes that "the sitter was probably a servant brought back from the Antilles by the artist's sailor brother-in-law." The timing of the work's execution—"during the brief period between the emancipation decree of 1794 and the restoration of slavery in 1802"— strongly indicates an antislavery inspiration, yet Honour is surely correct when he observes, "Whether or not Benoist saw the woman as an embodiment of 'liberty,' she portrayed her as an individual, living, feeling, fellow human being."

The exceptional quality of the painting highlights the fact that until that moment, and for a long while thereafter, "[f]ew, if any European images of non-Europeans are as calmly and clear-sightedly objective." The late eighteenth century seems, in that regard, to have marked a fairly dramatic turn in Western perceptions of non-Westerners.

Given that any portrait of a black person was remarkable, let alone one with the qualities in the Benoist painting, it is difficult to know how to evaluate Henry Laurens's offhand remark in 1755 that he had had a picture drawn of one of his slaves, a house servant named "Old Stepney." Laurens, a future "Founding Father," was by 1755 already well on his way to becoming one of colonial South Carolina's most respected and wealthiest planter-merchants. He refers, parenthetically, to the picture in a letter he wrote to a former business partner of his father's, offering (by way of update and explanation) that although Stepney "too often . . . gets dead drunk, he is our principal hand in the Garden."

Stepney, according to Philip Morgan, was one of five slaves with whom Laurens "had relatively close contact." Whatever other purposes the portrait was intended to serve, and whatever other motivations Laurens had for ordering the drawing, his objective seems consistent with a later observation about Stepney that Laurens made to one of his overseers: "[I]f you will speak to him he will not allow anybody within his sight to rob you."[17]

The phrase "if you will speak to him" states explicitly what is elsewhere so often only implied, that is, that recognizing a slave's individuality was often useful and necessary for successful plantation management. Indeed, it would be easy to interpret Laurens's offhand suggestion in the most literal sense—as meaning that Stepney was the sort of person whose loyalty was easily assured, if not taken for granted. In that regard, the drawing could be considered merely an extra bit of flattery.

Nonetheless, the act of recognition and the nature of the flattery offer a dramatic counterpoint to what we know about the experience of enslavement from surviving records, including the relatively voluminous collections of personal papers and business records such as those generated by Laurens, as well as to what historical scholarship has made of those records. So rare is the recognition of black subjectivity that even indirect, offhanded references like Laurens's have a jolting quality.

Acts of recognition stand out in the record even though most large planters, like most of those with fewer slaves, had unavoidably close contact with at least a few of their bondsmen and women. Yet Laurens was the only one we know of who had a picture drawn of one of his slaves. Others of course may have simply not left any record.[18] We know, for instance, that a number of planters had pictures drawn of themselves or their families with slaves in attendance; several left brief written sketches of blacks they had known well. Most of these fragments of recognition obscured and distorted the image of the blacks they made reference to, but some offer very closely observed representations.

Ads for runaway slaves are of the latter type, and most of the extensive collections of papers that deal at length with plantation management include scattered, brief references and asides that offer similarly observant reflections on the personality or behavior of a particular slave or black slaves in general. But even the most illuminating of these remarks offer fleeting and fragmentary images and are almost always the unintended by-product of a perspective that could be both keenly observant and stunningly myopic. In Laurens's papers and those of other slave owners who left a daily record of their lives in the colonial era, we can see the authors occasionally straining to see beyond themselves, but none of them appears to have concerned himself in more than a parenthetical way with the self-reflective presence of blacks, not even those closest to him. Stepney's portrait is a striking symbol of what slavery sought to repress in the colonial South. Fittingly, the portrait has not survived.

In 1819, by contrast, the artist and renowned collector of curiosities Charles Willson Peale completed on his own initiative a portrait of a former slave then living near the nation's capital. The subject of Peale's painting, Yarrow Mamout, was reputedly born in Africa during the first half of the eighteenth century, probably before 1730. He was a professed and practicing "Mohammedan," an assertion supported, according to historian Charles Sellers, by the "strongly Semitic cast of the features," observable in Peale's painting of Yarrow.[19]

Intrigued by reports that Yarrow might have been as old as 140, Peale sought him out and painted his portrait (paying him, apparently, $1.50 to do so), even though Peale determined that Yarrow was probably not nearly as old as the rumors indicated. He was, however, sufficiently intriguing and, perhaps more important, sufficiently interesting visually to warrant not only a portrait by Peale but also a subsequent one "by Simpson, an accomplished artist and portrait painter of the town [Georgetown, Maryland]." Sellers describes Peale's portrait as a "delightful" picture of "a slouching, chuckling old Negro, with a greatcoat wrapped about him and a striped woolen cap on his head." The painting was for many years erroneously identified as President George Washington's servant Billie Lee. Prior to that it languished unexhibited or unpromoted, because, Sellers speculated, Peale was suspicious of the former slave's age. Had he been 120 or older, the vitality conveyed in his portrait would have undoubtedly been an attraction; at eightyish he was perhaps easily overlooked or better promoted through his association with the still revered Washington.

Both Peale and Laurens sought to portray or have portrayed likenesses of black men who were slaves for most of their lives in the colonial South. We have no way of knowing how either subject felt about his portrait, but we have to assume that Laurens hoped and intended that Stepney would be pleased by his, that the old man would see something of himself in the picture that appealed to him. As a work of art, Peale's portrait resembles Géricault's *Portrait of a Black Man (Joseph)*, painted around the same time. Though the Géricault portrait is of a brooding, dark figure (both literally and figuratively), the antithesis of Peale's Yarrow, both images are of men who intrigue us because they seem so self-expressive and self-expressing, qualities that appear to have been captured rather than created by the artists.

Maybe this judgment reflects a purely subjective impression. Still, the paintings highlight an aspect of black individuality that slavery actively sought to repress. By so doing they foreground one of my central concerns. They portray black people, who are missing entirely from other surviving sources. Perhaps for that reason very little of the scholarship on slavery in America has sought to capture, or been able to convey, the very characteristic that seems so important in these paintings. The portraits represent individuals for whom enslavement and racism are insufficient explanations. Neither sympathy nor contempt is the primary sentiment evoked. Instead, what comes through is something more interior and self-reflective and defining of the subjects. We are invited to contemplate a dimension of the represented subject and by extension the represented subject's lived reality—a reality that slave owners either could not see or felt obliged to ignore.

THE MISSING SUBJECT

The few portraits I have discussed remind us of how difficult it is to "be yourself" while posing or sitting for a painting without appearing self-conscious about being closely observed. Some of the artists, and some of their subjects, handled this problem better than others. Yarrow is especially interesting in that regard. In Peale's portrait, his awareness of holding a pose, although not obvious at first glance, becomes clear when one observes the painting closely. He even seems to be slyly observing others and his surroundings while he is posing.

To be a slave in the colonial South was to be under close observation and scrutiny. Slaves, like subjects sitting for a portrait, were expected to present themselves in a certain way, to maintain the image that others imposed on them. Unlike the subject of a portrait, however, a slave was an object devoid of subjectivity and thereby incapable of participating in a meaningful recognitive relationship with other human beings. When one considers that nothing is more fundamental to human development than the process of mutual recognition between individuals who are involved in a relation of interdependence, the effects of representing blacks as objects and so perceiving them on a routine basis can be easily imagined. Similarly, it is not hard to understand why the protocol developed in the colonial South governing how and when, or whether, blacks could look at others. The effect on blacks of being denied recognition by those who controlled so much of their lives would have been mitigated by the recognition they received from a wide range of others, including especially family members and friends. But the systematic denial of their subjectivity, a denial that was built into the master/slave relationship, would have served to reinforce and perpetuate a process of subjugation initiated by other means and embodied in the violent expropriation of their labor. Slaves could look *to* their owners (and to others to whom they were expected to be subservient). Indeed, it was necessary and required that they do so. But it was not expected that they look *at* them. Some looking that was not entirely submissive in character was unavoidable and allowed. A degree of harmless insolence from a people not considered fully human was seen as inevitable or natural, a symptom of the group's innate inferiority and therefore tolerated. Insolent glances or stares, however, rarely went unnoticed, and generally served as an occasion for warning the offender, and all others who might make the same mistake, that there was a very definite limit beyond which behavior considered impudent would not be tolerated.

Some sense of the extremes to which slave owners went to keep blacks from broaching that limit may be gathered from ads for runaway slaves, notices that describe fugitives as having "down" looks, nervous twitches, and a variety of speech impediments. Even when we consider only those ads that describe a fugitive's response as having been made in direct reply to the actions of others, the frequency of such references is alarming. Common examples include descriptions such as "much scared when strictly examined," or has a "down look when any ways examined," or simply "looks down when spoken to."[1]

Cato, according to one typical ad, could not "look at anyone in the face with confidence," but was "quick in his language, and when spoken to is apt to stammer." Similarly, David, his owner reports, "is apt to turn himself sideways and look down," when any one talks to him. Binah's "eyes would shake when you look attentively at her." Eve, on the other hand, "when sharply spoken to," especially if in a manner "expressive of anger," would hesitate "in answering, with an appearance of her face drawn awry." In yet another ad, the advertiser (or subscriber as they often referred to themselves) remarks that "when spoken to [the slave] speaks quick, and is apt to turn her face a little to one side and casts her eyes towards the ground." Another runaway "when spoken to has a small impediment or speaks confused."[2]

Stephen, meanwhile, is described as being "very apt, when any person is talking to him, to be shaking his hands." Another ad explains that, when spoken to, the fugitive becomes greatly agitated, "and keeps his fingers, in continual motion." Another ad seeks the return of a fugitive who is described as having "a Stoppage in his Speech, and if strictly examined, or suddenly asked a Question, cannot directly give an Answere."

Not surprisingly, the ads also show that more than a few slaves resisted being objectified, illustrating the process of objectification by defying it. John, for instance, "a negro man" who was "bread to the sea," "looks you full in the face when he speaks." Jack meanwhile is described as being a "bold, fierce looking Fellow," and Peter had "an impertinent Look, and speaks boldly." Sall, for her part, has "an impertinent look and talk, when examined, and likewise swears hard," whereas Betty is "proud in her Carriage," and Isaac valued "himself much on account of his bodily strength and activity." Isaac represents only one of a small but significant number of runaways who are described as possessing an inordinate amount of self-confidence or self-regard. More frequent, however, are those fugitives who were described as bold or brazen. One slaveholder, for instance, wished to sell a remarkably sensible young woman because "of the perverseness of her temper." In another ad, the slave Nann is termed "very brazen," whereas in yet another, Lucy is described as not having "the most pleasant countenance, unless she speaks, which is very free, and sometimes impudent."[3]

Looking back defiantly undermined the assumption on which slavery was based by making clear and unavoidable the slave's subjectivity. The flash of recognition at the moment of intersubjective eye contact between a slave and his or her owner dissolved the illusion on which enslavement by means of objectification was based, both for the individuals involved and for others who may have noticed that instant of mutual recognition. Thus, instead of portraits like those drawn by Benoist, Copley, Peale, and others, the paintings with blacks in them that were commissioned by slave owners in the colonial South depict blacks as servants or in servile postures and positions. The slaves in those paintings serve visually as adornments, like drapery or furniture or jewelry. In many of the paintings they share the focal center of the painting with the featured subject or group, but in a few instances they appear so much in the background or so near the edge of the painting that they are barely noticeable, literally obscured or enshrouded by shadow.[4]

This shadowy presence is especially pronounced in paintings of George Washington by John Trumbull and Edward Savage, in which his longtime body servant Billie Lee is shown literally in Washington's shadow dressed in full livery, holding the general's favorite steed and awaiting his command; or he is seen standing in attendance at the very edge of a painting of Washington and his family, who are seated at a table at the center of the painting.

By contrast there is the painting by Charles Phillips entitled *A Family Group* (ca. 1745), in which a neatly dressed mulatto housemaid is positioned at the focal center, close enough to the others to be mistaken on first glance for a part of the group, yet ever so slightly removed to the rear of them, and distinguished by her servant's clothing, her at-attention posture, and the color of her face which sets off and is set off by the almost bright white of most of the others.

In the majority of surviving paintings, the placement of blacks, when they are featured at all, resembles that of Billie Lee in the Trumbull and Savage paintings. For example, in Charles Bridges's portrait of William Byrd II's daughter Wilhelmina in 1735, "an indian basket and negro boy servant" are placed as American features. An even earlier illustration of this pattern is Gerard Soest's portrait of Cecilius Calvert, the second Lord Baltimore, which was completed at some point prior to Baltimore's death in 1675. In that painting a black attendant is partially obscured by the drapery at the rear of Calvert and by an unidentified white child, who, based on his or her dress, was undoubtedly "a close family member." The black attendant, a young boy, appears to be looking directly at a piece of paper being held jointly by Calvert and the child, and directs the viewer's attention to the paper. The paper upon closer observation turns out to be a "map of the Calvert holdings in Maryland embellished with the family coat of arms." Subsequent paintings of Calvert children in Maryland—descendants of Cecilius or his younger brother Leonard, who served as the first governor of Maryland—replicate the positioning of the black attendant in Soest's portrait, as does the late-eighteenth-century painting by an unidentified limner of the grandchildren of one of Virginia's most notable royal governors, Alexander Spotswood.[5]

These portraits and the tradition of portraiture that they represent were of course created to reflect the self-image of those who commissioned them. In doing so, however, they very effectively capture the way in which blacks are more generally represented in surviving written records from the colonial South, records kept or generated in most instances by elite members of colonial society like the people featured in these paintings. Blacks are placed in shadows, a dark, blank space that would not have existed visually except for the light cast by others.

As the framers of the Constitution suggested, when the black presence in the colonial South was represented at all, a portion was always missing.[6] James Madison, for one, made this point explicit by observing, "The Federal Constitution . . . decides with great propriety on the case of our slaves, when it views them in the mixt character of persons and property. This is in fact their true character." On the one hand, he explained, it recognized them as "inhabitants" and "as a member of the society," but it also defined them as having been "debased by servitude below the equal level of free inhabitants." The regrettable condition of slavery, from Madison's point of view, required the Constitution to regard "the slave as divested of two fifths of the man."[7]

Leading slave owners like Washington and Jefferson occasionally indicated what the missing fraction represented. Washington, for instance, noted on a number of occasions his belief that as a result of their condition, blacks lacked both the moral and intellectual capacity necessary for self-respect. They were so deficient in this regard that even though they could feel pain and loss as deeply as others, they could not feel shame or experience disgrace to the same extent, and therefore could not be expected to have developed fully as human beings. "Blacks," he once noted, "are capable of much labor but having (I am speaking generally) no ambition to establish a good name, they are too regardless of a bad one." How, he asked on another occasion, could "the mind of a slave be educated to perceive what are the obligations of freedom"? By contrast, Washington once indicated to a fellow planter that it was "as much against my inclination as it can be against your's, to hurt the feelings of those unhappy people by a separation of man and wife, or families." Yet, like most of his slave-owning contemporaries, he was convinced that blacks lacked, or had been deprived of, some fundamental attributes shared by other human beings.[8]

Jefferson's views about blacks are better known and have been more fully discussed and analyzed by historians. Blacks, he wrote, were deficient both in reason and in imagination, though not in memory. In Jefferson's view they were certainly feeling beings, capable of bravery and possessed of human souls, but they lacked the capacity for reflection and thus the "refinements and restraints of thought." They were, in consequence of that fundamental deficiency, "emotional, instinctual creatures" and inferior to all others as such. Moreover, an "eternal monotony," he claimed, existed in their "countenances, that immovable veil of black which covers all the emotions." On the one hand, he observed, they lacked the creative means to give effective expression to their essentially emotional nature, unless in a form that was "wild and extravagant" or "incoherent and eccentric." On the other hand they lacked the physical beauty to manifest their humanity at the more basic level of appearances.[9] Black people, in other words, were not merely consigned to a shadow existence by their enslavement but conceived as shadow figures, lacking the essential substance of humanity.

Jefferson's concerted dismissal of the humanity of blacks can be seen, according to historian Rhys Isaac, in Monticello "as it was being constructed by the stories that its founder and others brought to it." According to Isaac, even though blacks were a central component of Jefferson's earliest memories, they were consistently absent from the "complex storied worlds" he constructed throughout his life, the narrativized worlds that served as reflections of his personal development and of his vision of himself, of others, and the world around him. Moreover, although we cannot know the extent to which Jefferson himself was "involved in the life of the home quarters" during his formative years, Isaac notes that we do know that his "younger brother, Randolph, did develop in his childhood sufficient rapport with the African-American folk to be able in later life to go away from the main house and mix 'among black people; play the fiddle and dance half the night.'" We know as well, Isaac adds, that his "elder daughter, Martha, also had an ear attuned to the singing and storytelling of such occasions."[10] Indeed, in later life Jefferson would observe that "they [blacks] are more generally gifted than the whites with accurate ears for tune and time, and they have been found capable of imagining a small catch."[11] Apparently, this talent that was presumed by Jefferson to be an innate characteristic was something he had observed for himself, yet he offered no hint that he had. From other sources, Isaac makes clear, we know that Jefferson's childhood was "suffused with the sounds" of blacks singing and performing, all of which communicated to him "versions of the imaginative universe of the numerous African-Americans whose labor provided the wealth and sustained the routines of the Jefferson" household, as well as the others he grew up in.[12]

As a young man, according to Isaac, Jefferson wrote at least two "enslavement stories," one an ad for a runaway slave and the other a freedom suit for a black man, who claimed his freedom on the grounds that his great-grandmother had been white. These texts, Isaac observes, like his later views on slavery, are contradictory, but they also provide a stark counterpoint to the majority of the stories he created as a young man, "dream-narratives" that told of "charming philosophic evenings with gentlemen and ladies sharing sensibilities, [and] the nights of familial merriment by the fountain at 'the new Rowanty.'"[13] In his *Notes on the State of Virginia* he recreated this sharp contrast. However, in that work he explicitly denied (albeit in a few lines of detached analysis) the subjective presence of blacks in his life: "Their love is ardent," he wrote, "but it kindles the senses only, not the imagination. Religion indeed has produced a Phillis Wheatley, but it could not produce a poet." Yet in those same lines, Isaac reminds us, "he had written over the top of that repressed African imagination— over the remembered sounds indeed of his childhood—the compressed but unmistakable story of his cherished 'inner' conjugal household."[14]

There was much irony in this, of course. Though he denied African Monticellans the capacity for "[r]efined and refining love," the reality was that "refined and refining love were what made Monticello an idealized center of all that was most civilized in the world [for Jefferson]—an estate house distanced from, and in moral opposition to, the city and its corruptions."[15] And what made Monticello possible for Jefferson, both as a physical reality and as an imagined one, was, like virtually everything else in his life, his access to the labor and human resources of large numbers of black slaves. In his thought the influence of their presence is never recognized, yet it is hard not to believe that the model of slavery that was their birthright did not somehow inform his view of British tyranny over American colonials. It could not be coincidental that slavery was invariably the metaphor he and most other Founding Fathers used to illustrate their felt sense of grievance (witness "A Short Story"). Isaac suggests another possible influence in a related context. "Where," he asks, "did the young Thomas Jefferson's recurrent aspiration for an extended communal house-hold, made up of co-resident couples, come from? Since this kind of house-hold was contrary to centuries-old English norms, may it not have come to him as a possibility unconsciously suggested by African stories, and indeed by the actual way of life in the slave quarters all around him?"[16]

Whatever the influence that blacks exerted on Jefferson's thought and life, it could not have been incidental even if it was not profound. Yet, in his *Notes on the State of Virginia*, according to Isaac, Jefferson denied "the African part of his upbringing" by writing "a denial of the oral-cultural storied richness" of the households he was raised and nurtured in. In doing so as a young man he laid the foundation for later writing blacks out of the storied worlds he would create, or attempt to create, for his family, his state, and his nation.[17]

In his survey of West Indian accounts of slave life in the eighteenth and nineteenth centuries, Roger Abrahams provides a clear indication of what was so consistently missing in the references to blacks that survive in records from the colonial South.[18] Unlike Jefferson and virtually all other Southerners of his class, the West Indian planters, who left some account of their observations and experiences in the islands, seem positively fascinated by the behavior of the blacks in their midst. Their writings are filled, relatively speaking, with descriptions of just those aspects of the black presence that are so glaringly absent from Jefferson's papers.

According to Abrahams many of those who wrote about black life in the West Indies equated "cultural difference with inferiority." Moreover, because they held that view, Abrahams theorizes, they were able to write relatively openly about the experiences of the blacks they observed. As a result their writing provides descriptions of black life that are "replete with accurate, if highly selective, descriptions of cultural practices of the stereotyped groups." David Brion Davis makes a related point in comparing the writings of Jefferson, Bryan Edwards, and Moreau de Saint-Méry in terms of what they had to say about slavery and issues of racial difference. He notes in conclusion that whereas "Edwards and Moreau were relatively free from Jefferson's aloof distaste for Negroes, they were far more unequivocally opposed to antislavery."[19]

Southern slave owners like Jefferson were as observant and perceptive, as voyeuristic and curious, as any of their West Indian counterparts. They had, moreover, equal, if not greater, opportunities to observe their slaves. Yet none of them left the sort of detailed accounts that "plantocrat journalkeepers" in the West Indies did. In an examination of the latter literature in terms of what it reveals about "speech activities" among blacks in the Caribbean, Abrahams concludes that the journal keepers often made clear "the importance [blacks] attached to all manner of speech: the use of talk to *proclaim presence of self*, to assert oneself vocally in the most anxious and the most unguarded situations."[20] By contrast, Southern record keepers either hid, obscured, or denied efforts by blacks to proclaim a sense of self.

Viewed in that light, what is missing from what we know about the lives of black people in the colonial South, and thus in the materials that have survived from that period, is not the physical presence of blacks. As objects of interest and concern they are often ubiquitous in the records, but their sense of themselves, and more broadly their subjective being, is absent unless denied.

A more commonplace illustration of the absence that blacks represented in the colonial South can be found in virtually any extensive collection of private papers generated by virtually any member of the gentry class. The earliest date from the late seventeenth century, but George Washington's diaries and correspondence, the bulk of which were written during the second half of the eighteenth century, are typical. The pattern can also be seen in any number of other surviving manuscript collections, including those generated by Robert "King" Carter, who was a contemporary of Washington's father.

Generally identified by historians of the colonial Chesapeake as a charter member of the "self-conscious ruling class" responsible for transforming colonial Virginia into a slave society, Carter is one of the few members of his generation of large land and slave owners for whom a significant quantity of personal papers, including a diary, has survived. Also, he was far and away the largest slave owner of his era and one of the largest in Virginia's history as a colony or a slave state. Thus, a good deal of our knowledge about slave life, at a formative moment in the institutional development of slavery in America, especially from the perspective of a participant observer, comes to us through his papers.[21]

Carter provides us with a relatively early point of reference for gauging the extent to which, and the consistency with which, blacks as subjective beings are absent from the gentry's papers and from their expressed image of themselves and their society. Here, for instance, are a few of his early entries in the diary he kept from 1722 to 1727 that make reference to blacks. On November 20, 1722, he notes, among other things: "My sloop set out for the falls carrys 13 Negros to the Burwell Quarter"; "Nassau this Night told me he had Carted to the Landing 26 Load of wood." The next is dated November 26, 1722: "Billy was whipped and branded."[22]

In April, 1724, a rather lengthy entry details the purchase of slaves from a number of different individuals: "I bought of mr Austin Moor 41 Negros," it begins, "to wit 6 men and 4 women that Harrison had for Seating the Land I boot of Tho Randolph." Much of this entry runs on without clear breaks and is often illegible, but near the end Carter identifies a number of slaves by name in a manner that suggests a detailed knowledge of them: "Joe and his family Simon his Son Scipio his Son Robin his family Montross his wife Hannah his daughter Old Jack Beck his wife Jonny his Son Robin his child Nero a boy all valued by Pratt at 148 Pound and Ebo Natt . . . 18 in all 180:10s."

A few other entries will suffice to give both a flavor of his style as a diarist and an illustration of his concerns and interests with regard to blacks. January 13, 1725: "Court Harry Judged for his running away for his stealing the Conoe of Nassau for his Charge in taking up etc." May 31, 1725: "Negro Ship came in yesterday." June 8, 1725: "I [s]ent my flatt Oyster Shell getting [I sent my flat to get or collect oyster shells]." January 20,

1725: "My Son Robert Negros went away." June 20, 1726: "Sold a Negro Girl to Burrel for 2400 Tob." On April 4, 1727, a long entry reports the abuses of an overseer, including the accusation that he sold something to blacks. July 15, 1727: "Capt Donlen [?] Arrived with 140 Negros." July 17, 1727: "I had 7 of my new Negroes run away in Nassaus Cano." These latter two entries begin a series of related ones that offer an extremely rare glimpse of how large slave owners like Carter purchased "new Negroes" and some of the problems they encountered in that process.

Carter's papers, even more than those of his much more prolific contemporary, William Byrd I, provide the most detailed and extensive references to blacks, and to the business of slave owning, to be found in the records left by colonial slaveholders of their era.[23] The point of importance here, however, is that his interests and concerns regarding blacks and the way in which he seems to have observed them were typical not only of others of his generation, but of virtually all those who would record their observations on such matters throughout the remainder of the eighteenth century, whether in the colonial Chesapeake or further south in low-country colonies such as South Carolina. He consistently noted their presence by way of keeping track of them, but like slave owners of subsequent generations in both the upper and lower South, he never seems to have recognized them as self-aware human beings. Or, if he did (and one would think that he must have), he did not record that awareness.

Washington's surviving papers not only are much more voluminous than Carter's but take us through the remainder of the eighteenth century and offer perhaps the best example of the pattern of reference to blacks that Carter's foreshadow. We can begin to see this pattern by noting that the editors of Washington's diaries, as would be expected, draw on a variety of sources to clarify and supplement his observations and the record he kept of where and how he spent his time. "No one," the editors explain, "holding the long-prevailing view of Washington as pragmatic and lusterless, a self-made farmer and soldier-statesman, would expect him to commit to paper the kind of personal testament that we associate with notable diarists." In practice this meant that his entries were generally very spare and unrevealing, brief if not terse reminders of things done or things he needed to do. At times, the editors note, a reader might even feel as though he or she had "got hold of an eighteenth-century guest book rather than a diary."[24] As a result, the editors insert explanatory notes on virtually every page of the diary, as a sort of shadow narrative, either in the text or at the bottom of each page, notes that are often more extensive than the diary entry for a particular day. The need for this extensive commentary arose partly because of Washington's understandable "preoccupation with other matters," but also because of his literary style, understood as an extension and as an expression of his personality.

Despite the brevity of his remarks and the frequent need for extensive elaboration, the editors point out that his diaries have a quality that is often missing in his more verbose correspondence. In his diaries, they note, "he is not on guard . . . for he seems unaware that any other eyes will see or need to see, what he is writing." In that sense the sparseness of his entries seems economical rather than overly evasive or unduly reserved: "Good enough for his purposes; it was what happened on that day." The place for expressions of emotion, whether brief or extended, "was in communications to friends, not in the unresponsive pages of a memorandum book."[25] The editors, therefore, were not required to spend much time speculating about his intended meaning or to account for things he carelessly overlooked. Their primary concern was to make clear for those unacquainted with Washington and his world the many relations and inferences that he had no need to explain.

Indeed, it is possible to argue that Washington was a rather skillful or gifted diarist and that he often managed with great economy to distill the events and occurrences that mattered to him on any given day or that in his judgment summarized its essential character and significance. Washington's diaries leave no less a sense of the person than the more fulsome diaries of Landon Carter, his contemporary and a son of Robert "King" Carter.

Unlike Washington, Landon Carter frequently rambled or described in laborious detail what others might summarize in a sentence or two.[26] Also, unlike Washington, Carter often used his diaries to vent his feelings about others or to defend himself against what he perceived to be their judgments of him. Despite these differences, however, the two diaries achieve a similar effect. One of the features that have made Carter's diaries so valuable to historians and so interesting to others is the expansive sense of the writer that they convey, in combination with the wonderful sense of time and place that his writings when viewed collectively provide. Washington's diaries and other personal writings are equally revealing, yet the revelation they offer is achieved in a very different style and manner.

Washington, like most other slave owners who left a written record of their lives, rarely went out of his way to mention blacks in his diaries. But as with the many other people who frequently entered his life on a given day or those who were involved in it on a more regular basis, he seldom failed to mention their presence when in his view that presence was notable. His entry for January 12, 1760, captures an almost uniform characteristic of the private papers written by slave owners. He says that on that day he set "out with Mrs. Bassett on her journey to Port Royal," which, the editors tell us, is a small port town on the Rappahannock River. From the same source we are told that "Mrs. Bassett, the former Anna Maria Dandridge (1739–1777)," was "the younger sister of Mrs. Washington." In the course of their trip they were required to cross Occoquan Creek by ferry, which they did without incident, much to Washington's relief, because, he says, "the Wind was something high." He does not tell us that the ferry, which was owned by George Mason, "was run by one of [Mason's] slaves." He does tell us, however, that they "Lodgd at Mr. McCraes in Dumfries" and that "Here I was informd that Colo. Cocke was disgusted at my House, and left it because he [saw] an old Negroe there resembling his own Image." Cocke is identified by the editors as Catesby Cocke, who "served successively as clerk of Stafford, Prince William, and Fairfax counties." No reference is made to the "Negro" who guided him safely across a windswept creek, although another black man is mentioned because he bore the likeness of one of his business associates, a gossipy morsel that Washington apparently found interesting (and amusing?) enough to record.[27]

The entries in his diary regarding blacks for January 1760 appear to be typical of those recorded while he was resident at Mount Vernon as a full-time planter and farmer. In fact, they begin his record of that part of his life following his return from the French and Indian War. If the references to blacks that he recorded during that month are abstracted and summarized, a portrait of their presence in Washington's life can be glimpsed.

On the third, a slave named Morris is reported to have caught a cold at work the previous day. Washington notes in the same context that "several of the Family were taken with the Measles," although no serious symptoms had yet appeared. On the evening of the fifth, which was very cold and windy, "Mulatto Jack arrived from Fredk. With 4 Beeves." On the eighth, in a single sentence unrelated to other entries for that day, he records that "Carpenter Sam was taken with the Meazles." The following day mention is made of "Colo. Bassetts Abram [who] arrivd with Letters from his Master." Also he apparently brought with him "some things from me that Lay in Mr. Norton's Ware house in York Town." The following day we learn that the cattle that Jack had brought down from Fredericksburg were killed and that two of them were "tolerable good."[28]

Many times, of course, as might be expected in a life as full and varied as was Washington's, blacks are not mentioned in his diaries, even though it would be logical to assume that they were present. Thus, initially it is not surprising to find them virtually absent from his account of his tour of the South during the late spring and early summer of 1791, a time during which he was still contemplating whether he would allow himself to be reelected to a second term as the new American nation's first president. Certainly it was a precarious moment in the nation's young life whether viewed in terms of domestic concerns or foreign affairs.

The absence of blacks in the diary Washington kept during his tour becomes both more apparent and more unusual, however, when one considers how important the issues of slavery and the slave trade were to the new nation's efforts to create a stable union both during and after the American Revolution, and as one reads the notes the editors provide to augment his account of his Southern tour. Frequently, for instance, the editors make use of the 1790 federal census to indicate the number of black slaves owned by the many different men and women in whose homes and ordinaries he stayed or who hosted his visit in other ways.[29] For example, on Monday, April 18, Washington "Set out by Six oclock—dined at a small house kept by one slaughter 22 miles from Halifax and lodged at Tarborough 14 Miles further." The editors then observe that "Slaughter's tavern was probably operated by James Slaughter (died 1799) of Halifax County, who was listed in the 1790 census as head of a household of 12 whites and 20 slaves."[30]

On Friday, April 29, having reached the northern border of South Carolina, he records that "We left Doctr. Flaggs about 6 oclo[ck] and arrived at Captn. Wm. Alstons' on the Waggamaw to Breakfast." He goes on to note how wealthy "and esteemed" "Captn. Alston" was: "His house which is large, new, and elegantly furnished stands on a sand hill, high for the Country, with its rice fields below; the contrast of which with the lands back of it, and the Sand & piney barrens through which we had passed is scarcely to be conceived." The editors then explain that "William Alston (1756–1839)" was "a veteran of Francis Marion's partisan brigade, bought 1,206 acres on the Waccamaw River in 1785 and developed it into the prosperous plantation he called Clifton. Below his two-story mansion, his marshy rice lands were cultivated by work gangs from his force of 300 slaves, the largest holding in All Saints Parish and one of the largest in the state."[31]

In addition to numerous references of this sort, the editors on one occasion use the journal kept by Robert Hunter Jr., a Scottish traveler who had visited Wilmington, North Carolina, in 1786, to supplement Washington's relatively lengthy (April 24) comments on that small but growing and commercially and strategically important city. Though the general took no notice of the blacks in that low-country town, Hunter had reported, "The inhabitants, white and black, are estimated at 1,200—the proportion four blacks to a white."[32]

Of course the editors' objective in using these references and many others like them was not to illustrate how frequently blacks were involved in Washington's life; rather their purpose was to supplement Washington's comments by providing as much contextual information about the places he visited and the people with whom he interacted as possible. In doing so, however, they allow us to appreciate how relatively invisible blacks could become in Washington's diaries. Though rarely unseen, their subjective presence is so often invisible in surviving records, including those of people as different in temperament and style as Washington, Carter, and Jefferson, that their absence seems repressed rather than merely overlooked or consciously ignored.

CHAPTER 2

SHADOW CASTING

O ne of the most important purposes served by the pattern of reference in the diaries of "King" Carter and Washington was the same as the pattern we observe in paintings commissioned by southern slave owners. Emblems of the power, prestige, and complacent self-image of those who presumed to own them, blacks were of greatest benefit to the widest number and range of people if their subjectivity could be overlooked, thereby fostering the assumption that they were devoid of any capacity for self-regard or respect.

In Copley's now-famous painting *Watson and the Shark*, the figure at the center of the painting, and thus critical to its composition, is black. Similarly, blacks were often at the center of colonial life. To place them at the center of things was natural enough, as in the painting *A Family Group*, but to portray them as prime actors, as Copley did in *Watson and the Shark*, as well as in his historical painting *The Death of Major Peirson*, would have not only distracted attention from others but subverted the logic that enabled blacks to be regarded as less than human. It would have also greatly diminished their value to slave owners as both reflecting objects and beasts of burden.[1]

The period spanning the Soest painting of Calvert and those of Washington by Trumbull and Savage roughly covers the lifetimes of Carter and Washington, which in turn, if combined, nearly encompass the period between the early institutionalization of slavery in the colonial South and its

early national—that is, late-eighteenth- and early-nineteenth-century—
transformation into a trans-Appalachian and, ultimately, trans-Mississippi
cotton kingdom. This suggests either a continuity of self-image among the
ruling elite throughout the colonial period, or a shift in self-image that became increasingly noticeable by the late colonial era. If the latter were true
it would be consistent with the idea that slave-owning patriarchs evolved
over the course of the eighteenth century into slave-owning paternalists, a
more genteel and sentimental version of slavery's founding fathers. In
this view, whereas patriarchalism was the dominant "social ethos" of the
planter class in late- seventeenth-and early-eighteenth-century colonial
America, paternalism supplanted it in the decades immediately bracket-
ing the American Revolution. By then "contractual reciprocity rather than
rigid authoritarianism had begun to characterize eighteenth-century family relations, but the sway of the father was still powerful." Much had
changed but much had remained the same: "a profound respect for rank,
hierarchy, and status infused the very marrow of the early modern Anglo-
American world, and at its core lay the authority of the father-figure in his
own household."[2]

The Soest painting of Calvert and those of Washington by Trumbull
and Savage seem to capture this sense of change within continuity. The
black image functions similarly in the paintings, but everything else that
the two paintings represent has changed, the form of government, religious worldview, the ruling elite's self-image, the institution of slavery.
What the paintings do not convey, however, is that even though change
did occur, it was not uniform but varied from a softening of the prevailing
authoritarian style to an extension and exaggeration of old forms. Nor do
the paintings give us a sense of how change, where and when it occurred,
was experienced by those most affected by it.[3]

Using the second William Byrd and Landon Carter as points of reference, it seems fair to suggest that one measure of change, indicative of an
evolution in how the gentry perceived itself, was the degree to which
slavery had become a more explicit element of the ruling elite's expressed
self-image. Byrd's elaborately drawn self-portrait has become, for historians of the colonial South, a classic expression of the patriarchal self-image
that men like Byrd's father sought to import into or to replicate in that
part of the Americas they colonized. The portrait is presented in a 1726
letter he wrote to a friend in England, Charles Boyle, earl of Orrery. Writ-

ing from his estate on the James River in Virginia, not long after he had re-turned from England in search of a second wife, Byrd sought to explain to "his Lordship" some of the advantages of his portion of the New World. "I have," he wrote, "a large family of my own, and my doors are open to everybody, yet I have no bills to pay, and half-a-crown will rest undis-turbed in my pocket for many moons together."[4] This, one student has noted, "sounds as though it could have been written by Robert Filmer or Ben Jonson a hundred years earlier."[5]

"Like one of the patriarchs," Byrd continued, "I have my flocks and my herds, my bond-men and bond-women, and every sort of trade amongst my own servants, so that I live in a kind of independence on every one, but Providence." In such a world, however, Byrd acknowledged that all was not carefree: "I must take care to keep all my people to their duty, to set all the springs in motion, and to make every one draw his equal share to carry the machine forward. But then tis an amusement in this silent country, and a continual exercise of our patience and oeconomy." Secure in their property and free from poverty or crime, his family and their soci-ety sat "securely under our vines and fig trees without any danger to our property. . . . We are very happy in our Canaan if we could but forget the onion and flesh-pots of Egypt."[6]

By contrast, the self-portrait Landon Carter left of himself as the master of a vast estate in northern Virginia is much less dependent on biblical ref-erences and much more centered in the slave-owning realities of his life. The image that he sketched of himself, one that is perhaps better de-scribed as a snapshot of Carter and his "indoor family" than a formally composed self-reflection, not only is more noticeably explicit in its refer-ence to those who served and depended upon him—abandoning the terms "bondsmen" and "women" for "slaves"—but, significantly, ex-cludes those present who, according to the social norms of his day, owed Carter deference rather than subservience.

At some point "between 1 and 2 o'clock [on Saturday afternoon, April 17, 1773] whilst reading" in his parlor, Carter tells us that he was "seized with a sudden nervouse tremor" after hearing what his "man Tom" de-scribed as "a rubbing upstairs with the brush of thunder at a distance." In an instant "a noise was heard resembling more the mighty burst of a bomb than anything else."[7]

Lightning had struck his mansion, Sabine Hall, located in the Northern

Neck, an area in colonial Virginia that was home to several of the wealthiest families and largest slave owners in colonial America, including John Tayloe of Mt. Airy and Carter's nephew, Robert Carter of Nomini Hall. As son and heir to Robert "King" Carter, one of Virginia's "first gentlemen," Landon Carter was one of that small and very exclusive group. Indeed, when the elder Carter died in 1732 at the age of sixty-nine, the *Gentleman's Magazine* in London reported that he left "about 300,000 acres of land, about 1000 negroes and £10,000 in money." Though Landon Carter was not his father's eldest son and therefore did not receive the lion's share of that estate, he received a substantial inheritance that enabled him to build Sabine Hall and leave his own heirs nearly 50,000 acres of land, "and perhaps as many as 500 slaves."[8]

Like other great homes of its type, Sabine Hall was constructed on high ground to give it prominence and added distinction and to command the most appealing and attractive "prospect" of the estate on which it was located.[9] One result of the gentry's preference for elevated sites was that many, according to scattered newspaper accounts, were struck by lightning. Those that were not properly grounded with lightning rods were damaged, in some cases substantially. Occasionally, lightning would spark fires that completely destroyed homes and other buildings. It was a fearsome phenomenon for most colonial Americans, and like fire bells in the night, signs of approaching thunderstorms triggered the deepest foreboding and apprehension ("nervous tremors") in most of them. Actually, the storm that passed quickly over Sabine Hall in the spring of 1773 did relatively little structural damage to Carter's home, but several people in the house were struck by lightning and for a frantic moment or two there was a general panic throughout.

In his diary, dated the day of the event, Carter summarizes the scene as follows:

> Reader, whoever thou art, picture to yourself this dismal sum. Grand-children many, though unhurt, with every sorrowful countenance, though ignorant of the consequences, Yet crying with Concern. A mother calling but for her babies though in her company, and going from place to place to be safe, through some confused expectation; and Poor slaves crowding round and following their master, as if protection only came from him, and yet quite void of

senses enough to assist me. But God was merciful, and I hope it will not be misplaced on anyone who saw this sight at least.[10]

Clearly, the storm had been a shocking, unnerving experience. Carter makes no effort to hide the fact that he was temporarily afraid. He marveled at the power of the force that struck his home and the miraculous survival of those who were injured by it. He minutely examines the damage it did and did not do to the buildings it hit as well as the people. That others panicked was entirely understandable, but he did not, at least not according to his recollection of the event, and that too was entirely understandable. He remained calm and rational throughout, though initially, as was to be expected, he had been frightened and trembled nervously. Later that day, or night, he was sufficiently composed to enter a fairly detailed description of the event in his diary (the first of only five entries for the month). That entry in turn would serve as the basis for a more formal account that appeared some months later in the *Virginia Gazette*.[11]

Though the lightning struck his cherished home and damaged it slightly, it did not threaten his person. It did, however, strike three of his black slaves and an overseer, who is mentioned in his diary but is not included in the account that was published in the newspaper, even though the overseer was on the piazza (according to his diary entry) when the lightning struck and was stunned slightly by the charge. The slaves, on the other hand, were apparently more directly hit and seriously affected. Characteristically, Carter's description is carefully, if not in this case obsessively, detailed.

The description of the storm that subsequently appeared in the *Virginia Gazette* is in the form of a letter, acknowledging Carter's election to the newly established Society for the Promotion of Useful Knowledge in Virginia, and is addressed to that group's secretary. In the letter, appropriate to its character and purpose, the personalities of the people involved in the incident are not emphasized. Instead, primary attention is paid to the phenomenon Carter seeks to describe, the remedies he prescribed to treat its victims, and the nature of lightning as a natural force.

In the newspaper account, Carter's servants appear as sympathetic but abstract figures, never referred to by name or status but only only by the most general indication that they were in his employ. However, in his diary, from which the newspaper account was adapted, they are clearly identified as his slaves. Their names are used, and there is a sense of them as individuals victimized by an extraordinary circumstance, but not as distinctive human beings who had meaning in his life apart from their involvement in the incident he is describing.[12]

The science of the event—i.e., why his house was damaged even though it had "points" on it, and how he was able to effect the recovery of those struck by the lightning—is the principal concern of the essay that appeared in the *Gazette*. The description in his diary is more personal, and Carter begins by announcing the great moral significance he attaches to the occurrence. It was, he begins, a circumstance that he hopes will never be forgotten. It should always be remembered, he says, "as one of those [events] which ought to correct the lives and behaviour of men." In Carter, it would seem, paternalism had eclipsed patriarchy in the same way and to the same extent as the Enlightenment had replaced his faith in the wonder-working majesty of Providence. The change was profound but not complete.

The transition to paternalism unquestionably required a modification of the traditional patriarchal self-image that the younger Byrd seems so clearly to manifest. Increasingly that image came to reflect the social complexity of the colonial South's slave-based society and thus the increased presence of blacks throughout the region. In the process, as objectified blacks became more important components of the elite's self-image, the blurred presence of the white nonelite population became more noticeable. The gentry's self-image fed on their obscurity, on denying them the spotlight of self-illumination and thereby making clear the social and cultural distinctions between the two levels of society. The deference of nonelite whites had never been unimportant, but the increased black presence heightened or encouraged recognition of its value and necessity. It was becoming harder and harder to entirely disregard or take for granted the mutuality implicit in social deference, however. How could the deference of the poor be maintained and their continued allegiance secured if the gentry denied them the same recognition it denied blacks, and in the same way?

Carter's diary and other writings are especially helpful in viewing and thus illustrating this dilemma. For instance, one intriguing manifestation of the dilemma reveals itself in an advertisement Carter placed in the *Virginia Gazette* several months after having proposed in the same medium the establishment of an association to encourage the manufacture of clothing in his home county of Richmond, on Virginia's Northern Neck. The ad, reflecting a heightened concern for self-sufficiency as the winds of revolution blew in late colonial America, is for a skilled workman in that enterprise.[13]

"I will give great Wages," the notice begins, "as well as agreeable Accommodations, by the Year, to any Person well skilled in managing Hemp, Flax, Cotton, and Wool for the Spinning Wheel, from the Growth." Prospective applicants, according to this advertisement, should also be "capable to instruct others, and conduct the Business of Weaving, and direct the making proper Looms, &c, for manufacturing such Materials into useful and decent Wear."[14]

In the letter he wrote to the *Gazette* two months earlier, the letter in which he proposed establishing an association for manufacturing clothing locally, Carter attempted to defend his motives for making the proposal against what he intimated were persistent, self-interested, and unwarranted criticism. His motives, he insisted, were entirely selfless, driven by a desire to provide a solution to a pressing public need, and born of "a compassionate tenderness ever entertained for the poor, not through a desire of tickling in their modes of a popular esteem, but because I love my country and fellow species." Failure to follow his lead, he argues, could have serious social consequences, for "if the poor do not soon meet with some such respect, too many of them will be under the necessity of growing out of conceit either with themselves or country, from their not having experienced among the pretty things that have been lately made to glisten before their eyes any of that golden humanity which from their very circumstances they must for ever stand in need of."[15]

His proposal itself, he suggests, was a modest one, the practicality of which could easily be tested and with relatively little expense to investors. Thus, he called on others to join him in forming an association to fund efforts to establish facilities and train workers to manufacture clothing for Virginians living in Richmond, his county of residence. Writing from his home plantation, Sabine Hall, on March 7, 1777, Carter promised to "gladly employ any skilful person to undertake the instruction of those who shall be put under him in the preparing of hemp, flax, cotton, and wool, in such a manner as to fit them for manufacturing; and to manufacture the same into a tolerable good wearing apparel, such as is generally produced from such materials." The machinery needed for such an enterprise—for example, "Hackles, wheels, looms, ginns, &c."—could be easily obtained; if not, "at least invention may be active enough in some proper succedaneum . . . when its parent necessity shall so loudly call for assistance, on so pressing an occasion as nakedness." His intent was "to see a publick spirit exerting itself in every county within this state to erect such manufactories, that might so encourage the poor among us to an active diligence in raising those materials for clothing, which are certainly in every man's power to do."

Already, he noted in conclusion, he had been contacted by "a certain mr. JAMES CROW from Augusta," who had heard of his intention, "and offered himself as a person fit for the purpose." They had reached a verbal agreement, but after their initial meeting in November 1776 he did not hear from him, although he was aware that Crow "had been in Richmond county not very long ago." Not uncharacteristically he was suspicious of Crow's motives, as he was of those of virtually everyone else he had ever known. In a veiled reference to the motives of unnamed others in the area, Carter sarcastically offered, as a "small hint out of compassion," the following observation: "I only hope mr. Crow has some very good reasons for such a treatment, but should be sorry to hear of one dated from any of the purlieus of malice, as it must argue a weakness not to consider that the perpetual dictatrix in all such places, ENVY, is a monster so double-headed as to wound as much in the advice she gives as she does in the detraction she uses to enforce her advice."

Envy, however, was not the only double-headed monster afoot in the Northern Neck, as Carter explaines in the subsequent ad, the second sentence of which begins: "Note, my Son on or about Saturday May 24, did, as he imagined, agree with a certain Orangeman, as he then stiled himself, a professed Manchester Weaver, at Hobb's Hole, in his Way to Williamsburg, to see a Half Brother by the name of Atwell, living near that City." It turned out, however, as Carter goes on to explain, that the person his son met with (and apparently agreed to hire) was "the same James Orange, who is advertised as a Deserter in Purdie's Paper of June 6."[16]

Ever leery of the motives of others, Carter even suspected that Orange had deceived the officer who was seeking his capture, implying that he had been as gullible as his son had been. Otherwise, "it wants some explanation, how such a Deserter could be enlisted, consistent with what is deemed our General's [George Washington's] Instructions, which seem to be issued with a View to remove a strong Impression prevailing among the Soldiers in our Enemy's Army, that, all the Deserters from thence would be made to take up Arms against their Country Britain." Orange had apparently told the officer advertising for his capture and return that he was "a Serjeant who came over with the 34th picket Guard from the British army, to General Washington's Camp about 5 Weeks before; and he had Letters of Passport from Gentlemen to the Northward."[17]

Characteristically, what Carter seems to resent most is not Orange's apparent lack of loyalty to his country, whichever one that may have been, but his failure to return to Sabine Hall after promising to do so. "Mr. Orangeman or Mr. Orange," Carter snips derisively, "seems to pay as little Regard to his private Engagements as he is advertised to have done for his public contract. . . . Nevertheless the unhappy Creature deserves to have his rare Virtue recorded; for he absolutely refused to receive Money from my Son to bear his Expences to and from Williamsburg for 5 or 6 Days, in which Time he was to come to Sabine Hall."[18]

Although in this instance Carter is expressing the contempt he feels for a virtueless individual, just as he did earlier regarding Mr. Crow, deciding which virtues should be recorded was a responsibility he took seriously on a personal level but also as a prerogative and obligation of his privileged status, of his wealth and education. It was in many ways the crowning distinction of his class, as well as a necessary obligation and function of the power they shared. Recording in this sense, however, meant not merely making note of, identifying, or listing, but also characterizing colonial life. The poor must be respected, according to Carter, even though their virtue could not be relied upon, especially when preyed upon and manipulated by unscrupulous and thus virtueless members of his own class. It is important to note, however, that both Crow and Orange were accused by Carter of lacking virtue, not of lacking the capacity to be virtuous. His attitude toward the truly poor or "indigent," to the extent that it can be discerned from the tone of his writing, is more condescending than sarcastic and thus similar to his attitude to blacks.

Especially revealing in that regard was his relationship with his multitalented, virtually indispensable, yet tragically alcoholic slave Nassau. An intriguing and illuminating parallel to the relationship with Nassau was the equally complex and tense association between Carter and his onetime secretary and accountant, a well-educated white indentured servant named Owen Griffith. He knew Nassau longer and probably more intimately than he did Griffith, but he saw in Griffith more of himself. Both Nassau and Griffith seem equal in their ability to anger Carter, to make his blood boil, and in that sense they shared much in common with Carter's daughter-in-law, who in his eyes was evil incarnate. But Nassau disappointed Carter more than he threatened him, whereas the reverse was true in Griffith's case. At some significant personal level, one is tempted to conclude, Carter felt threatened by Owen but not by Nassau. Both men held comparably strategic positions on Carter's estate and were therefore equally capable of exploiting and manipulating him. He clearly felt himself judged more directly and tellingly by Owen than by Nassau, and by what was known by others of his relationship with Griffith. He repeatedly makes references to the character flaws of both, while much less frequently acknowledging how useful they were to him.

Under his own signature, Carter placed a note in the *Virginia Gazette* in the late summer of 1770, seeking information about the whereabouts of a package that Griffith was expecting from his "brother at the Duke of Montague's." "It seems," the letter continues, that the "goods" believed to be in the package were placed there "by Griffith's father, who died presently after, and the contents of the package is not set down." Though no one knew for sure what the contents of the package were, Carter thought that Griffith was preparing to go home "to really a very good estate, [and that he] would be glad to [receive] the things, because they were possibly such as may fit him to appear again in character in his own country; which I [Carter] have seen attested under the name Montague, in a large hand, dated at Montague-House, May 26, 1770." The notice, dated August 23, 1770, appeared in the September 6 issue of the *Gazette*.

Less than three weeks later, a letter from Carter (appearing in a September 27 edition of the *Gazette*) attempted to answer the suspicions of "some Gentlemen" who felt that Carter had been deceived by Griffith regarding the letter "under the name Montague." That letter, Carter reasons now, was too detailed, involving such a wide range of specialized information, that its fabrication must have been the work of an extremely clever person, "[a]nd I am certain," he writes, "from the experience of five years, I cannot suspect Mr Owen of any thing so sensible, from a natural silliness that governs his whole conduct." Also, Carter asks, if Griffith had been responsible for writing the letter, why would "a man worth thousands" limit himself, as the letter did, to "drawing for 100£. if he wants it"? And why would he beg "his late master [Carter] to let him live in the family for such services as he can do, till the ship he is to go home in shall be ready; and asks for no other assistance than what will barely furnish a few decent necessaries, and put a little cash into his pocket for some accidental occasion"? This last query is by way of preface to Carter's admission that he agreed to advance Griffith a small sum of money "by indorsing one bill of exchange for 30£."

However, in his diary, dated March 22, 1771, Carter's confident tone and reassuring assumptions disappear. "Yester[day]," he writes, "Mr. Wmson. Ball told me Mr. Mills at Essex court read a letter from his nephew, John Mills, who went home either in the ship with Owen Griffith or about the same time; which told him that he had seen that rascal's father alive, that he showed my advertizement in the Virginia Paper to the Old man, who said the rogue must come to the gallows, for the whole of his great estate was a forgery." Moreover, based on Jack Greene's summary of a letter Griffith wrote Carter, Griffith had in fact " 'contrived' the entire hoax 'many months' before putting it into execution simply to outwit and embarrass Carter, to whom he referred as a 'Boisterous Tyrant' and an 'outwitted Cunning Man.' Griffith, according to Greene, "indicated that he had no intention of repaying [Carter] the 100 and expressed his intention of 'going to India to remain forever.' "

There was apparently no escape for Nassau, although he ran away frequently. Indeed, if we regard his alcoholism as an escape mechanism, running away from Carter (whether physically or into a sheltering intoxication) could be considered a central feature of his existence or part of what Rhys Isaac has termed "Nassau's rebellion against oppression."[19] Also, Nassau was brutally beaten for his transgressions, whereas Griffith was not. Nor is there any indication that Carter beat any of the other whites he mentions in his diary, even those dependent on him, like Griffith, and including those who lacked Griffith's veneer of gentility but who were, like Carter's slaves, accused of dereliction of duty, laziness or indolence, and dishonesty.

Relatively late in his diary Carter records a scene in which he confronts Nassau for a final, climactic time regarding the latter's alleged insobriety. The episode is powerful as a personal drama and symbolically reflective of the distinctions that separated blacks from whites throughout the colonial South. As a vivid dramatization not of how all whites regarded all blacks or of how all whites treated all blacks, but of how all whites were positioned socially in relation to all blacks, the scene allows us to see as well as to feel the inherent tension in that relationship.

When the scene opens, Carter remarks that it was "A fine day but still in the heat of bilious complaints; for I hardly remember more inveterate agues in my life and severe fevers that do attend the aged and the infant." As Carter's principal medical assistant, Nassau was greatly needed at such a time. However, according to Carter, "I have hardly a servant to wait on me"; he laments that "the only [one] to assist my endeavours after humanity is drunken Nassau who has not been sensibly sober one evening since this day fortnight." The previous day, Nassau had been sent to aid "my overseer at the river side [who] perhaps frightened to death with his disorder sent up to desire some assistance." Nassau, however, before going to the riverside plantation, managed to obtain some rum. For a while, "[n]obody could find him," but eventually he was found "at sunset a Sleep on the ground dead drunk." As soon as Nassau "got home," according to Carter:

I offered to give him a box on the ear and he fairly forced himself against me. However I tumbled him into the Sellar and there had him tied Neck and heels all night and this morning had him stripped and tied up to a limb and, with a Number of switches Presented to his eyes and a fellow with an uplifted arm, He encreased his crying Petitions to be forgiven but this once, and desired the man to bear witness that he called on God to record his solemn vow that he never more would touch liquor. I espostulated with him on his and his father's blasphemy of denying the holy word of God in boldly asserting that there was neither a hell nor a devil, and asked him if he did not dread to hear how he had set the word of God at nought who promised everlasting happiness to those who loved him and obeyed his words and eternal torments who set his goodness at nought and dispised his holy word. After all I forgave this creature out of humanity, religion, and every virtuous duty with hopes though I hardly dare mention it that I shall by it save one soul more Alive.[20]

Carter repeatedly felt betrayed by both Griffith and Nassau, and his admiration for each of them is clear, partly through his continued reliance on their skills and partly through his grudging admission. Explaining their betrayal of him and their human failings as he understood them therefore became an important part of his own quest for "inward satisfaction" and self-definition. That one man was black and the other white often seems to have made little difference to him, or certainly less difference than the respective roles they played in his life and the status ascribed to each of those roles. Yet at the same time it appears to have made all the difference in the world. It is the one distinguishing factor that seems to explain all the assumptions that undergird Carter's view of both men, the clearly stated yet unspoken explanation for why he identified with them differently.

Although his judgments of others were unfailingly self-serving and could be mean-spirited and vindictive, in relative terms Carter could be quite generous in some of his depictions of others. Though often sarcastically, he generally managed in the course of writing about others to give even those like Mr. Orange, whom he suspected of deception, their due. Nevertheless, Carter and other members of the inner gentry not only served as the most important, if not the sole, judges of what constituted virtue and virtuous behavior and who deserved credit for it but also controlled all of the means of formal representation in their local communities and throughout their colony more generally. Not surprisingly, form mattered immensely to them. Conventions and customs governing what one could say to another, where and when, and what tone or diction was appropriate were followed closely and enforced. Violations of the conventions governing the etiquette of social relations and the forms of its expression were rarely tolerated or forgiven. Some degree of drunkenness and eccentricity, and even rebelliousness, was allowed, but only if it was deemed essentially nonthreatening and could be classified as a regrettable but harmless flaw in an offender's moral character, or as insanity or in some way delusional, a loss of bearings in a social world requiring careful navigation.

For Carter, as for the planter elite more generally, form mattered because it spoke volumes about who they were, and thus its integrity had to be upheld and protected in order to safeguard and stabilize their society and nurture their self-esteem and thus their sense of themselves.

In such a world, sarcasm was especially useful as a medium for conveying pointed, heartfelt opinions without at the same time betraying the social conventions designed to maintain order and propriety in a rigidly hierarchical society. Only the better sort, those sufficiently well educated and cultured, could employ such tactics effectively. Others would invariably betray themselves while trying to appropriate the form. Sarcasm, however, as Carter so often inadvertently demonstrated, could be a two-edged weapon. When he used it against white servants, as in Griffith's case, he sought not only to express contempt for them but to deflate what was to his mind their inflated sense of themselves as cunning or shrewd individuals, not to mention whatever pretensions they may have harbored about their station in life. In Griffith's case we sense from the start that Carter felt largely defenseless. In other cases, he was more self-assured. Yet, ironically, even in those cases where his only weapon against a white dependent like Mr. Orange was sarcasm, the self-images of those he used it against were enhanced rather than diminished. Sarcasm, in other words, could be turned on itself and used to subvert or contest authority as well as to deflate or deflect attacks against it.

By running away, through cunning and deception, individuals like Griffith were able to impose themselves on Carter and thus enter his record keeping (even if at the time they might have preferred to remain unnoticed). Nassau, however, could only frustrate, irritate, anger, and perplex him. Griffith was only a step removed from Carter in all the ways that counted in colonial Virginia, a relationship close enough that Griffith could, and ultimately did, contest Carter's definition of him on his own terms. Nassau, though closer to Carter, represented a world apart and could never challenge what Carter thought about him, or how he treated him, without actually attempting to overthrow his world or escape it entirely. It would not be surprising to discover that Nassau was aware of this at some level of his consciousness—perhaps even that it was a conscious dilemma—and that his alcoholism was symptomatic of that realization. Yet even if substantially correct, such an explanation would oversimplify what appears to have been an extremely complex and tragic personal life.

Nonetheless, viewed through Carter's eyes, it is difficult not to make the connection. His frequent references to Nassau reflect, rather than explicitly convey, a blend of emotions and attitudes, including contempt and rage, tinged occasionally with pity, which itself is a mix of concern, resignation, and admiration expressed as condescension. Though convinced of the inferiority of blacks as a group, he recognized their humanity and held them to the same standards of morality by which he judged himself and others, though with more modest expectations. He reasoned that because they were inferior all that was expected of them was a responsible recognition on their part of that fact. Such a recognition, however, would constitute an act of self-abnegation like the one Old Stepney offered Henry Laurens (see chapter 9). Though made uncomfortable by his effusiveness, Laurens nonetheless felt, to use Carter's phrase, that "the unhappy Creature deserves to have his rare Virtue recorded."

Arguably Robert Carter of Nomini Hall, Landon's nephew, embodied more fully the ideal of the gentleman planter than any other colonial slave owner who left a substantial personal record of his life, yet he was only marginally more successful economically than Landon, a circumstance that can be partially explained by the fact that he received a larger inheritance than did his uncle.

Both Landon and his nephew Robert died wealthy and generally well respected by their peers. Although Robert served on the executive council, as had his grandfather, and even though Landon failed to gain reelection to the House of Burgesses after serving for thirteen years in that body as a relatively young man, Landon was a much more significant figure intellectually than his nephew in late colonial Virginia, making important contributions as an essayist to the public dialog regarding many of the most significant issues of his day.[21]

More to the point of this study, however, Robert Carter of Nomini Hall freed his slaves during his lifetime, whereas Landon Carter did not. Robert was clearly a more humane master than his uncle; and judged by what he wrote, he was also much less overtly racist. On a number of occasions, Landon either stated explicitly or strongly implied his belief that blacks were inferior to whites, whereas no such statement or inference appears in any of Robert's voluminous letter books or daybooks. Also, there is, in Robert's references to blacks, an absence of the condescension that is so characteristic of Landon's writings. Whereas Landon would on occasion express his contempt for, or anger at, a particular slave by referring derisively to that slave as "Mr. Ambrose" or "Mr. Guy" or "Mr. Jimmy," Robert never did.

For instance, in his correspondence, most of which is business-related, with particular reference to plantation management, Robert frequently reports having received information from one of his slaves. For example, "Negroe Jesse from the old Ordinary Plantation informs me that the nine following Negroes viz Harry, Daniel, Dick, John, Cate, Let, Pat, Barbara and Dorcas are bear of cloathing. . . . "[22] There is an unstated assumption of trust in all of his references to blacks, a recognition of the moral capacity for honesty and thus for a sense of honor and self-respect. This was not an uncritical assumption that presumed the contented loyalty of his slaves, but a reasoned belief that they trusted him because it was in their interest to do so, and because they could clearly judge for themselves whether or not he was fair and honest to and with them and would thereafter act accordingly.

By contrast, Landon seems incapable of trusting others, his slaves serving merely as the most numerous and often the most readily available focus for that incapacity and its expression. In his diaries he frequently reports having spoken to one or another of his many slaves, but very often it is clear that he did so in a manner that was demanding, threatening, reproachful, or accusatory. On numerous occasions he served as an inquisitor, and often even when he was not directly interrogating a slave, he was seeking information from one to compare with that he had received from another. Everyone who spoke to Landon Carter, or with whom he had regular communication, was potentially an informer on anyone else they knew in common.

In that sense he seems to have mistrusted everyone he knew, equally, including slaves, frequently questioning their character and their motives. He speaks at least as critically and unkindly of his son or daughter-in-law, or social and political rivals, as he does of his slaves. Indeed, he judged whites more harshly than blacks because he did not think whites lacked the capacity to be virtuous. Thus, whereas Landon makes a number of references or allusions to what he believed to be the inferiority of blacks, Robert's papers are barren of such allusions or references. Yet although Robert treated his slaves more humanely and regarded them more sympathetically, he did not describe them any more completely than did Landon. In fact, thanks to Landon's obsessive need for self-justification, we learn more about a few of his slaves, those he mentions most often and with whom he had the most difficulty, than we do about any of Robert's.

Thus, the transition from Byrd through Landon Carter to Robert Carter of Nomini Hall, and thus from the early institutionalization of slavery in the colonial South to the eve of its most profound transformation, was not an insignificant one relative to how blacks were represented by leading patriarchs. Yet at the same time, black subjectivity did not become more visible as a result of the change.

As a national figure, Washington, like Jefferson, had the opportunity that other Southern planters did not have to recognize the abilities of an exceptional black woman, Phillis Wheatley, an African-born poet. She would have been difficult for them to ignore because the debate over her talent as a poet became an important focus of the discourse about black intelligence that was a significant feature of the Enlightenment debate over slavery. Washington's recognition of Wheatley, however, came in response to a letter from her that was lavish in its praise for him, whereas Jefferson wrote about her and other gifted blacks primarily to support or demonstrate his theory that blacks were inferior to others, especially whites.[23]

Another notable instance of recognition on Washington's part involved one of his wife's maids, Olney Judge. After she ran away Washington exerted as much effort as he felt practical to have her captured, considering his position and the difficulties involved in the effort to retrieve her. The Washingtons were convinced that she had been brainwashed into leaving them by a French visitor. However, Washington reluctantly gave up his effort to recapture Judge after being advised that retrieval could spark a disturbance of some sort in Portsmouth, New Hampshire, the city in which she had sought refuge, and where she had been advised by black friends not to return.[24]

Neither Wheatley nor Judge, however, was typical of the blacks that appear in Washington's diaries and correspondence. Wheatley, especially, has a voice and was formally recognized by Washington, who responded to her letter by inviting her to visit him. When they met, as far as we know, she was received cordially and treated as a person worthy of his attention and courtesy. Judge gains a voice only once in New England. More typical of the black presence in Washington's life, as in that of most other members of the gentry, was the ubiquitous attendance of Billie Lee, who appears in the shadows or at the extreme edge of the paintings of Washington by Savage and Trumbull. We can see those portraits in greater depth, however, in the poignant description of Washington's death that his biographers have generally based on the observations of Washington's secretary (and fellow slave owner), Colonel Tobias Lear.

As he was dying, Washington required constant attention from sunrise on the morning of December 14, 1799, when his servants and staff were first alerted to the unexpected severity of his seasonal illness, until shortly after ten that night when he spoke his last "'Tis well." In addition to his wife, Martha, and his secretary, three doctors attended him before he finally succumbed to what various physicians subsequently speculated was either diphtheria or a virulent streptococcus infection of the throat. Numerous servants, all of whom were black slaves, were also continually involved in caring for the new American nation's most revered Founding Father. One of them, Christopher, his body servant (Billie Lee was still alive but no longer physically able to serve in that capacity), was apparently in constant attendance from first to last. He dressed the general and assisted him throughout the day to adjust himself to the pain he stoically endured with little or no complaint. The presence of the servants, however, is referred to only incidentally until Washington, by then fully resigned to his imminent demise, motioned to Christopher to be seated. Washington, with that gesture, recognized that Christopher had been standing at attention near the doorway throughout the long ordeal, except for those times when he was actively assisting the president.[25]

Beyond whatever else the gesture may have symbolized, it fleetingly drew Christopher out of the shadowed realm he inhabited as Washington's slave. By recognizing Christopher, however, Washington did not remove him from the shadows. His gesture, like all such gestures regardless of their intention, affirmed rather than removed the shaded boundaries to which people of African origin were restricted. Elsewhere in the handful of references made to Christopher in Washington's writings, the dual nature of Christopher's life as a slave is revealed: juxtaposed with his image as a loyal servant is that of a man poised for flight; while counterbalanced to his presence as the property of one person is his identity as the husband of another. What is not revealed is the extent to which each role reflected the other, how the images and perspectives they reflected were reconciled, if indeed they ever were or ever could be.

Few slaves, even house servants like Christopher, saw themselves depicted in paintings or in printed references, let alone portrayed by their masters in their diaries and private correspondence. Instead, they saw themselves reflected in the symbols of authority that they were required to respect, in the social distance placed between them and others, in the demands made upon them, in the things they were denied, in the contrast between themselves and others, and in the behavior of others toward them—in noble gestures or condescending asides.

For survivors each slave owner's projected self-image was a distillation of this symbolism, a concentrated reflection of the slave's subjective absence. Henry Laurens is interesting and instructive in this regard because he projected two distinctive images of himself as a slave owner. On the one hand, he pictured himself as an "absolute monarch" who ruled over "a little kingdome . . . on which the slaves were his 'Subjects.'" On the other, he portrayed himself as a "Factor" for his slaves, "buying the produce of their gardens and retailing manufactures to them on credit."[26]

These two seemingly but not necessarily contradictory self-images offer a picture not only of how Laurens perceived himself as a master of slaves but of the dilemma that slave owning patriarchs more generally faced in "the greater 'world system' of capital and exchange in which they were embedded." His slaves, however, have a subjective presence only in relation to the latter picture. In the former he speaks about them, or of them, as if they had no capacity to speak or think for themselves. He described for them how they should feel about him and what would happen to those who did not "love me."[27]

By contrast, in his persona as plantation and slave-owning capitalist, Laurens suggests a mutual relationship with at least some of his slaves that presupposes a self-interested capacity on their part to think rationally—that is, in ways that Laurens would consider rational—and to respond accordingly. In a letter written to one of his overseers in 1765, Laurens notes that he has enclosed "an Account of sundry articles sent to be dispos'd among the Negroes for their Rice at the prices mark'd to each article which I hope they will take without too much fuss & trouble that I may not be discouraged from being their Father another Year."[28]

The response of Laurens's slaves to these two personas, or the response of slaves more generally to the images that their owners had of themselves and sought to project onto their relations with their slaves, not surprisingly mirrors the slaveholders' dilemma as suggested by Laurens's two-sided self-image. At one extreme was the fawning, embarrassingly obsequious greeting that slaves like Stepney sometimes gave their owners and that Stepney gave Laurens upon his return from England. At the other was Laurens' recognition that "his slaves defended and asserted the 'law of the market' and of market relations whenever they were able."[29]

From Laurens's point of view he was merely indulging his slaves, as he had Stepney. What he gave he could take away. But in his own account of his commercial dealings with them his slaves seem to take for granted that within obvious limits theirs was a negotiated relationship and even that the limits themselves had been included in their agreement. Clearly the light in which slave owners insisted on casting themselves was not always as flattering or self-revealing as they hoped it would be, and thus not always the barrier to self-expression by others that they hoped and needed it to be. But it was always shadow casting and consistently effacing in its character.

Whether standing in the shadow of this light or in its reflected glare, blacks were seldom unseen, but judged by the way in which they were most often portrayed, they were virtually invisible as subjects. Both the light and the shadow extended even into their private lives where their efforts at self-proclamation were inhibited by the requirement that they express themselves openly, and live their lives freely, only in secrecy and that it never be revealed.

The risks connected with self-revelation were immense. Christopher's plan to run away involved such a risk. His presence at the scene of Washington's death suggests a negotiated settlement of some sort, the terms of which required Christopher to remain fully contained within the limits of his marginalization. Washington had drawn him out of the shadows of his life and into history's spotlight, if only fleetingly, but Christopher's relation to Washington, like that of all blacks to slave society, was not one-sided. Washington had needed Christopher to stay, just as Martha had needed Olney Judge.

If the Washingtons, for whatever reason, could not or would not allow their slaves to share the spotlight with them, except ornamentally, they nonetheless did have to recognize their presence as more than objects and as beings important to their lives. The relation of Christopher and Olney to their masters, George and Martha—its intimate and personal nature, combined with its impersonal and objectifying character—meant that the two slaves saw their owners in a distinctive way and from a distinctive vantage point that was largely, if not entirely, unrecognized by either owner. Olney, as a consequence, was able to escape Martha's shadow entirely and to establish her own place in history. Christopher, like blacks in general, was able to negotiate a self-sustaining life for himself in the shadows and the glare of exceptional inhumanity cast by both the thoughtful and generous and the cruel and even barbarous shadow casters.

AMBIGUITY

Using the second William Byrd's diaries as a starting point, our focus now shifts from the projected self-images of slave owners to the patterns of reference to blacks by slave-owning whites that can be discerned in surviving records. Byrd's diaries are intriguing as an illustration of the pattern because, as we have seen, they are at times distinctively ambiguous in their references to perceived racial differences among the servants and slaves whose presence Byrd records. But the diaries are not consistent in their ambiguity. Also, they are no doubt much more ambiguous to us than they were to Byrd or to those to whom he refers. The term "my people," for instance, is always used in reference to dependents outside his immediate household. These included people who were not black, but the primary reference was increasingly and unquestionably to blacks.

There is also some level of racial ambiguity in his references to the racial identity of those of his dependants he sought to discipline. One of the individuals he mentions most often in that regard is never explicitly identified racially. Nor is there any internal evidence within his diaries or his other papers that allows for a reliable identification. It seems likely, however, that the woman in question was black, as some historians have argued. Nevertheless at least one other house servant, Nurse, who was probably white, received similarly brutal correction. Both are distinguished from Byrd's wife by the physical nature of their correction and by his wife's own authority over them, but not in the intensity of his efforts to subordinate them.[1] However, outside of this close immediate circle of dependants, a circle of relationships that literally vibrates with domestic intrigue and undertones of sexual tension, the ambiguity lifts considerably.

Byrd, like many other leading planters of his day, was heir to a considerable slave-based fortune, including vast amounts of land on which large numbers of black slaves produced the region's primary cash crop, tobacco. The generation before his had initiated the substitution of black slave labor for that of white indentured servants. The process was largely complete when the second Byrd took over the estate his father had built, but in some important respects his earliest surviving diary, like Robert "King" Carter's, reflects the latter stages of the process rather than its aftermath. Most important, from our perspective, is the fact that his early diary was being kept during the first extended period during which Virginia planters were acquiring large numbers of slaves directly from Africa.[2]

Chronologically, Byrd's life experience as a slave-owning patriarch nearly parallels that of "King" Carter's. Indeed, when Washington was born in 1732, the year Carter died, Byrd was an elderly man by the standards of that period, only twelve years short of his own demise. Thus the slave-owning experiences of the younger Byrd encompassed all but the most embryonic period of its institutional development and a good portion of the early maturation of slavery in the area of that region where its institutionalization first occurred.[3]

As with "King" Carter's diary, Byrd's journals are full of references to blacks, but as an extensive day-to-day account of his life Byrd's diaries resemble Landon Carter's more than "King" Carter's. Landon Carter's diaries, "unlike similar documents of his contemporaries," have, according to Jack Greene, "a reflective quality and an openness that provide, perhaps better than any other single source, a suitable vehicle for a journey into the mind of one member of Virginia's eighteenth-century plantation gentry." Byrd's diaries are much less reflective, but they are undoubtedly the most nearly comparable to Landon Carter's that have survived from the era dominated by men like "King" Carter and Byrd's father.

Indeed, Byrd left a larger and more expansive literary legacy than did any other member of his or his father's generation of slave-owning patriarchs. Like others who sought to describe Virginia in the late seventeenth and early eighteenth centuries, including his brother-in-law Robert Beverley, who like Byrd had been born in Virginia and had inherited a relatively large slave-owning estate, Byrd spent "much time describing the characteristics and customs of the Indians of Virginia but gave extraordinarily little attention to blacks." Indeed, readers have difficulty in distinguishing between Byrd's white and black servants.[4]

Also distinctive were his views on slavery. He shared with Beverley a sympathetic view of the native population, stating in his *History of the Dividing Line* a belief in the "natural dignity" inherent in all "nations of men." That sentiment certainly seems to have included blacks, especially in light of his observation that "we know that very bright talents may be lodged under a very dark skin." Yet it is likely (given the fact that he never makes references to blacks whom he considers talented but frequently notes admirable qualities in Indians) that he has Indians in mind and not blacks when he makes this statement, and the salacious one he made elsewhere regarding the beauty of a woman he describes as "a dark angel."[5] Nonetheless, his explicit critique of the negative effects of slavery on whites, an analysis that Thomas Jefferson would echo in his *Notes on the State of Virginia* half a century later, make him unique among his contemporaries in colonial Virginia, although not among the officials planning the settlement of Georgia. Indeed, it was to one of them on the eve of that project that his views on slavery were addressed.[6]

There is little about his references to blacks, however, that was distinctive. He is solicitous of their health and generally sided with them in disputes with overseers.[7] He made it a practice, often a daily one, to walk about his plantation and observe those he generally referred to as "my people." Interestingly, in the diary that covers the early years of his experience as a plantation patriarch, he writes merely of having walked about his plantation, occasionally recording what he observed, whereas in the diary that survives from the last years of his life he writes of having talked with "my people." The health of his people, as much as their work, is a primary focus of many of his references to blacks. Discipline not surprisingly was another important concern. For the most part his comments about slaves are minimally descriptive, as they are of most others he made note of, and matter-of-fact in their tone and contextual implications.

In his diaries there are a number of references to the purchase or sale of slaves. He notes, for instance, on October 12, 1709, that "Mr. Holloway

sent me two negroes of Colonel [Walker's] estate for part of my debt."
And on May 26, 1710, he records that while eating "milk and strawberries
with Captain Posford for breakfast," he was told "that a ship was arrived
with negroes" and that Posford had "offered to fetch my wine from
Williamsburg." A week later he reports that "[I]n the evening [of June 1,
1710] I took a walk and met the new negroes which Mr. Bland had
bought for me to the number of 26 for £23 apiece." And the next day
there is this: "About 5 o'clock Robin Hix and Robin Mumford came to discourse about the skin trade. We gave them some mutton and sallet for
supper. In the evening I did not walk because of my company. Robin Hix
asked me to pay £70 for two negroes which he intended to by [sic] of
John [Evans] which I agree to in hope of gaining the trade." Three days
later he records having given a note for another "negro." The following
day we learn that "[t]wo of the new negroes were taken sick" and were
given "a vomit which worked well." Two days after that we hear that
"[t]he two new negroes that had been sick were well again." But then on
June 12, 1710, Byrd reports that "[t]he sloop was unloaded. Several of the
new [Negroes] were sick and I ordered them a vomit, which worked very
well."

In the midst of all this Byrd also records a drama involving a runaway
slave, a black woman named Betty, whom Byrd at times incorrectly, and
inexplicably, identifies as a boy. Byrd records on June 24, 1710, that when
he returned home from Williamsburg at "8 o'clock in the morning [he]
found all well except that a negro woman and seven cattle were gone
away." The next day he notes, "My people could not find the negro
woman but found her hoe by the church land." Two days later, "The
negro woman was found again that they thought had drowned herself."
On July 1, 1710, Byrd reports, "It was exceedingly hot. The negro woman
ran away again with the [bit] on her mouth." The next day he elaborates
on that report by stating, "The negro woman ran away again with the [bit]
in her mouth and my people could not find her." On July 8 we discover
that "[t]wo negroes of mine brought five of the cows that strayed away
from hence and told me all was well above, but that Joe Wilkinson was
very often absent from his business. It rained all the afternoon, that I
could not walk. The negro woman was found and tied but ran away again
in the night." She was captured again on July 15, ran away again, and was
caught again, according to Byrd's diary dated July 19. Not quite a month

later, on August 10, we learn that "[m]y cousin's John brought home my G——l [Betty] that ran away three weeks ago."

Typically, in none of this do we learn very much about Betty, except of course that she was by any measure an extremely determined individual. We can also infer that the motivation driving her determination must have been great. And this we know not because Byrd saw fit to tell us but because Betty's actions forced him to report it, forced him in that sense to recognize her humanity.[8]

Betty's anonymity, if not her saga, was typical. Indeed, there is only one reference to a black person in Byrd's diary that is more revealing than these entries he made regarding Betty. And the one exception is barely that: "Colonel Digges," he notes on November. 13, 1710, "sent for a white negro for us to see who except the color was featured like other negroes. She told us that in her country, which is called Aboh near Calabar, there were many whites as well as blacks."

For a brief, fleeting instant, and only for that instant, we glimpse a black person, who ironically was not black, at least not in color, with a life of her own and an awareness of it. She was, moreover, a person who was not anonymous, and who had a conscious sense of herself and her history. Like Mr. Shirley's slaves, this woman—this "white negro"—identified herself by reference to a place that was still vivid and fresh in her mind. Ironically, on the same day that her presence is noted in Byrd's diary, November 13, 1710, Byrd also records that he received a letter informing him that Betty had been found dead.

Byrd, of course, like Washington and other slave owning patriarchs who left an extensive written record of their lives, was not consciously withholding information about blacks when he wrote about them in his diaries and correspondence (at least not as a general practice). Indeed, Byrd's "secret" diaries were written in a shorthand code that would have relieved him of that need or obligation even had he felt it. Rather, the pattern of reference to blacks in his surviving papers consistently renders them as absent in any self-reflective sense and by so doing reflects the distinctive nature and history of slavery in the colonial South.

Throughout the colonial era, as at other times and in other places, references to, and discussion of, the black presence in surviving records was roughly proportional to its demographic significance. Historians have been able to chart the formation and evolution of slave societies with ever-increasing precision through records that matter-of-factly reflect those developments.[9]

When there were few blacks in the region there were relatively few references to them in the records that survive, and needless to say there were also no plantation records. As their numbers increased, indicating the rise of a plantation economy based on their labor, so too did the number and variety of the references to them. It is also true that the descriptive detail in the records increased progressively in tandem with the increase in the numerical presence of blacks. Yet the increased detail seems to have been a function of the greater occasion for record keeping, rather than of a change in perspective. The essential character of the records, in other words, remained consistently enumerative, managerial, commercial, legislative, or legalistic throughout.

The key factor in shaping the pattern of reference we have been observing, however, was not the number of slaves present at any given time, or even economic reasons for their presence, but the composition of the society into which slavery was introduced. Where and when the black presence increased significantly in the colonial South, the increase was never coupled with the total extinction of the native population as was the case throughout virtually all of the West Indies. Nor did the black presence replace the white presence as a dominant social (or laboring) factor, even in those areas where blacks became a majority of the population.

However, black slaves did replace white indentured servants as the principal source of labor for the large-scale production of the staple crops, thereby transforming all aspects of colonial development. Very early in that process, even before large numbers of blacks began to be brought into the colonies on a regular basis, formal legal or legislative discriminations between whites and blacks had been made. One of the first occurred in the 1640s when "black women were first subject to the payment of tithes, a yearly tax which frequently took the form of levies upon their masters, husbands and fathers." Though both white and black men were counted for purposes of taxation, white women never were, "even when the colony was in serious financial difficulty and in need of additional tax revenue." Legal discriminations of this sort were of course overlaid on those the colonists had already made through violence and conquest of the native population they had initially encountered. Clearly racial discriminations based on attitudes regarding perceived racial differences were evident from the very beginning of the colonial process, and just as clearly those discriminations evolved from a time of relative social fluidity to one of greater rigidity, from a time when the black presence was relatively small and economically insignificant to one when it was pervasive and defining.[10]

It is often difficult to see where and when this process of discrimination took on the form that would come to be identified much later in American history as racism. Inga Clendinnen offers a helpful description of how general perceptions of cultural difference during the early stages of colonial contact between the Spanish and the Aztec evolved to a point at which each side saw the other almost exclusively in highly objectified terms. Both groups, she contends, encountered each other full of self-assurance, discovering the otherness of the other in the process of their struggle for survival and dominance. Consequently, when Cortes's "strategy . . . to treat all men, Indians and Spaniards alike, as manipulable" failed, when his efforts to terrify and subdue the Aztecs "proved phantasmal, when killing did not lead to panic and pleas for terms, but a silent pressing on to death," he was faced with a "terminal demonstration of 'otherness', and of its practical and cognitive unmanageability." Otherness, especially as a function and process of domination, is in this sense not only a product of how we (all of us) know what we know (whatever that may be and however it becomes known to us), of how we make sense of our very different and distinctive worlds, but also and especially it is a product of terror, the experiential fire in which our rationalizations—our symmetry of self-understanding and cultural awareness—become belief that is both necessary and defining.[11]

Clendinnen's reading of the Spanish conquest of the Aztec appears to share much in common with Edmund Morgan's interpretation of the evolution of relations between the first permanent English settlers and the Indians they encountered in colonial Virginia, as well as those they had contacted earlier on Roanoke Island off what became known as North Carolina. The Indians, he concludes, "presented a challenge that Englishmen were not prepared to meet, a challenge to their image of themselves, to their self-esteem, to their conviction of their own superiority over foreigners, and especially over barbarous foreigners like the Irish and the Indians." They were challenged by the Indians' own sense of themselves, and by the obstinacy of the Indians when confronted by the superiority of English technology.[12] Meanwhile their own sense of self was threatened by their dependency on Indians for sustenance and therefore their very survival. Difference, in the sense discussed by Clendinnen, became otherness as terror begat terror and especially "when killing did not lead to panic and pleas for terms, but a silent pressing on to death."

Byrd's experience with blacks and slavery occurred during a time when the patriarchs of an emergent gentry class in the upper South were involved for the first time in the acquisition of large numbers of captive Africans. His father and Robert "King" Carter, as indicated earlier, were charter members of this group. The younger Byrd not only continued the practice of acquiring "new Negroes" but had been part owner of a slave ship, "the William and Jane . . . [that] was captured by a vessel of the French Senegal Company on March 1, 1699, off the coast of Africa."[13]

Though men like Byrd left little record of their involvement in the processes of acquiring and seasoning "new Negroes," enough is known from a variety of other sources to assure us, if we had any doubt, that both processes involved extreme cruelty.[14] Such a process, intent as it was on the total submission of one human being to another, and on subservience as a sign of self-abnegation, was a powerful and unavoidable expression of the discriminations that many whites were making regarding the rapidly increasing numbers of blacks in their presence. In that raw and terrifying experience there was little room for ambiguity about perceived racial differences.

For the most part Byrd's diaries reflect a world in which "an individual's status was dependent not on his or her ascribed rank (even that of wife), but on the actual influence which an individual could exert on events," a world in which it was possible for Byrd to "continually [imagine] his slaves to be American equivalents of the Old World poor," only better off.[15] In such a world ambiguous references served a useful purpose as a strategy for maintaining personal authority. However, Byrd's considerable inheritance reflected a society that was being radically transformed by a black and largely alien presence. Slave-owning patriarchs like Byrd were therefore pressed much more than their ancestors had been to make clear to the many dependents they relied on the difference between deference and subservience, a distinction that was becoming increasingly unambiguous and racially defined in the American South during the late seventeenth and early eighteenth centuries. Whether patriarchs were consciously aware of that need or not, some means of distinguishing between those required to be subservient and those from whom deference was expected was necessary to guard against any ambiguity that might in any way encourage group solidarity as a foundation for class consciousness. A them-against-us mentality served neither patriarchs nor paternalists, yet at the same time it was crucial that none be unclear about the difference between them and the many ranks of others in a given community.[16]

However, because the black presence was so strikingly distinctive both visually and culturally, it was relatively easy for Byrd and similarly inclined members of the ruling gentry to be ambiguous, without at the same time being unclear about the intent or meaning of a reference.[17] The unambiguous nature of patterns of reference that may at times seem relatively ambiguous to us becomes apparent when we consider the few descriptions or indications of how Byrd sought to force black slaves to become a completely subservient and submissive group. The racial discriminations that emerge from such a consideration are also useful in suggesting how important it was for the ruling elite to make clear, and socially resonant throughout the patriarchal social order they sought to establish in their multiracial and multi-ethnic communities, the difference between deference and subservience. In the colonial South that difference was peculiarly racial in its reference, whether it was implied, as it most often was, or explicitly stated.

If the recognition of cultural and physical differences in Byrd's world had not yet become otherizing, in the racializing sense we associate with modern forms of racism, it was surely on its way. Betty's experience is a graphic illustration of the violence required to enslave some blacks, and probably many more than surviving records allow us to imagine. It is also worth noting in that regard that even though both blacks and whites in Byrd's household were beaten, of the four references to people punished by means of placing a bit in their mouths, three were black and one, "Redskin Peter," was presumably Native American. Betty, of course, was one of the four, and her story can be read as a distillation of the experience more grandly played out by Cortes and Moctezuma. Byrd's efforts not merely to capture her but to muzzle and control her, to break her will and destroy any independent sense of self she may have managed to maintain despite her enslavement, vividly dramatize the objectifying process as described by Clendinnen and Morgan. The symbolic meaning of the effort, pressed directly and relentlessly against Betty, though denied by her death, could hardly have been lost on Byrd's "people," including those relatively privileged blacks in his household or in the larger community he dominated by virtue of his standing as its largest slave owner. Betty's experience, moreover, suggests that in that community being black had long since become a sign of difference and subjective absence.

Ironically, ambiguity of racial reference surrounding cases like hers (as well as in less extreme ones) served to accentuate and thus to highlight, for participants and observers, for victims and victimizers, and for all those others for whom the distinction was important, the stark reality of real-life racial discriminations in the world that Byrd and his contemporaries inherited and dominated. Although racial references, of necessity, became less ambiguous as black slaves became more of a defining aspect of colonial society the need for ambiguity did not cease. In some ways it became even more essential in the late eighteenth century because the black population had become less African and more creolized throughout most of the South and because the leveling and democratizing currents that swept through late colonial and revolutionary America posed a challenge to patriarchy.[18] Paternalists, unlike their patriarchal forebears, were rarely ambiguous about the racial identities of their dependents. They rarely left unclear the most obvious external differences between them.

Much more than in the British West Indies where absentee ownership of estates, including slaves, was the norm, the self-image of slave owners in the colonial South like Washington and Carter was tied to, and dependant on, the deference they received from free, nonelite members of their communities, a deference they expected and demanded but that they also very often needed to court. They could and did use coercive measures to guard against or punish deviance from expected norms, but mutual consent was always implied in the relationship. The logic of deference, in that sense, was primarily consensual. Jonathan Prude, for instance, has speculated that working people in the late colonial era "may have been increasingly pressing against the lack of attention polite observational strategies afforded them," noting as one example that "contingents of the urban nongenteel . . . were charging by the 1770s that gentlemen candidates were actually 'looking at them' only during elections."[19]

However, in the colonial South, whether during the time that was of interest to Prude or during earlier periods, blacks, whether free or enslaved, male or female, were not courted for their votes or invited to participate in society as citizens in any other way.[20] Moreover, those missionaries or evangelists or social visionaries who appealed to whites on behalf of blacks were quickly convinced of the error of their ways. David Ramsay's brief foray into electoral politics in post-Revolutionary South Carolina clearly illustrates the cost of such deviance. A successful physician, passionate patriot, and South Carolina's first historian, Ramsay was twice defeated in elections, first in 1788 and then again in 1794, both times because "his views on slavery undermined him."[21]

A more ironic illustration of how blacks were regarded differently from others, and thus how their subordination served to distinguish them from others, can be found in the runaway ads for unfree laborers in colonial America that Prude has analyzed. Aside from the most obvious distinctions of gender, race, or status, indications of differences in how the fugitives were perceived are difficult to pin down, except by means of statistical analysis. With the aid of such an analysis it becomes possible to suggest "that in subtle but chronic ways—in ways varying across social, physical, and clothing descriptions—females, blacks, and slaves were less known to their masters than males, whites, and nonchattel laborers." Is it possible, Prude goes on to ask based on his analysis of nearly two thousand ads, that "even the impolitely intense depictions in fugitive notices enclose[d] biases that distorted perception itself? Did masters actually see some workers less clearly than others"? As Prude observes, answers to these questions are not explicitly apparent in the ads, "yet the runaway notices are surely freighted with these implications."[22]

However, to find explicit expressions of racial or other bias, it is generally necessary to look elsewhere in colonial newspapers. For instance a few want ads indicate a preference for whites only, or demean the ability of blacks relative to whites. Ads such as this one also express a desire not to be treated or regarded as blacks were: "A Young Woman from Geneva, of a good character, who can be well recommended, wishes to be employed in some respectable family, (where she may be treated kindly and not be placed on a footing with Negroes) as a Nursey Maid, or an attendant on young ladies."[23]

Expressions of racial bias or animus against blacks can also be found scattered throughout the commentary that appeared in colonial newspapers, as in the following criticism of a law that, according to one essayist, gave no value to "a Master of a Ship's Word or his written Order," valuing it and "them as little as their Sailors, nay worse or as mean as Negroes." Similar expressions can also be found occasionally in court records, as in the deed of "John Dibdall, minister," giving his grandson, among other things, "one black two yeare old heifer called Neger Nose." Or, again, in the deposition of a Joseph McKeels in a case involving a dispute he had with another man at a "merry-making," a dispute that became so heated that McKeels alleged that his assailant insulted him by comparing him to a Negro.[24]

But one reads extensively within the records before encountering such expressions. Yet it is easy to find examples of profuse, and at times wonderfully imaginative, swearing. Conversation among whites was often laced, especially at "merry-makings" of various sorts, with terms such as villain, scoundrel, rogue, whore, "sorry dog," "Indian," "glister pipe," or "blink-eyed son of a bitch," and slander was one of the most common offenses in surviving court records.[25] More often than not, however, whites slandered one another, as such expressions graphically indicate, rather than blacks (at least not in writing). Yet it seems clear that negative assumptions about black character and status were taken for granted throughout the slaveholding South. That racist assumptions were taken for granted seems clear not only because of what historians of slavery in colonial America have told us about the nature of that institution in the Southern colonies and in particular the ways in which blacks were treated, but also because when explicit expressions of racism are encountered in surviving records, they appear as offhand remarks or are stated in ways that suggest no need for further elaboration.

Though it may seem surprising that more Southerners did not publicly express their views on blacks in the open and unqualified manner that West Indian planters like Edward Long did, the fact that whites slandered one another more than they did blacks is not. Given the role Southern society had assigned to blacks and the characteristics it ascribed to them, how could blacks be effectively slandered, except of course in the way Jefferson had done, by judging them inferior to all others, or as Jefferson and his fellow record keepers did, by denying or ignoring their proclamations of self, by looking closely at them but never seeing or recognizing them?

As demeaning and offensive as jokes about sailors often were or as hurtful as satiric references to mechanics or others thought to be uneducated or uncultured sometimes could be, such comments affirmed rather than denied the status of other whites, generally males, as human beings. They were considered by virtue of having been slandered to be implicitly capable of possessing a value that could be demeaned. As such they were recognized as members of a social hierarchy in which deference given to superiors was in some sense a reward for that recognition.

By contrast, blacks existed either in the anomalous position occupied by free blacks, who though free were neither welcomed nor recognized as participants in society, or as members of slave-owning families in which dependency more than deference was the central and defining feature of social relations. Moreover, their subordination and the degree of subservience required of them served to enhance the self-image of all others. The advantage of having a group that was considered to be beneath slander or slandering was not inconsiderable in colonies that at times were described as "the best poor man's country in the world," colonies that consistently sought to convince the poor in England and elsewhere to indenture themselves as servants in America or to lure potential immigrants with promises of fair treatment and promising opportunities. Yet at the same time, the colonies sought to replicate the deferential traditions that bound, no matter how uncomfortably, rich to poor in England.

The problem of maintaining deference from one group while insisting on subservience from another equally dependent one was further complicated for the gentry by variations and potential divisions within its own ranks. Jack Greene has noted that in Virginia, for instance, within the broad social category that "the dissenter James Reid, an obscure but effective social satirist," characterized in the 1760s as accessible to any person who had "Money, Negroes and Land enough," there was "an inner gentry," representing "a much smaller, cohesive, and self-conscious social group, at the core of which were about forty interrelated families that had successfully competed with other immigrants for wealth and power through the middle decades of the seventeenth century" and had consolidated their position between 1680 and 1730. This category, Greene estimates, was a very small fraction of the more numerous group of large plantation owners and their families, which was itself a very small percentage of the total white population.[26]

The gentry's founding generation, spurred on by a desire to "outdistance their fellows," focused their energies and concerns on acquiring wealth, whereas "the third generation found that their desire to excel could best be realized in the public sphere." In that arena, according to Greene, leadership in Virginia's House of Burgesses divided into two groups: traditionalists and realists. The traditionalists "insisted upon a strict adherence to the traditional ideals of politics," and as "disinterested patriots par excellence," were "the ideologues of virtue and independence." The realists were "the pragmatic politicians, whose primary emphasis was upon accommodation, moderation, deliberation and control, and whose most fundamental commitment was to the continuing stability of the polity." According to Greene, division within the gentry, who were generally harmonious and unified and bound together by shared values and shared concerns, reflected disagreements as to "how the game should be played," rather than "over the rules of the game." The achievement of political power by the local gentry, based as it was on the consent of free adult white males, was one development that, by the 1740s, opened an internal division. Other developments—the Great Awakening, increases in migration or immigration, shifts in commercial relations, economic problems, vacillations in royal governance—would reveal similar divisions. Yet unity held because it was essential not only to the maintenance of social stability and order but to the continuance of the gentry's rule and their way of life: "It was perhaps because the stakes were so high that the gentry learned to play the game so well."[27]

Few issues were more unifying than slavery. For all those who sought to improve their condition, as well as for those who hoped to maintain what they had, the ownership of black slaves was essential. Security, however, required extreme discretion in what slave owners said about slavery and when and where they said it. Indeed, just as there were always good or necessary reasons for paying close attention to blacks and recording their presence, there were also always good reasons for not mentioning them, or referring to them only in a very limited and narrow way. This also meant, of course, that whites were expected to be careful about what they said in the presence of blacks.

Landon Carter, for instance, describes in his diary for Sept. 24, 1772, a domestic dispute in which a local farmer told his neighbor, the local "Pastor," that "his riding horse had got into his cornfield." After hearing the neighbor's denial, the disputant, according to Carter, "went away cursing and in the hearing of the negroes swore that he would not come to complain again but he'd do for the horses; And so he did[,] for one of his horses was shot in his own pasture[;] for a creature so wounded could not have jumped over any fence to get into his own Pasture again where they found him."[28] Carter, like most Southern slave owners, expected that disagreements between whites would not be aired in front of blacks.

A more serious breach of this etiquette occurred in the early years of the nineteenth century, in the aftermath of the discovery of Gabriel Prosser's planned insurrection. The circumstances surrounding the incident are described in a letter to the public published in the *Virginia Argus* on July 17, 1802. The author, a "doctor" Robert De Graffenreid of Lunenburg County, Virginia, starts the letter by noting, "It has been reported in various ways that I have been concerned in promoting an insurrection of the slaves." The gist of the case against him was that De Graffenreid, when intoxicated, "said to Capt Waddy Street, that the negroes were by nature as free as he was, and it could be proved by scripture, law, and reason." In the room when he made that statement to Street "there was a negro boy, who probably heard him." Later, "in the piazza, and after some idle expressions, which shewed he was not in his right reason, [De Graffenreid] called out your negroes, do you hear, you are entitled to your freedom, I will carry you through and let them hang me." At that time, according to his summary of the case against him, he "was alone and not a negro nearer than the boy, in Capt. Street's room, and Mr. Smith's negroes about forty yards off in his kitchen." Mr. Smith, apparently, then "went out and told his negroes to shut the door, go to sleep, and not go where the Doctor was, and one said he believed the Doctor had drank so much he was a fool."

Finally that night De Graffenreid found shelter at a Mr. King's house, where he stayed all night. In the morning at breakfast, King's wife asked him why he looked troubled, and he agreed to confide in her if others left the room, whereupon "two young ladies who were present left it," but he indicated that "it was the servant girl he wished to leave the room"; and when she did, "He then said he had been drinking at the court house, and talking about the right of negroes to freedom and was very much afraid Mr. Smith's negroes had heard him." He added that even though "he thought the negroes by nature as free as the white people, yet he would not say so to them for five hundred pounds."

Others testified that "whenever he had been heard to speak on the subject in his sober hours, he always expressed himself very much like other rational men," opposing any extralegal efforts by the slaves or others to gain their freedom. He was a slave owner himself, and was known to require "as much from them as in reason and justice he should; [and] that he has always been very strick with his neighbours negroes." In short, when sober he was "a man of good conduct." The court apparently agreed, unanimously discharging him "from any further prosecution."[29]

At the other beginning of the colonial era, a very different but related inhibition can be seen. Historians of early American history have often been frustrated by the extremely meager information that has survived regarding the first documented arrival of blacks in colonial Virginia. Early English settlers in that colony, according to Wesley Frank Craven, were not only preoccupied by questions of survival but also constrained by what they could say about the presence of blacks among them during that crucial period in the colony's history. Thus we know virtually nothing more about the beginning of the first permanent black presence in colonial America than that twenty or more of them arrived at Point Comfort, Virginia, in a Dutch man-of-war named the *Treasurer* in 1619. This lack of information is due, Craven explained, to the fact that their arrival was so intimately bound up in a controversial issue—"the encouragement of privateering against the Spaniard." For that reason, according to Craven, any detailed reference to events linked to the *Treasurer*, and thus any mention of blacks, called "for discretion in reports to London."[30]

The point of course is not that these reasons were contrived but that there were always good reasons not to say very much about the black presence in the colonial South, or to be extremely circumspect about what one said. In that regard the reactionary response of the gentry to the proselytizing efforts of missionaries, or the even more threatening, leveling implications of the messages preached by evangelists, is not surprising.[31] Nor is it surprising to learn, after reading through the deeply personal and often very moving correspondence of Rosalie Stier Calvert, the "Mistress of Riversdale" in late-eighteenth-century Maryland, that her husband had fathered a large number of black children apparently before he married Stier. Though this would seem to have been a hard-to-overlook part of his life, Rosalie manages never even to hint at it in her voluminous and otherwise revealing personal correspondence. We know about Calvert's other life only because the editor of Rosalie's correspondence was able to reconstruct parts of it from legal records regarding manumission proceedings.[32]

The pattern of reference in colonial South Carolina was apparently quite similar to that in the upper South. There were, however, important differences. Unique in the colonial South, Charleston's large size, diverse and often transient population, and its region-wide cultural and economic importance allowed for the presence of a distinctive and influential merchant class. Their presence, perhaps, is the clearest symbol of one scholar's belief that "beneath the veneer of paternalism and the sheen of patriarchy in the low country were always the talons of the market, their hold sure, their mark deep." It seems clear, however, that even if a "market ethos" penetrated the low country more fully and from an earlier period than other parts of the colonial South, a large segment of the ruling elite nevertheless shared the patriarchal view of society that animated and bound together other elites elsewhere in colonial America.[33]

For instance, despite the time and effort slave owners devoted to plantation management, we have virtually no explicit descriptions of how "new Negroes" were seasoned. We know, however, from comments such as this one by Henry Laurens that it involved extreme cruelty: "I have been largely concerned in the African trade. I quited the profits arising from that gainful branch principally because of many acts from the masters and others concerned towards the wretched negroes from the time of purchasing to that of selling them again."[34] Thus, though few men had a better vantage point than Laurens from which to observe those "acts," and few men in the colonial South left a more detailed account of their lives, especially their lives as merchant planters, he never described in his papers any of the "acts" that caused him to quit "the profits arising from that gainful branch."[35]

An even more striking instance involved the conversion, in the late 1730s, of Hugh Bryan "to experiential religion through his brother Jonathan and their contacts with the Wesleys."[36] Thereafter, in the early 1740s, Bryan became one of George Whitefield's earliest and most ardent supporters in South Carolina. Indeed, his passion was such that he wrote a letter to the *South Carolina Gazette*, which appeared on January 15, 1741, that warned, as Whitefield had, that recent disasters that had befallen South Carolina, including the Stono Rebellion, were a sign of "God's just Judgments." For this he and the paper's editor were arrested. Whitefield was also charged and ordered to appear before the chief justice. "South Carolina's ruling elite," historian John Scott Strickland has pointed out, "could not tolerate such a direct challenge to its hegemony and acted quickly to stem the swelling emergent culture of evangelicalism."[37]

Even before Bryan "fell under the spell of Whitefield's evangelism," according to Strickland, he "had become interested in the religious wellbeing of his slaves." Meanwhile, authorities religious and civil had become concerned about Whitefield's critique of local society and his efforts to reach out to blacks and thereby include them in his vision of a reformed society. It was in this context that authorities became aware of reports that "there had of late been frequent and great Assemblies of Negroes in the Parish of St. Helena." Subsequent information suggested that Bryan was involved in stimulating these gatherings. Especially damning was the discovery of "a Book or Paper signed by" Bryan in which were apparently contained "sundry enthusiastic Prophecys of the destruction of Charles Town, and the deliverance of the Negroes from their servitude." Bryan was arrested again and sufficiently brought to realize the consequences of his behavior that on March 1, 1742 he addressed a letter to the authorities recanting his actions, claiming the equivalent of insanity and begging forgiveness. Strickland notes in conclusion that the St. Helena planter never again engaged in zealous propagation of evangelical religion though he remained a loyal Whitefieldian until his death.[38]

CHAPTER 4

THE VIEW OF STRANGERS

It should be clear by now that we are interested in the portrayed or expressed self-image of planters not only for what that image reflects about their—and their society's—attitudes toward and about blacks but also because such images and attitudes reflect an important aspect of the enslavement process. The assumption throughout the preceding discussion has been that the gentry's expressed self-image embodied factors and forces that demanded the complete submission of blacks to the will of their masters, as well as to all other whites. Thus the gentry's self-image—projected in bearing and attitude as much as in other more direct ways—served as a primary means of perpetuating the cultural and psychological assault on blacks that enslavement originated.[1]

Enslavement, however, as a process of objectification, is perhaps best seen not in terms of how slave owners portrayed or failed to portray blacks but rather in terms of how those from outside the colonial South saw them. The absence of blacks from writing by members of the gentry becomes much clearer when blacks are observed through the eyes of visitors to the region. The difference is apparent when we contrast what we learn from Robert Carter's papers about life at Nomini Hall with what we learn from the journal kept by Philip Vickers Fithian, a Princeton-educated tutor Carter hired to supervise the education of his children.[2] We do not gain a more detailed knowledge of that life from Fithian, but we are given humanizing glimpses of a few of the blacks mentioned by the tutor, relatively brief references that bring them into closer and more revealing view.

Much of what Fithian recorded about blacks in his journal, as well as about others, is not the sort of information one would expect to find in papers like Carter's, most of which are concerned with his commercial interests and slave management. The absence of observations like those that appear in Fithian's journal would be more conspicuous in the diaries of William Byrd or Landon Carter, or the more topically expansive papers of Jefferson.

Fithian was a young man, fresh from college, and new to the plantation South. Also, he was writing to entertain himself, and with an eye toward what others might also find interesting. Many of his letters home drew heavily on entries he made in his journal. Carter as a writer shared none of these motivations or characteristics.

Regarding black slaves, however, the two did share one thing in common. Fithian was opposed to the institution, and Carter, who would later become a born-again Christian, would free all his slaves in 1791 after being converted. In mid-September of 1774, however, Fithian reports hearing a "very practical Sermon against the common vices here in particular against the practice of abusing Slaves." Carter, he observers was one among several planters in attendance who were "not pleased with" the sermon's message. Yet we also learn from Fithian that Carter was not unconcerned about the vices of which the sermon complained. "At Breakfast," on Thursday, March, 24, 1774, Fithian reports that "Mr Carter entertained us with an account of what he himself saw the other Day, which is a strong Representation of the cruelty & distress which many among the Negroes suffer in Virginia." While at a fellow planter's house for dinner Carter had found another guest's coachman sitting chained to "the Chariot Box, the Horses off." Paraphrasing, and also commenting on, Carter's account of the incident, Fithian says, "The fellow [was] inclined to run away, & this is the method which This Tyrant makes use of to keep him when abroad; & so soon as he goes home he is delivered into the pityless Hands of a bloody Overseer!"[3]

The outrage is Fithian's, not Carter's. In fact, it is not clear that Carter related the information as a condemnation or merely as part of his description of a recent visit to a friend of the family. In his papers Carter, like many other slave owners, frequently entertains complaints from his slaves about the treatment they received from overseers, not infrequently siding with them in the disputes. But there is little if any of the outrage expressed by Fithian in Carter's records. When he does indicate his displeasure with an overseer's behavior, it is for exceeding his authority or for dereliction of duty. The story, however, is one that would not be surprising to find in Carter's papers. A more conspicuous absence are references to the musical and recreational life of blacks on his various estates, especially his home quarter. Though music was one of his passions, we would not know that at least some of his slaves were also passionate about it were it not for Fithian's occasional remarks indicating that they were. "This Evening [January 30, 1774] the Negroes collected themselves into the School Room, & began to play the *Fiddle*, & dance." And then a few days later: "This Evening in the School-Room, which is below my Chamber, several Negroes [with Carter's sons] are playing on a *Banjo* & dancing!"[4]

Fithian, however, appears more attuned to the lives and concerns of blacks as individuals only by comparison with Carter. The tutor, compared with some other visitors to the colonial South, or travelers to other British colonies in the New World, was not unusually observant of the black presence. For example, historian James Sidbury has suggested, referring to a boat race attended by Fithian, that Fithian's description of the "unusual event" "revealed the seductive quality of the gentry's competitive world of display and luxury." His "lack of interest in the slaves who participated in this event," according to Sidbury, "best reveals the power this display of gentry values had upon him." Though he showed "great interest" in the blacks he encountered in Virginia elsewhere in his journal, "he almost erased the Black presence" in his account of the boat race. Blacks played a crucial role in the festivities and not just as rowers in the race, yet the rowers were the only blacks Fithian specifically identified. No doubt, Sidbury adds, blacks in the area took the occasion to have their own party, "a gathering those at the 'big' party knew about but ignored." To provide a sense of what such "shadow" parties were like, Sidbury, like other historians faced with a similar reconstructive problem, has to use the "traces of the slaves' different world" that are scattered throughout Fithian's journal and other similar sources.[5] For there is little of use in the surviving papers of natives or longtime residents in the region, especially those who owned slaves or who benefited from slavery.

Carter's references to his more than five hundred black slaves are, as we have seen, no more revealing of blacks than those extant references made by other large slave owners in colonial Virginia. Unlike the papers of most others, however, Carter's papers lack any gratuitous negative evaluation of black character or intellect. Not even Washington's papers are as generous as Carter's in that regard. Like Washington's papers, Carter's provide invaluable information about the presence of black people on his extensive holdings, but they seldom if ever present blacks in the self-proclaiming sense that can be observed in descriptions of slavery by planters and others in the West Indies. Indeed, without the evidence from Fithian's journal, the black presence on Carter's vast holdings would resemble Washington's body servant Billie Lee in the paintings by Trumbull and Savage.

The difference being suggested is particularly noticeable in the observations offered by a "Stranger" about life in Charleston in 1772. Not only do his observations vividly illustrate what is so often missing from references to blacks by American-born whites or longtime residents in the Southern colonies, but they also bring into sharper focus the issues of perspective and vantage point without which it would be hard to gauge the extent to which this lack was actually perceived or felt by blacks themselves.[6]

"At my first coming to this Province," the "Stranger" confesses on the front page of the *South Carolina Gazette* in the late summer of 1772, "I was not a little surprised at the Number of Black Faces that every where presented themselves; but my Surprise was so greatly heightened when I reached Charles-Town, that, had I not seen some few of those People before, as I passed through the other Colonies, it is my Opinion, I should have been weak enough to suspect, that my Guide, instead of shewing me the Way to this Town, had conducted me to Africa, or Lucifer's Court."[7]

The "Stranger" quickly acknowledges that local residents would have found his initial impression of their teeming, half-black city "very outré."[8] In fact, by the time the "Stranger" first visited Charleston in the early 1760s, longtime residents of Charleston, and of the low country more generally, had not only come to expect such reactions from first-time visitors but seemed almost to relish them. They had, over the preceding century, adopted an indulgent rather than a defensive attitude toward those who were frightened or disoriented by the low country's alluring yet threatening environment and the multitude of black people whose ubiquitous presence was one of its most striking and characteristic features.

The residents of Charleston were not unconcerned about the many dangers that threatened their well-being. But they knew that showing fear was the surest way to increase the danger they faced. Also, as the colony became more secure from external as well as internal threats, they became more confident and proud of their ability to survive. After all, they and their ancestors had survived the region's notorious disease environment and the explosive and unnerving rise in the black population, reflective of an ever-deepening dependency on slave labor. They had survived numerous slave conspiracies and an actual slave rebellion, not to mention several death struggles with local Indians and attempted invasions by the Spanish. Indeed, they had not only survived but become hardier for it. Moreover, they had also prospered, transforming a region that shocked or terrified others into "the most opulent and flourishing colony on the British Continent of America." They had made it a source of wealth beyond any prior expectation, and to their mind a virtual paradise of cultural refinement and civility.[9]

To suggest that the slave-owning population in late colonial South Carolina was fully at ease with the large number of captive Africans and people of African descent who lived among them, or that they were unconcerned about the security threat their presence represented, would grossly misrepresent the attitudes of most low-country whites. Just as they had learned to cope with and overcome all the other threats that faced them, they had managed to survive the persistent anxiety generated by their dependence on the close and often intimate presence of so many alien people among them. Survival and success, not unexpectedly, had bred confidence and self-assurance.[10]

This was especially true in Charleston, according to Philip Morgan, and increasingly so as the eighteenth century progressed. Suggesting that "the latitude, diversity, and fluidity of urban slavery were as much a strength as a weakness" in eighteenth-century Charleston, Morgan has argued that subordination was maintained by the military preparedness of the entire adult white male population, and "in a number of more or less subtle ways—from the habitual arrogance of whites to the naked power of an armed watch, from the masters' fine clothes to the arbitrary power of individual slaveowners, from the etiquette of the street to the powers invested in all whites to assault blacks almost with impunity."[11]

Despite the shocking presence of so many blacks in Charleston and his misgivings about what he had seen or been told about their behavior, the "Stranger" became an ardent admirer of the city and the region as a whole. His letter indicates that he even intended to make South Carolina his permanent home, "provided your many excellent Laws . . . be so observed and enforced, as to render the Health and Security of the People less precarious than they appear to be at present." Apart from the behavior of blacks in Charleston, he thought South Carolina had "many Superior Advantages" to "all the other Colonies" he had observed in his travels. On an earlier visit to "North-America" in 1763, he explains, he "passed thro' every Colony from Quebec to West Florida," but he lived in South Carolina after returning to North America in 1770.

The "Stranger's" misgivings were shared by prominent Charlestonians. He acknowledges, for instance, that "the greatest Part of the Knowledge I have acquired relating to this Province" was received from two local informants, including "a Gentleman here, who was descended from a French Refugee of some Rank; a Person blessed with a liberal Education, and as liberal Principles; clear Perceptions, and a sound Judgment; who had read both Men and Books, enjoyed an excellent Memory, and possessed an extraordinary Share of Affability and Humanity." Through this acquaintance, he explains, he was introduced to yet another informant, "a Planter" who "had been in the Commission of the Peace, as well as in divers parochial Offices." This latter individual, in fact, is the person who apparently encouraged the "Stranger" to find out for himself the extent of the lawlessness that he believed characterized black behavior in Charleston: "The horrid Vice of Blaspheming," and the "equally abandoned, and unrestrained . . . Gaming, Drunkenness and all Manner of Lewdness." The "Stranger," his informant advised him, was well placed to make such an investigation. He was "known to few," he was told, and thus he could "with great Facility and Success, by either disguising [himself] in the habit of a common Sailor, or putting on the Appearance of Indigence and Distress," easily meander about "the Town on Sundays, early and late." He could thereby observe how lax enforcement of the colony's laws regarding the behavior of blacks in Charleston had become, owing largely, according to the "Stranger's" informant, to the collusion, indifference, or incompetence of local constables.

Responding to his friend's challenge, the "Stranger" disguised himself "at Four different Times, the last in the Easter Holidays," and sought to observe black life in Charleston from a vantage point presumably unavailable to other local whites, especially those who were neither indigent nor sailors. Yet reading the "Stranger's" report, or the *Gazette* more generally over an extended period of time, it is hard to determine precisely who would have been unaware of what he found. Certainly not his informants nor the whites accused of being in collusion with many of the offending blacks, or those who wrote the laws the "Stranger" was concerned to have more rigorously enforced, or those who read the presentments of the grand jury that were published periodically in the *Gazette* and that frequently pointed out and lamented the same sorts of behavior that the "Stranger" reports, albeit in far less detail.

Few in other words were unaware of what blacks were up to, and some at least were incensed enough to call for reform. What the "Stranger" did not apparently recognize "was that maintenance of the system may have depended partly on its looseness."[12] Indeed, unless one was indigent, in distress, or a sailor (or a stranger capable of disguising himself so as to gain a closer view of things), it was not easy to observe blacks in contexts where they did not feel themselves being observed. Moreover, as the "Stranger's" report would demonstrate, even for those individuals, those who could walk among them without arousing undue suspicion, there were limits to what they could see or overhear.

To see blacks as they saw themselves, one had to get close enough to them to hear them speak openly among themselves, without at the same time being observed by them. The "Stranger" was only partially successful in this regard. As long as they remained in public view, blacks could be easily observed by those who had an interest in them, especially if that person, like the "Stranger," disguised himself for that purpose. But what was one to do when they sought to conceal themselves? The "Stranger" was at first perplexed. By concealing himself in a deserted hut that was adjacent to their meeting place he learned that blacks had "their private committees," but their deliberations, he says, "were carried on in too low a voice, and with so much caution, as not to be overheard by the others."

Ironically, his ability to observe the meeting without being seen was unintentionally aided by "the humanity of a well-disposed grey-headed Negro man," who gave him shelter, "pitying his seeming indigence and distress."[13]

Here was a world rarely seen by nonblacks, though there are numerous references suggesting that its existence was widely suspected by slave owners. Virtually from the beginning of English settlement in the low country and before that in the British West Indies, whites had complained about the gathering together of large groups of black slaves. They complained and/or legislated against the noise they made, their music, especially their drumming, their dancing, the "babel" of languages they spoke, and the suspicion that clandestine plotting took place at such gatherings. The "Stranger's" report no doubt confirmed those suspicions for many who read the *Gazette*, but it also opened up to view a private unobserved world in which blacks appeared more fully rounded as human beings, a world, that is, in which they appeared as seeing subjects rather than ambulatory objects. Thus, the "Stranger" offered readers of the *Gazette* a view of black life in Charleston that they rarely if ever saw portrayed in public mediums, and never, when mentioned or discussed by whites who had been born in South Carolina, to the extent and from the perspective offered by the "Stranger." Everything that he reported about the public activity he witnessed had been pointed out and decried by others long before he first arrived in the colony, but no resident had ever described it in the sort of detail that he provided. That level of description, when it appears in the written record left by natives, is always fragmentary and thus disconnected in some way from any purposeful or extended effort at observation and understanding. As such, it is usually offered parenthetically, as brief asides rather than as the focus of discussion or description.

This was true not only in South Carolina but also throughout the colonial South. Whites and blacks could easily observe one another on the farms and plantations and in the small towns they inhabited, in the face-to-face world that existed, necessarily, even in a place like Charleston, which was until relatively late in the colonial era the only real town of any size and cultural and economic significance in the entire region. Not only did blacks and whites work together and in many instances live together in the same structures, the range of their social interaction in other contexts was substantial. There were few social gatherings among the elite at which blacks were not in attendance as servants, and they were always present, as were most other members of a given community, at public events such as court days or musters, at horse races or worship services. They can also be located during moments of social unrest or at political gatherings. At war and in peacetime blacks and whites from all walks of life lived and worked and died literally side by side.

Moreover, slave owners like Landon Carter, one of colonial Virginia's largest and most successful planters, could and did on occasion order the homes of his slaves searched, as when Carter had an apprentice plantation manager "search all their holes and boxes" in an effort to discover a missing butter pot. He also had access to, and assiduously cultivated, a wide range of sources of information, both black and white, regarding his slaves. Indeed, opportunities for close observation of his black dependents were numerous and routine. As a resident patriarch he saw them frequently in the various roles they played. As their taskmaster he rode out to the fields to inspect their work. As provisioneer he dispensed or oversaw the dispensing of supplies. He also functioned as a physician for his slaves, either by proxy or in person, as patron and prosecutor, as father confessor or avenging angel. There was in short nothing regarding his slaves that was beyond his concern or theoretically beyond his capacity to observe. Thus, he could write of a slave he suspected of malingering: "I am clearly of opinion he had chilled himself by lying in bed without his cloths and getting up and setting without his breeches which it seems he and his Lady too are fond of[?]"[14]

Yet only strangers, as travelers or visitors or temporary residents, wrote extensively for publication about blacks and black life. Even in their private papers, Southerners rarely offered the sort of detailed, close-up observations and descriptions of private, non-work-related aspects of black life that the "Stranger" provides in his various letters to the *Gazette*, although it is clear from their papers that slave owners like Carter saw much more than they recorded.

One measure of the disparity between how strangers represented blacks and how locals portrayed them are the incidental references scattered throughout the latter's extant records. For although it is generally through the eyes of strangers that we see the black presence as more than merely a physical one it is from the records kept by members of slave-owning communities that we gain the fullest sense of how ubiquitous their presence was. In many instances, as we have seen, and as we will continue to see as the study progresses, local record keepers could not avoid noting the presence of blacks, as for instance when slaves ran away.[15] A sense of the pervasiveness of the black presence throughout southern slave societies derives in part from those records. However, a fuller impression of the ubiquity of the black presence emerges when it is encountered on those occasions when it did not force itself onto the records. Reports of damage from natural disasters, for instance, very often make passing reference to blacks, as did Landon Carter's description of the storm that struck his mansion. Similar references occasionally also appear in descriptions of public events.

Indeed, a Hogarthian sense of the presence of blacks in colonial society can be gleaned from references to them that are incidental to the primary focus of surviving records, and also from observations of unusual or bizarre occurrences.[16] We learn, for instance, in a notice forbidding the public from making use of land owned by the advertiser, that the plantation he lived on "has been for many years unoccupied and left open, and thereby become a haunt for several persons to make use of it as a landing place from the river, their negroes waiting for many days together with their horses."[17]

A few years earlier in the same paper, in a letter to the editor, a complaint "By a Lady" is made of the "Gentlemen who last Muster day delivered their Fire Arms to Negroes to carry home (and which they charged and discharged several times as they went along the Streets, to the great Terror of many Ladies)."[18] Other references give us brief glimpses of the quotidian presence of blacks, similar to those found in some of Henry Latrobe's sketches of life in the early national South. Latrobe, an architect and engineer, began an extended visit to America in 1795.[19] Distinctive in Latrobe's drawings is the occasional, matter-of-fact appearance of black figures. They are not often featured as primary subjects, but rather are situated where they would be expected to be seen in a mature slave society, throughout the landscape, as boatmen on the river, women plowing while being observed by a perched white overseer, wagoners and servants, etc. Indeed, their presence defines the landscape more definitively than any of its other features. It alerts and orients us to the geographic and historic particularity of the worlds conveyed in Latrobe's drawings. There are other clues, but none so dramatic and centering as the presence of black people: the two black watermen steering a small canoe through rapids in the James River; the three other boatmen navigating the more turgid rapids on the same river; "Nelly" Custis and Martha Washington with child and black servant in attendance; or the black wagoners struggling up a difficult incline framed by a spectacular rainbow.[20]

In incidental references to blacks appearing in newspapers and other records, both public and private, we gain a semblance of the presence evoked in Latrobe's drawings when, for instance, reference is made to place names that identify a black presence. A sampling of such references include the following: "Negro Head Point," "mulatto alley," "Guinea bridge," "Guinea creek," "Negroe-Creek," "Guinea road," "Cuffee Town-Creek," "Negro Ground," "Negro Hammocks."[21]

More often a Latrobe-like or Hogarthian sense of presence is found in reports of disasters such as fires, epidemics, storms, or accidents of various sorts. The following is unusual in terms of what it describes but typical of the type of reference to be found in reports of local calamities: "There had like to have been a Number of broken Limbs last Sunday fe'n-night at the lower Church in Lunenburg Parish, Richmond County, by some Part of the Gallery where the Negroes sit giving Way." The alarmed congregation, the report continues, "made the best of their Way out. Many were violently squeezed, some fell down and were trod upon, particularly a poor Negro Woman big with Child, who was so much hurt that her Life is despaired of. A Negro Man likewise had his Legs much torn and bruised."[22]

Even more unusual, but again typical of one of the most frequent incidental ways in which blacks appear in surviving local records, is the following report from Camden, South Carolina. "A few days ago," it begins, "as a negro fellow of Mr. Chesnut's was driving one of his master's oxen from one plantation to another, and passing through the town, it ran at a child that was sitting by the door of Robert Tulloch, and gored it very much." When this happened, the newspaper account explains, "[t]he grand-mother, (Mrs. Tolloch) ran to the door to drive away the animal; [but] the ox immediately pitched at her into the house, and with his horns crushed her against the floor, and for some time continued goring and tossing her in the house." Meanwhile, the black man "dismounted [from the cart he was driving], snatched up an axe, with which he ran into the house, knocked the ox down, killed him on the spot, and saved the woman's life."[23]

Naturally reports of destruction caused by fires that make reference to blacks are much more commonplace than accounts of dramatic ox-killings in surviving records. Most often the references are to their involvement in causing (or culpability in starting) the fire, or to their efforts to help (or reluctance to help) put it out, or to their death or injury as a result of the fire. Also, generally, the reference locates slaves on their master's property, where we would expect to find them. For that reason the following is relatively unusual in that it apparently gives us, albeit tragically, a look at a black family in their own home: "Friday Night Last, a small House about seven miles from Town [Annapolis], where one Mulatto Betty liv'd, which had a Wooden Chimney, took Fire while she was from home, and was burnt down, and seven black Children which were asleep in it, all burnt to Death, the eldest of them about 9 Years of Age."[24]

Reports of accidents are frequently boating related. For example the following report locates "10 Negroes" on a boat that sunk "North of New-River in North-Carolina" when it came to anchor with "the Breakers running very high." On board with them was "John Abbot, of Little River in Craven County . . . , with his wife, Child, [and] a Blacksmith with his Daughter and 10 Negroes." The white passengers carried with them "several Goods and Effects [including the 10 black slaves], in order to go off this Province, and to defraud his Creditors." When the boat "fill'd" Abbot's "Wife, Child, the white Man, his Daughter and 6 Negroes were drowned; the other 4 Negroes were seized, and he left to make his Escape by himself."[25]

Much less often reports like the following one appeared in local newspapers, no doubt because they were more commonplace and much less dramatic: "On Friday last, as Mr. David Dott, a young man, a carpenter of this city, was shingling a house, the scaffold gave way, by which means he fell to the ground, broke his neck and expired immediately.—Two negroes, who were on the house, likewise fell, but are not dead—their lives are despaired of."[26]

Damage from lightning like that described by Landon Carter on April 17, 1773, was frequently reported. The following account reflects the pattern represented by Carter's report, except that the black woman who is reported to have been struck by lightning is not identified in relation to her owner or, assuming she was free, to her status. "By a gentleman from Dumfries we learn, that on Tuesday fe'nnight there happened some very severe thunder and lightning, which struck a ship lying at the mouth of Quantico, and shivered her foremast to pieces, but fortunately killed some of the crew; a negro woman who happened to be at some small distance from the ship was killed dead on the spot."[27]

By contrast, the black victim mentioned in the following account is clearly identified as to who his master was. The situation in which he is found rather than how he was identified is its unusual characteristic A brief newspaper account explains that while "people were assembling in the church at Sunbury to hear the examination of the scholars of the Academy, the building was struck by lightning, which entering the church killed two young men, named Cubbage and Cole, and a valuable negro man belonging to Capt. Peacock, named Peter."[28]

We learn very little about Peter from this report, as is generally the case regarding the blacks that are represented in such reports. Their appearance in the accounts we have been sampling captures our attention because the context in which we encounter them is, to use a familiar journalistic term, of human interest (rather than for its news value alone). In other surviving records, except when seen through the eyes of strangers, blacks are encountered in contexts that encourages or reflects their objectification. The humanizing effect of their appearance in reports of accidents and other catastrophes is generally minimal at best, as in the case of the unnamed woman who was struck by lightning. However, in a scattering of other disaster or odd-occurrence reports, we are able to gain a slightly fuller sense of the person. For example, severe flooding in the Richmond area in 1771 generated a lengthy report of the devastation wrought by the flood. In the middle of the account we are unexpectedly introduced to "Old Joe, an honest and well known negro Fellow at the Falls of James River, who is intimately acquainted with the Remains of an Indian Nation that has resided there for Ages." Joe, according to this report, said that "he was shown by their old Men the Marks of the greatest Fresh [flood] handed down to them by Tradition, and that upon his carefully measuring, it wanted near fifteen Feet of the late dreadful One."[29]

Encountering an individual like "Old Joe" in records other than those

that were intended or expected to keep track of blacks for the slave owning community is rare, but not singular. Indeed, given the nature of the
event that was the occasion for the report that introduced him to us, his
presence in the report seems eminently logical and thus in some sense un-
exceptional. It is much more surprising to see blacks as they are portrayed
in *The Old Plantation* or as the "Stranger" saw them in their secret meeting
place, in records kept by members of local slave owning communities.
Nowhere, as has been suggested earlier, is the contrast between what
strangers tell us about the presence of blacks in the colonial South and
what local residents recorded about them more striking than in the
sources of our knowledge about the slaves' expressive culture.[30]

Recall, for example, the contrast that was made earlier between Robert
Carter and Philip Vickers Fithian, as well as the one that was suggested
between Jefferson and his brother, Randolph, and his daughter, Martha.
In Randolph's case we know about his interest in the slaves' music not
from the younger Jefferson himself but from one of Thomas Jefferson's
slaves, Isaac Jefferson, who recalled in his memoirs of life at Monticello,
"Old Master's brother, Mass Randall used to come out among black people; play the fiddle and dance half the night."[31]

We know even more about Jefferson's eldest daughter's interest in the
expressive lives of blacks but again only indirectly, not, that is, because
she left a record of her own, but because in 1841 a man named Eugène A.
Vail published a book (*De la littérature et des hommes de lettres des États-Unis
d'Amérique*) in Paris "in which he included Martha's songs and tales. Most
of them," according to historian Elizabeth Langhorne, "came directly
from Monticello." Their source, according to Langhorne, was "Mammy
Ursula, who had nursed Martha and then Martha's children."[32]

As valuable as it is, Martha Jefferson's remembered African American
folklore represents an extremely modest collection, dimmed considerably
by time, and is notable only because so little else has been left to us from
the colonial era about the songs slaves sang and the stories they told
themselves. In that sense perhaps it is appropriate that the "most remarkable evidence of the vigorous music and storytelling tradition in the Monticello quarters survives because of an interested foreigner."[33] That the
same could be said more generally about evidence of the expressive life of
blacks who survived enslavement throughout the colonial South is accen-
tuated by the following extremely rare glimpse of a vital part of that life

that has come down to us in the form of a thumbnail account of yet another lightning storm: "A Negro Quarter of [unclear] Lee's, near Goose Creek, was lately struck by lightning, by which two negroes were killed, and 6 or 7 wounded; one of the wounded has after died. They had assembled for the purpose of prayer, and were singing hymns at the time of this awful visitation!"[34]

PART 2

THE TURNING

"HE IS FAST, HE CAN'T GO."

$\mathbf{L}$ate in the eighteenth century, at a ferry crossing on the Tar River in North Carolina, William Attmore, a Philadelphia merchant who had come "to North Carolina to collect debts owing to his firm and to obtain new business," engaged in conversation with the "two Negroes" who rowed him across the river. "Being fond of remarking upon the tempers of Men and upon human Nature in general," Attmore explains in his journal," ... I thought proper to interrogate Polydore[,] one of the [two] Negroes ... , in respect to his condition."[1]

The brief interrogation, which is presented with no further comment, begins with the following question: "Where was you born, boy?"[2] Polydore responded, "I was born in Guinea." Attmore then asked, "Don't you want to go back to your country?" Polydore's fellow slave answered first, "He is fast, he can't go." Polydore then elaborated, "I have learnt another language now, they will kill me if I go back to my home."

Apparently, for Attmore, that was a satisfactory or self-explanatory answer, because he then asked, "How came you brought from yr. Country?" Polydore explained that he had gone "with many more to attack a town, where they were too strong for us, they killed a great many, and took 140 of us prisoners, and sold us." "Had you not better have let them alone and remained in peace at home?" Attmore wanted to know. "No," Polydore responded, "My Nation always fight that Nation." "And what would you do," Attmore asked, "if you return'd to your Country now, wou'd you be quiet?" "I go there," Polydore said, "and fight 'em worse than ever."

Shortly thereafter, just as the sun was setting, they reached Attmore's destination on the other side of the river. He gave the "two ragged Ferrymen a small present, for which they were thankful—and Galloped up the Shore to [his] former Quarters."[3]

Polydore's responses to Attmore's interrogation are important here for what they allow us to imagine or infer rather than for what they actually tell us about the issue of interest to this section of the study. Especially intriguing is his explanation of why he would not go home if that were possible. His answer leaves us wondering, puzzling over apparent contradictions not only in his reply to that particular question but in other information he related in response to other queries from Attmore. Why, for instance, would learning a new language serve to inhibit his return? Had he forgotten how to speak his native language? Or (and this is the possibility of interest here) had his enslavement, requiring as it did the learning of a new language (and with it a new framework for self-awareness), changed him in some fundamental way, an alteration that he did not think he could disguise, cast off, or explain away?

This chapter makes an effort to explore the perspective-altering nature of enslavement for blacks in the colonial South, using one particular category of sources as a focus for the exploration. It focuses on the relationship of self-awareness (consciousness-of-self) to the experience of enslavement. It is premised on the assumption that, at some point in the process, a shift in the meaning of survival—in the framework of self-reference and awareness—was necessary. Polydore's cryptic answer to Attmore's question—cryptic because it was left unexplained and thus unexplored—is not clear or full enough to carry the weight of such an assumption, but its expressed concerns are sufficient to point us toward other responses that when considered collectively are much weightier.

Slave narrators were of two minds regarding the possibility of returning to their homelands. One group, made up of those who had been converted to Christianity, was disinclined to return unless they could do so as missionaries. The reverse was true for the majority of Muslim narrators.

For them, returning home would have been morally and spiritually restorative rather than corrupting.[4]

Polydore stands out from these narrators because he apparently does not fit neatly into either camp. He seems, by comparison, notably conflicted, thereby suggesting the dilemma-inducing nature of forced acculturation. What seems suppressed, unspoken, or hidden beneath the surface in slave narratives by African-born narrators is more apparent in Attmore's description of their conversation.

Of course, the slave owners who hosted Attmore during his tour of North Carolina and who indulged his cautiously stated reservations about slavery (concerns that seem to have had more to do with the institution's current and potential impact on society than on the slaves) would not have been inclined to ask Polydore if he wanted to go home. Moreover, if, out of curiosity, some of them did question their recently imported slaves (Byrd, for instance, who often noted in his diary, without further explanation or elaboration, that he had visited his "people"), none left a record of that fact. They did, however, have frequent occasion to distinguish between slaves like Polydore and those who had not yet attained his level of adjustment and reconciliation to his enslavement.

To them, he had become a "sensible Negro," as distinct from an unassimilated "new Negro," by virtue of having learned the language necessary for his enslavement, that is, the language he needed in order to understand what was expected and required of him and to respond accordingly. The ability to engage a literate white man or woman in conversation, rather than merely responding to his or her commands, would have marked him as admirably, if not exceptionally, "sensible" in their eyes. Whether they would have been surprised by his answers to Attmore's questions is less certain, but from what we know about their judgments of "sensible Negroes," it is unlikely that they would have been. Such slaves, they knew, did not run away for the same reasons as did unassimilated or unseasoned slaves. "Sensible Negroes" ran for "sensible" reasons—that is, "sensible Negroes" reasoned, using terms of reference that were intelligible to the slave owning community. Freedom for such slaves meant returning not to their homes in Africa, but rather to a previous home in the colony in search of friends and family, or to some more distant or remote area (possibly even outside the colony) where they could "pass for free." By contrast, recently arrived "new Negroes" frequently could not be reasoned with. Although slave owners understood their desire to return to their homes, their determination to do so, to defy all logic to do so, identified them for slave owners as not being fit for slavery, in much the same sense that Indians native to the colonized region they were enslaved in had proved unfit. Until acclimated to the inescapable nature of their enslavement, they could not be reasoned with as slaves.

Punishments, reprimands, or corrections that would have evoked a number of possible and predictable responses from "sensible Negroes" could trigger extreme and unexpected responses from unacclimated "new Negroes." This was especially apparent when "new Negroes" committed suicide. The observer of the following incident, for instance, was at a loss to explain its sudden and decisive nature. "A few Days ago," according to the brief report that appeared in a local news section of a mid-eighteenth-century newspaper, "a fine Negroe Man Slave, imported in one of the late Ships from Africa, belonging to a Wheelwright, near this City, taking Notice of his master's giving another Correction for a Misdemeaner, went to a Grindstone and making a Knife sharp cut his own Throat, and died on the Spot."[5] That he was a recently imported captive, and that he had cut his throat shortly after witnessing his owner correct another slave for what was to the observer a minor offense, expressed the limits of the observer's capacity to understand the action of a fellow human being not recognized as such by those who had enslaved him, and a failure of the observer's imagination when confronted by an alien perspective.

Though much too vague to read with any certainty, an overseer's report of another suicide in Virginia, much earlier in the eighteenth century, suggests the problems of understanding that "new Negroes" posed for those whose job it was to fit them for slavery. The report involves a slave who was found hanging in a tobacco-curing barn and was thought to have killed himself because he had not been allowed "to keep other mens wives" in addition to his own. In making this explanation to his owner, however, the overseer also reported that he had ordered that the man's head be cut off "and Stuck on a pole to be a terror to others." What would have been the terror imparted to others? Would it have been the realization that the slave's suicide had not resulted in his physical transmigration to Africa? Even if slave owners believed, as many apparently did, that their slaves' belief in transmigration was limited to the physical body, why would that belief be relevant in this case, if the cause of his death was understood by blacks in the area in the way that the overseer explained it to his employer? Decapitation and public display in this case make sense only if the overseer interpreted the slave's suicide as an act of defiance and if he assumed other slaves would also read it in that way.

In his letter to his employer, the overseer characterized the slave's behavior as petulant and entirely indefensible by any moral standard, an extreme and irrational response to his not being able to have his way. If, however, the slave was as immoral and self-interested as he was described, why would he have committed suicide? "Sensible" slaves were skilled at finding ways around an overseer's rules. Indeed, that is one reason why the word "sensible" was most often used in conjunction with the words "cunning and devious." And why, if the slave had acted out of pique, would the overseer be concerned to point this out to the slaves who knew him? Could it have been that the overseer knew or suspected that other slaves did not read the suicide in that way, seeing it instead as a matter of honor? Had the slave committed suicide because he experienced his overseer's prohibition as a shaming act intended to dishonor him?[6]

Most slave owners and overseers, however, understood that until they had been fully seasoned, "new Negroes" were prone to behave in unexpected ways. Some would commit suicide for reasons owners could explain only by reference to their own ways of thinking; others would try desperately to return home. "King" Carter's matter-of-fact juxtaposition of entries announcing the arrival of a slave ship just offshore from his estate and noting that seven of his "new Negroes" had run away is suggestive of the generally held expectation that flight was the first instinct of recently arrived captive Africans. Carter's response is also indicative of that understanding; he notes on July 15 that a ship arrived with 140 blacks and then on July 17 that "7 of my new Negroes" ran away in a canoe that belonged to another slave of his.[7] It appears to have been taken for granted within the slave-owning community that a certain level of loss was to be expected during this critical early stage of the enslavement process. Some captives would inevitably die or be killed, whether from disease, from suicide, from running away, or from being killed by others while they were runaways.

Polydore's responses to Attmore's questions regarding his desire to return home are very telling when viewed against the behavior of those not yet fully reconciled to their enslavement. Seasoned slaves calculated their behavior: weighed and considered its consequences and/or how it would be perceived from the perspective required to come to terms with their enslavement. In doing so, they reflected an irrevocable change in the persons they had once been, the persons slave owners called "new Negroes." Part of what makes Polydore's answers to Attmore's questions so intriguing, and so inviting as a source of speculation, is that they suggest a consciousness on his part of that change in himself.

Polydore's response would have distinguished him in another, related sense. Only for recently arrived captives from Africa was the hope of returning home an active and pressing concern, and for them it remained so apparently only for a relatively short period. For an indeterminate, though clearly significant, number of captives, we know from runaway ads that the desire to return home remained a powerful compulsion until they reached that stage in their adjustment to slavery that Polydore has served to illustrate. "Sensible new Negroes" would not have attempted to return home, even if they still desired to do so, as many undoubtedly did. Acting on such a desire would mean that they had not been fully acclimated. The impracticality of the desire had not yet sunk in.

The following ad, though unique in its details, gives a sense of the extent of the compulsion to return to Africa, a sense that is missing from other less dramatic references: "TAKEN up on the high Seas, the 26th of September, 1758 [on] . . . an uninhabited Sand Island bearing S. by W. . . . a short well-set *Angola* Negro Man, branded on one Shoulder T. W. He was lying in a small Canoe, half full of Water, in a wretched helpless Condition, having a very deep Wound on the hind Part of his Neck, and another on his right Hand; and that the Loss of Blood, Fatigue, and Fasting, was [unclear] and insensible, and continued so for some time after he was taken up."[8]

More often, ads merely noted that a fugitive was attempting to return home. They were "supposed to have gone an East course as long as they could, thinking to return to their own country that way." Or they had been captured trying to do so: May, "A NEW negro[,] . . . was paddling in a canoe when taken up, and by what they could understand from him, his intention was to return to his own country."⁹ There are only a scattering of such ads in surviving newspapers, but none of them gives the impression that such efforts were viewed as unusual. By contrast, a large number of ads that make reference to recently imported, runaway "new Negroes" are understandably silent as to where they were expected to run, and why, a silence that distinguishes such ads from most others. "Sensible new Negroes" had developed connections and patterns of behavior, an experiential history and an awareness of the possibilities available to them that made it possible for slave owners to speculate about where they might have gone and why.

Because they were "new" to the colonies, the behavior of "new Negroes" was much harder to predict. Such slaves might try to return home, but having no real idea where they were, they found it impossible to know which way to go. Moreover, they were much more likely than were "sensible Negroes" to run away impulsively with no clear idea of where they were going.

For "sensible Negroes," however, flight was most often premeditated and tied to a specific motivation and expectation. For instance, if they had been recently sold, which was often the occasion or triggering event for running away, it was highly likely that they would seek to return to the area and the people they were familiar with, especially if they had left behind family or friends. Such attachments anchored them, in much the same way as "thinking sensibly" did.

At one point in their enslavement, from all that we know of slaves' behavior, returning home, however daunting the prospect, did not seem entirely impractical, or its impracticality was overridden by the impulse to try. At another point, however strong the desire may have remained, the obstacles and risks involved became so clear to them that the idea no longer occurred as a meaningful option. Unlike "native Africans," according to slave narrator Charles Ball, who was born a slave in Maryland around the time of the American Revolution and who experienced slavery in virtually all of the original Southern states (those, that is, that had been former British colonies) before obtaining his freedom by running away, "the American negro[s]" "discontent works out for itself other schemes, than those which agitate the brain of the imported negro. His heart pants for no heaven beyond the waves of the ocean."[10] For "sensible new Negroes," however, the issue ceased to be purely a matter of whether they wanted to return. Returning was not something that they, as successful survivors, could realistically contemplate.

Undergirding their new realism was the emergence of a new way of reasoning, a Copernican turn in perspective and thus a new basis for calculating (weighing and considering) their actions or expressed intentions from the reoriented perspective required to come to terms with their enslavement. In time, they came to share in the meanings of those who had enslaved them (to be able to reason as they did). Once turned—that is, once they had become 'sensible'—seasoned captives sometimes made fun of "new Negroes." They ridiculed or played practical jokes on them. More often, however, according to the runaway ads, they sympathized with, or shared in, the "new Negro's" efforts to escape. Even into the twentieth century, former slaves—often many generations removed from their nearest African ancestor—continued to admire the African's tenacious effort to maintain an independent sense of self, to admire, that is, the thing about the African that slave owners feared most.

Not surprisingly discriminating between those who had been turned and those who had not was extremely important to the slave-owning community and an essential part of the enslavement process. How this was done, however, is not apparent, in any obvious sense, in surviving records. But when the runaway ads, for instance, are read closely (and repeatedly) the vocabulary used for that purpose becomes clear.

The term "new Negro" was of limited use in that regard. It was used most often as a generic term to identify both newly arrived captives and fully "seasoned" slaves (although most often for the former purpose). It was in that sense a synonym for African-born. The more seasoned a captive became, the less often the term was used, although the pattern was not consistent. Therefore, terms other than "new Negro" were needed to discriminate among the large number of captive Africans who lived in the colonial South, an extremely diverse group, who, as we have seen, could range in their degree of acculturation from the "unintelligible," to borrow a word from one of the ads, to the recognizably "sensible."

The word *sensible* was in fact often used for that purpose. But *sensible* was more often used to identify "country born" or Creole blacks than it was to identify acculturated "new Negroes," thereby to an extent serving as the reverse of African-born. However slave owners must have shared a common store of assumptions about what "new Negro" and "sensible" meant, unless otherwise modified. If that was not the case, the inclusion of those terms in ads that offered few other details would have been of limited use in distinguishing fugitives for the purpose of recapture.

In newspapers published in the low country—that is, in that part of the coastal plain devoted primarily to the production of rice, stretching roughly between the Cape Fear River in colonial North Carolina and the St. Johns River in East Florida—relatively detailed and unambiguous descriptions were offered for most "new Negroes." The term was generally modified in ways that made clear the individual's inferred stage of adjustment. Elsewhere a variety of terms other than "new Negro" were sometimes used—"salt water" or "granddywater" slaves, for instance. But like "new Negro" they merely indicated that the person so labeled had been born in Africa.

The term "outlandish," however, which was used most often in the upper South (Virginia and Maryland, primarily, but also in parts of North Carolina),[11] frequently carried with it a meaning that, unlike "new Negro," would have distinguished Polydore as "sensible." If understood in that way, "sensible" would have meant the opposite of "outlandish" and thus both terms could have been used to qualify "new Negro." This seems likely even though "outlandish" was sometimes used synonymously in place of "new Negro." More often it carried the added inference that the person so identified had not yet become fully acclimated to his or her surroundings or condition. "New Negroes" who survived their enslavement became by virtue of their survival "sensible." Thus, we often encounter individuals who were identified as "new Negroes" and who were also described as being "sensible" or more typically as having skills or other attributes that were understood to be the mark of a "sensible" slave. When the latter was the case with those identified as "outlandish," the term "outlandish" was used as a synonym for "new Negro." In many cases, however, this is not clear because "outlandish" was used in lieu of any other description.

Also, in the low country, where for a longer period during the colonial era the black population comprised a greater percentage of African-born slaves than was true of colonies surrounding the Chesapeake Bay, advertisers developed a greater capacity to discriminate among newly imported "new Negroes." They did so by specifying the ethnicity of newly imported slaves from Africa and describing them in greater physical detail than was characteristic in the upper South, where the term "outlandish" generalized for slave owners in that region what was more fully described or particularized in low country colonies. In those colonies, a description of a fugitive would typically identify him or her as a "new Negro" from a specific "country" (e.g., "Ebo" or "Guinny" or "Jalunka") followed by a description of physical characteristics, including "country marks" (native scarification). This pattern was also followed in the Chesapeake but not as routinely as in the low country. In the upper South the "country" of the "new Negro" was rarely given in ads, whereas it was typical of references in the low country. In the Chesapeake, "outlandish" would often be used without elaboration as a label denoting those characteristics that were more often described in the low country.

Gerald Mullin, who was the first scholar to systematically survey runaway ads printed in newspapers published in eighteenth-century Virginia, indicates that "outlandish" referred to "native African slaves" who "were strangers to the English language and seldom trained as artisans. . . . Thus they were usually purchased by smaller planters from the large slaveowners, who were slave traders as well as retailers and manufacturers." At the most general level of discrimination, according to Mullin, "there were only two kinds of blacks: those who were 'outlandish'—born in Africa—and those born in America."[12]

But for some, and probably for a majority of advertisers, the term "outlandish" did more than identify a point of origin or linguistic capacity. It embodied, as did "new Negro" and other similar terms, a range of opinions and attitudes held by the slave owning community relative to Africans. Though rarely stated as clearly, the core distinction expressed in the following ad appears to have been understood and shared by most advertisers to one degree or another. According to the advertiser, whereas "Bob [was] . . . a Ferryman for many Years, and from his Ac-

quaintance with Gentlemen has assumed an immoderate Stock of Assur-
ance . . . Bristol [was] an outlandish Fellow . . . and . . . as ignorant as the
other is artful."[13]

A similar distinction is offered in depositions taken for a late-eighteenth-
century court case in North Carolina. The case involved a dispute among
deponents over a black slave. One of the parties argued "that a certain
Negro Woman Named Hagar . . . had as Much Sense as is common for
New Negrows to have and that said Negro Was Never counted Silly,"
whereas another deponent said that, while he had known many "new
Negroes," he had never known a Negro as dumb as she. The woman had
not sense to know where she was raised, or where she came from, or
whom she belonged to before her last owner claimed her. Moreover, this
deponent asserted, she did not appear to have any more shame in her
than a brute.[14]

However severe or, conversely, open-minded an individual slave
owner's judgment of blacks from Africa may have been, all agreed that in
order to be productive, captive Africans had to be made "sensible." Thus
the difference of opinion in the quoted deposition relative to their innate
intellectual and moral capacities is somewhat misleading. For the diver-
gence of opinion among slave owners, assuming there was a substantive
one, was not about the moral or intellectual capacity of Africans, but
rather about the degree of their incapacity. This distinction no doubt
would have had little meaning for most blacks, but undoubtedly it was
important to some slave owners and to the slaves who benefited from
concerns for their moral uplift or more humane treatment. Nevertheless,
whether slaves were considered ignorant and brutish or less radically dis-
advantaged, all agreed that there was a very definite limit to the human
potential of black Africans and their descendants. For slave owners advertising for runaway slaves, as for those few who commented on the morality of the institution itself, the intelligence and moral character of "new
Negroes," and of Negroes more generally, was measured on a scale of incapacity, rather than on one that comprehended a full range of human
possibility.

On the one hand most ads describe "sensible" slaves as rogues who
were cunning and devious and therefore not to be trusted under any conceivable circumstance. The assumption behind this elaboration of the
term appears to be that blacks were inherently flawed such that when

overly acculturated they were prone toward antisocial or immoral behavior. A smaller number of ads employ modifying adjectives such as tractable, submissive, honest, civil, and the like to describe those "sensible" slaves for whom the edifying intent of enslavement as an acculturating (and thus as a civilizing) process had presumably succeeded. Indeed, it is not unusual, but also not typical, to find a fugitive described in very positive terms. Peter, for instance, had "from his Infancy, been a waiting-Man, and drives a Chair very well, has a smiling Countenance, and very complaisant . . . is a good Plantation Waggoner, careful of his Master's Horses, as a waiting Man, and very honest." Such was his character, the advertiser says, that "I can assign no Reason for his running away, but quarreling with his Wife."[15] If ads of this sort are to be believed, these slaves, unlike the majority of runaways who were invariably characterized as being inherently cunning and devious, recognized their limitation and made the best use possible of their acculturation. The majority of the ads, however, offer a very different opinion of "sensible Negroes," something which should not be surprising given their nature and objective.

In plantation records, with the exception of Landon Carter's, characterizations of the sort that appear in runaway ads are infrequent. Most surviving plantation records were kept by planters who owned large numbers of slaves and referred to only a small number of them in more than passing ways. When those planters advertised for runaway slaves, however, they used the same typology. Jefferson, for instance, in the only ad by him to appear in surviving issues of the *Virginia Gazette*, itemizes the skills his "Mulatto slave called Sandy" possessed, the clearest symbol, along with language proficiency, of how "sensible" a slave was considered. Yet Jefferson then notes that "[Sandy] is greatly addicted to drink, and when drunk is insolent and disorderly," and that "in his conversation he swears much, and in his behaviour is artful and knavish."[16]

Like the quality "sensible," the love of "drink" strained or symbolized the inherently limited capacity of blacks to moderate their behavior. Along with other roguish behavior, becoming drunk was what happened when blacks were confronted with their innate limitations. Becoming "sensible" represented just such a confrontation. When drunk, as when they became "sensible," slaves confirmed for many slave owners the deficiency that required their enslavement. "Sensible" in that way marked the limit beyond which black incapacity could not be ameliorated. At base this was the justification that governed thinking about the morality of slavery in the colonial South. Slave owners, as well as clergymen, differed over whether, given the innate incapacity of blacks, anything more could be done for them beyond restraining their baser instincts by means of their enslavement.

For some slave owners like Landon Carter, no matter what tack one took in managing black slaves, they lacked the capacity for "virtue," a term that embodied the highest aspirations of the planter elite and was used by them as a measure of their own self-worth as well as that of others. Those who lacked the capacity for virtue could never be considered the equals of those who possessed it. However, for other members of the planter elite, like Landon's nephew Robert Carter, there was a direct correlation between the type of management used and the way slaves behaved, an attitude that allowed the younger Carter, after becoming a fervent Baptist, to consider a black man his "brother."

George Washington leaned toward the younger Carter's view, as did Henry Laurens. Like Jefferson, Washington wrote only one ad for runaway slaves, but in the one he did write Washington managed in his typically concise way to capture the essence of what it meant (in his view) to become a "sensible Negro" in the colonial South. Though quite lengthy, the ad is compact in terms of the information it includes.

Washington identifies four runaways from his *"Dogue-Run in Fairfax"*—Peros, Jack, Neptune, and Cupid—and devotes a paragraph of description to each of them. Indeed, the ad's composition could serve as a model of the genre. Peros, the first named of the four, for example, is described as, "35 or 40 Years of Age, a well-set Fellow, of about 5 feet 8 Inches high, yellowish Complexion, with a very full round Face, and full black Beard, his Speech is something slow and broken, but not in so great a Degree as to render him remarkable. He had on when he went away, a dark colour'd Cloth Coat, a white Linen Waistcoat, white Breeches and white Stockings." After describing the three other escaped slaves, Washington then distinguishes between them: "The two last of these Negroes [Neptune and Cupid] were bought from on *African* Ship in *August* 1759, and talk very broken and unintelligible *English,* the second one, Jack, is Countryman to those, and speaks pretty good English, having been several years in the Country. The other, Peros, speaks much better than either, indeed has little of his Country Dialect left, and is esteemed a sensible judicious Negro."[17]

Washington then notes that because he was unable to determine why these slaves had run away, "'tis supposed they will hardly lurk about in the Neighbourhood, but steer some direct Course (which cannot even be guessed at) in Hopes of an Escape." However, the two who had been in the "Country" the longest, Jack and Peros, might conceivably attempt to return to the areas they were most familiar with. In Peros's case that would have been "about *Williamsburg*, and *King William County*," and for Jack it was "*Middlesex*" County. To have done so would have been characteristic of the majority of "sensible Negroes" who ran away, especially those who had established families and friendships in a particular area. The other two fugitives, by contrast, fit the description, or lack thereof, of "new Negroes," who were classified as "outlandish" because they spoke "unintelligible *English*" and because they had run away with Peros and Jack. These factors, as well as the unexplained nature of their flight, made it difficult to predict where they might be headed. Alone or together, the behavior of either Jack or Peros could have been reasonably anticipated. But because of their association with two "outlandish" slaves, and especially considering that Jack was a "Countryman" of theirs, it was difficult for Washington to determine to what extent Peros and Jack remained residually "outlandish." Had they run away individually or together, Jack or Peros could have been expected to try and return to those places most familiar to them and where they were most likely to find support from friends and family, "relations" as advertisers often termed them. 'Sensible Negroes' were intelligible and, hopefully, judicious, just the opposite of "outlandish New Negroes."

For "new Negroes," the quality of being "sensible" was an acquired characteristic, and one generally involving a period of indoctrination, whereas for "country born" or Creole blacks, like Jefferson's Sandy, the quality of being "sensible" was by comparison inherited in that they were born into a tradition (and a condition) they could not escape. The outcome, however, was generally the same. Once an "outlandish" slave became "sensible," he or she became as a consequence very similar to "country born Negroes."

Whether one was born to it or gained it by inheritance, a "judicious" nature was, from a slave owner's perspective, the ideal outcome of the enslavement process. It not only made slaves productive and predictable (that is, of course, in the eyes of slave owners) but raised them to an awareness or acceptance of their innate limitations. That so many blacks in this view became "devious and cunning" instead of "judicious" in their behavior and thought was proof of their inherent incapacity. However, in purely practical terms, "devious and cunning" slaves, no matter how frustrating and infuriating they might become to planters (and they seemed at times capable of pushing Landon Carter to the very edge), were infinitely more useful to slave owners than were "outlandish" captives, and there was always the hope that they could eventually be reformed. For the slave owning community, reform meant a recognition by "sensible" slaves of their innate limitations as human beings, or, at a minimum, an accommodation by them to their condition and an appreciation of the opportunity enslavement had afforded them.

For instance, throughout most of his voluminous diary Landon Carter consistently questions the character and honesty of his slaves, including Jack Lubbar. He even laments having "suffered him [Lubbar] to follow his own will" as a reward after a lifetime of service. However, ten years later, thinking that Lubbar is about to die, Carter eulogizes him as a person deserving his respect: "Farewell to as honest a human creature as could live; Who to his last proved a faithful and a Profitable servant to his Master as every remembered Conduct must testify." As generous and thoughtful as this gesture was, no other benediction of that sort was offered by Carter for any other of his slaves. More typical is his assessment of Lubbar eight years earlier: "Jack Lubbar is a most lazy as well as stupid old fellow grown. All is my own fault to think a drunkard could be reclaimed, or a negroe honest enough to carry on any business long enough for more than one year." "A negroe," Carter exclaims a few days earlier (with Lubbar in mind), "can't be honest." Lubbar was a "Profitable servant," just as Nassau had been, before falling "into a most abandoned state of drunkenness."[18] Though they may have been cunning and devious, there was profit to be made from "sensible Negroes," no less than from judicious ones.

Carter, of course, in this as in much else, was an extreme case, as indicated previously, and useful primarily for the explicit nature of his comments about a subject that was more often ignored. Most ads were less venomous than the one Carter wrote seeking a replacement for Nassau. At his most sarcastic, Carter declares that he has resigned himself to the incorrigible nature of Nassau's "most abandoned state of drunkenness . . .

which he cannot be cured of" and would "as soon as I can, send him to some of the islands, where no doubt he may get his liquor with less pains than he now seems to take."[19]

For Carter, apparently, the term "sensible Negro" was something of an oxymoron, though he occasionally intimated that he wished things were otherwise. Nonetheless, the difference between his reflections on Lubbar, as Lubbar neared the end of his long life, and on Nassau suggests the dual nature of the specification "sensible Negroes," as it was generally elaborated in the ads.

It is also important to note, however, that although the devious/judicious dichotomy was generally the same for "sensible Negroes," whether they were African or "country born," not all recently imported Africans were labeled as "outlandish." Some ads for "outlandish" slaves, for instance, indicate that certain captive Africans were already "sensible" before being brought to the colonies. Likewise advertisements announcing the sale of "new Negroes," perhaps not unexpectedly, frequently indicate, in apparent contradiction to the runaway or taken up ads, skills or knowledge on the part of recently arrived captives that would have made them especially useful to prospective owners, skills or knowledge that when acquired through acculturation were always understood as a sign of having become "sensible" or certainly of moving in that direction.

Some ads, for instance, indicate that the "new Negroes" to be sold were from "a rice growing country," thereby implying that they had knowledge of rice growing or that such knowledge was an indigenously acquired expertise. In this use, however, the suggested expertise is offered as an indicator of potential rather than of achievement. In runaway ads, references of this sort are less ambiguous. In one such ad, the slave is unnamed, presumably because he had only recently arrived in the colony, having been "Imported in 1760," which, the advertiser notes, accounts for the fact that he "scarcely speaks any *English*." Nonetheless, the ad continues, the captive could "work at the Smith's Trade, having been employed in his own Country in that Way."[20]

Such ads, however, were rare. The majority of ads that identify "sensible new Negroes" indicate that "sensible" was an acquired characteristic, one, moreover, that captive Africans would not have possessed unless en-slaved by Christian slave owners. As in Washington's ad, language was the first indication that an "outlandish" slave had become or was becom-ing "sensible" and the surest measure of their advancement throughout the process. "[S]peaks tolerably well of an outlandish Negro, and appears very sensible," one ad reads, while another refers to "a young Negro Wench, of the Eboe Country . . . [who] speaks exceeding good English . . . and being an artful wench . . . may have directed her course southwardly, where she may attempt to pass as free." Nowhere is this point made more forcefully than in the ad that describes "a likely young artful negro fellow named Peter, of the Angola country, [who] may pass for country born." Again, "Jehu, an African, about 25 years old," is described as, "very likely; artful and sensible, speaks very proper, and would be taken for a country born."[21]

Ultimately, "sensible," when used to identify a "new Negro" who had become so fully acculturated that he could, like Peter and Jehu, pass as a "country born slave," was an indication that a slave possessed the awareness and perspective necessary to be considered useful to an owner and thus necessary for the slave's own survival. However, whereas its meaning for slave owners, like the meaning of "outlandish," depended on a negative framework of understanding of the moral and intellectual capacity of Africans and their descendants in the colonial South, its meanings for blacks themselves were as unlimited as the exigencies of their enslavement.

For some like Titus, a "native of Africa," who, it would appear from his owner's description, had become inordinately "sensible," redefining one-self by new terms of reference also involved the ability to mock, and thereby to reconceptualize those terms, to open them up to the possibility of new meanings. "He will probably alter his name," the ad speculates, and even though he could still speak only "bad English," he could "(tho' very cunning and artful), pass for a fool." Jack, by contrast, was a "coun-try born" fugitive and "by trade a blacksmith." But he too appears to have gained the capacity to alter significantly, for himself, the meaning that being "sensible" was intended to denote. Indeed, Jack had attained a level of sensibility that allowed him to parody the concept itself. Of course, ac-cording to the advertiser, he was both "fond of Liguor," "artful," and de-vious. But so "artful" had he become that he could be expected not only to "use every method to deceive and effect an escape," but "with much facility" to act "the cripple and Guinea negro, [and] is very active and fond of having his little tricks."[22] Like Titus, Jack had become outlandishly sensible, and as unintelligible to slave owners, albeit in a different way and for a different reason, as "outlandish new Negroes" were often considered to be.

CHAPTER 6

BEING HAILED

But how, in practical terms, were captive Africans, whom slave-holders called "outlandish," to be turned into "sensible" ones? The answer unfortunately can in no way be definitive or comprehensive, but the effort to make some sense of the process, however fragmentary and unsatisfactory that sense may in the end turn out to be, is necessary for the concerns of this study. The attempt will help to bring forth in more concrete terms what was described in the previous chapter as a turn in the survivor's framework of self-awareness, by which survivors were able to rationalize their experience of enslavement as a process of racial subordination.

Unquestionably, becoming "sensible" involved for many "new Negroes" physical violence, and even though the violence was less brutal for some than for others, the terror, caused by the degradation of those who resisted the demands made on them, was shared by all. Despite indications that violence was widely used, however, its scope and details, perhaps not surprisingly, are difficult to document.

This is true especially of the violence that undoubtedly had the greatest reverberation in slave life, the sexual violence committed against black women. Too often this has been obscured in discussions of miscegenation that focus on experiences that occurred outside, or in the aftermath, of the conditioning or seasoning process, the inference being that sexual violence was a consequence of enslavement rather than one of its founding abominations.[1] The presumption continues despite Olaudah Equiano's testimony, as an African-born slave, that as a seaman he frequently had "different cargoes of new negroes in my care for sale; and it was almost a constant practice with our clerks, and other whites, to commit violent depredations on the chastity of the female slaves. . . . I have even known them to gratify their brutal passion with females not ten years old."[2]

As with the sexual exploitation of slave women, or mixed race sexual relations generally, information about other forms of violent assault involved in the "seasoning" of slaves was repressed, or obfuscated when avoidance at one level or another was not possible. In colonial newspapers, however, unlike plantation or court records, in which references are rare and scattered, there was need on a fairly regular basis to discuss captives who were undergoing what might be termed a demonic rite of passage designed to initiate them into their new reality. But, despite the regular and ongoing appearance of ads that contained references to aspects of the experience, details and explanatory descriptions, even of the most modest sort, are virtually nonexistent, so much so that at times it seems that there was a conspiracy of silence at work.[3] More often, however, the sense is that many things that were left unexplained, as well as those that were left unsaid, simply did not require explanation or mention, either because they were not thought to be relevant, or because they were taken for granted by advertisers, who assumed that they would also be taken for granted by their readers.

Of course either of these reasons would have been very convenient for those who placed the ads and those who had a special interest in reading them. Remember in that context Henry Laurens's strategy of leaving unsaid the "many acts from the masters and others concerned towards the wretched negroes from the time of purchasing to that of selling them again." Avoidance such as that reflected in this quote was necessary especially when one deplored the "business," as did Laurens, but nonetheless profited from it. Advertisers rarely identified, described or explained, those "acts" as such. Apparently, it was not in their interest to be explicit about such matters.

Both in the ads for runaway slaves and in those reporting their capture, advertisers apparently relied on knowledgeable readers to fill in the blanks. Hidden in virtually all of the ads are clues that help explain, though not conclusively, many of the marks and physical deformities on the faces and bodies of most fugitives, including, with great regularity, those on "new Negroes." These marks were often so distinctive and noticeable that it was not possible to avoid describing them without defeating the purpose of the ads. However, we are rarely told the source or cause of the markings, except, on occasion, when the explanation is that they were the result of an accident, or were in some sense self-inflicted (for example, due to frostbite incurred by the advertised fugitive during a previous flight). Often there were no explanations offered at all.

In many cases, however, even when not attributed to accidental causes, we can assume that the marks were not marks of correction or intimidation. Brands, for instance, were often used, as they were on horses or other livestock or other property like canoes, in order to identify newly arrived and recently purchased captives. According to slave traders, captives were sometimes branded on the coast of Africa before being shipped to the Americas, and some slaves reported being branded on board the ship that brought them to the colonies by its captain. For instance, the slave referred to in one ad is said to have "a brand on his right arm like [diagram] [and] by what can be learnt from him, it was done on board the ship at sea." In another ad, we find the remark that there were "some small signs of a brand on the left arm [of Will, a "new negro man, of the *Mandingo* country"] that he says was done by the Captain on board the ship."[4] In other cases the trading firms that sold slaves in Charleston had them branded when they arrived.[5] Other ads indicate, however, that the brands were those of the slave owners themselves. Thus, we find such statements as "branded upon his shoulder PI," or "branded on the breast IC," or "mark'd either upon the shoulder or Breast with a W."[6] In general there are few indications, in the runaway ads, that "new Negroes" were branded as a form of punishment. But it should be borne in mind that in ads that specifically acknowledge a punitive motive for marks on a slave, no indication is ever given to suggest that the practice was uncommon.

The most explicit references to the use of branding as a punishment or mark of criminality appear in ads for runaway "country born" slaves. "He is notorious for running away," one ad explains, "having constantly practiced it since he was Six Years of Age, in return for which he has received Two remarkable Certificates; the first, Stripes, by Whipping; the other, having the Letter D branded on his A——se, which, however, may be now wore out, as he only received a slight Impression." The following notice for a fugitive "new Negro," and a number of others like it, could describe instances of punitive branding, but could just as logically have been unrelated to any disciplinary action: "A new negro fellow, Mandingo born . . . is branded on the left buttock [cR?]."[7]

Explicit acknowledgments in the ads that the physically deforming marks on the fugitive(s) being described were inflicted for punitive or disciplinary purposes are extremely rare. The few acknowledgments that are made generally refer to blacks born in the colonies rather than captive Africans, reflective no doubt of the fact that there were many more ads for "country born" runaway slaves than for fleeing "new Negroes."[8] Another possible explanation is that for the slave-holding community, it would have been logical to think that turning "brutes" (i.e., "outlandish" blacks) into "sensible Negroes" required that they be treated as brutes. If this were so, there would have been little need to describe or acknowledge what was generally taken for granted.

Conversely, "sensible Negroes" were expected to act accordingly, and when they did not, it was useful to let others know by describing the corrective measures needed to keep them in line. Brutes had to be treated as brutes, and everyone understood what that meant and was apparently reconciled to it, whereas "sensible Negroes," when they misbehaved, violated the norms of behavior that their survival required and by so doing symbolized a threat to the logic those norms were intended to maintain.

In either instance, however, there were restraints working against specific acknowledgments, and conversely encouraging oblique references. Though necessary to the objectives of slavery, punishing slaves, whether "outlandish" or "sensible," reflected badly on the institution and its moral rationalizations. At some level, the general silence regarding the uses of violence against blacks raised a difficult question for slave owners. Given the recognized necessity for the use of violence against slaves, did open discussion or acknowledgment of it serve any public interest? If such violence was more corrupting of public morals than beneficial to them, as men like the second William Byrd and Thomas Jefferson indicated, would not a public airing of its practice exacerbate its corrosive impact on society?

Regardless of the questions raised by the almost total silence surrounding the "seasoning" process in general and its brutality in particular, it is important to keep two factors in mind in order to put the larger issue of brutality in perspective. Both are obvious and commonsensical but easy to overlook. The first is that the slave trade was a vast and often violent enterprise from the moment of capture through the Middle Passage. Thus much that was brutal and brutalizing was done to the slaves during that phase of the trade. So much so that one could virtually choose at random any account of the Middle Passage from Elizabeth Donnan's collection of documents illustrative of the slave trade and find numerous examples.

One captain of slave ships, who criticized other commanders for their cruelty, accusing them, among other offenses, of beating slaves without provocation, notes that captives often fell into despondency out of fear and dread of what lay ahead for them in the Americas. Such was their despair and melancholia, according to the captain, John Barbot, that some refused to eat though beaten to force them to do so. To save them, Barbot adds, some of their teeth were broken in order that they might be force-fed.[9]

Given the many hazards of the trade and its practical requirements, and despite the relative abundance of evidence like that provided by Barbot, captives were no doubt more often injured by accident than by malicious intent. This was also true of plantation slavery itself. Nonetheless, even accidental or work-related injuries, it must be kept in mind, were the result of the coercive and violently disruptive nature of the two enterprises.

Whatever happened to a "country born" slave on a plantation in the colonial South, even burns or "scalds" that were attributed to his carelessness with fire, or to a captive on a long march from the interior to the western coast of Africa, in the holding pens after arriving there, or on board ship, happened to him because he had been enslaved. In the former case, sources of warmth were lacking; and in the latter, he had been forced to march and was held against his will. Practical considerations, in other words, cannot be isolated from the intent of the process that made them necessary.

The seasoning process in the region of interest to this study was in that sense merely an extension of the sort of conditions Barbot laments. No doubt few captive Africans who were enslaved in the colonial South would have been surprised by the recollections of Quobna Ottobah Cugoano, a contemporary of Olaudah Equiano who "was born in the city of

Agimaque, on the coast Fantyn" in West Africa, and was shipped from a nearby coastal region to Grenada. Like most other African-born narrators he did not dwell on the brutality of his enslavement experience, stating that "it would be needless to give a description of all the horrible scenes which we saw, and the base treatment which we met with in this dreadful captive situation." Before being delivered from Grenada, Cugoano recalled that he spent "eight or nine months, beholding the most dreadful scenes of misery and cruelty, and seeing my miserable companions often cruelly lashed, and as it were cut to pieces, for the most trifling faults." For what seemed to him minor offences ("eating a piece of sugarcane") some of his companions "were cruelly lashed, or struck over the face to knock their teeth out." And he was told by some of them that "they had their teeth pulled out to deter others, and to prevent them from eating any cane in future."[10]

Though Britain's southern colonies on the North American mainland were not sugar colonies, we can assume that the cruelties that Cugoano reports were experienced by many captive Africans throughout the colonial South, including those who arrived there by way of Grenada. Certainly, as we will see further on in the study, blacks in that region bore the same markings and deformities as described by Cugoano and others. But because no eyewitness left a detailed account of how these signs of their enslavement were gained or inflicted on them, distinguishing between injuries and deformities that were the result of accidents and those that were inflicted purposefully to discipline or punish captives is generally not possible. Thus the physical marks left unexplained in the sources that offer the most extensive and continuous inventory could be as easily attributed to accidents as to other causes. But again, the frostbite and burns that resulted in missing or deformed appendages, and the scars and scalds, often occurred during flight, on the run from enslavement, in the woods or other hiding places; whereas those deformities that are said to have been work-related happened while the slave was being forced to work by owners, overseers, drivers, or other supervisors. The difference between accidental and punitively inflicted injuries was often, if not always, largely a matter of semantics.

Likewise the underlying interests being served by the process of enslavement must be kept in mind. However mean-spirited and vicious, or humane and caring, an individual slave ship captain or a plantation manager may have been, it was in his interest to transport and acclimate the captives in his charge as safely as possible. Certainly, he should have been highly motivated to keep them as damage free as possible. They were, after all, more valuable if healthy and undeformed than if maimed and crippled.

Captive Africans, however, were often so concerned with escaping or defending themselves against the dangers they faced that they could not be counted on to accommodate the objectives of their enslavers. As a result, slave owners and their employees often had to settle for minimizing rather than avoiding injury to their property, forcing compliance from reluctant and resistant captives with as little damage as possible to their labor and market value. This could involve startling acts of brutality against an incorrigibly defiant captive as a necessary object lesson to others. Such captives were of little use as slaves, and in that sense more trouble than they were worth. From a slave owner's perspective, a slave who was becoming increasingly difficult to control was of less value than a slave who bore a gruesome but not incapacitating injury and deformity.

From that perspective the deformities described in the runaway and taken-up ads that appeared routinely in colonial newspapers represent the ways in which planters of varying dispositions and personalities responded to the inherent tension within the slave owning enterprise itself. At the same time, they reflect, in their most extreme physical form, the brutalization involved in the transformation required of captives who survived enslavement as well as those who did not. Change for captives, whether cultural or perspectival, occurred literally in the course of a life and death struggle that was built into the process of making them productive slaves.

The first response of many captives to that logic was flight. This impulse is evident in West Africa throughout the history of the Atlantic slave trade, and as we have seen, a number of ads note that newly purchased "new Negroes" ran away within a day or two of purchase. "King" Carter's diary, it will be recalled, records similar instances. But the slaves' first confrontation with efforts to initiate them into an accommodation with their new condition, and to force a transformation in their sense of self, took place when planters assigned new names to them and attempted to have them respond to those names.

Equiano's experience in that regard would have been familiar to many captives in the colonial South. On board the "African Snow" that took him to Virginia he was named Michael. His master in Virginia then named him Jacob. However, on board the ship captained by the man who bought him in Virginia (as a gift for a friend) and was taking him to England he was named "Gustavus Vassa." "I at that time," Equiano explained, "began to understand him a little, and refused to be called so, and told him as well as I could that I would be called Jacob; but he said I should not, and still called me Gustavus: and when I refused to answer to my new name, which I at first did, it gained me many a cuff; so at length I submitted, and by which I have been known ever since."[11]

In addition to their new slave names, captives were also required to learn and to give upon request the name of their master, and/or their overseer, or in some cases that of a black driver. Like Equiano, many recently imported captives were reluctant at first to do either. It is less clear, however, whether they could not or would not give their own or their master's name as an act of defiance or as a stratagem to make it difficult for owners to reclaim them when recaptured by others. In most instances where refusal occurred, even among the most "outlandish new Negroes," both objectives were probably involved to some extent. However, the ads suggest that the more "sensible" a "new Negro" became, the more dominant the latter objective was.

From the slave owners' perspective there were several necessary and therefore practical reasons for requiring a prompt response from their new slaves. It was hard to give orders to individuals who did not respond when called, and if they wandered off, got lost, or ran away, the possession of a name would help those seeking their return. If a slave could be convinced or persuaded to tell others his or her name and that of his or her master, and, preferably, to give some indication of where he or she lived, the chances of a speedy recovery were greatly improved.

The fact that "new Negroes" were given new names, even though allowing them to keep their "country" names undoubtedly would have made it easier to condition a newly purchased captive's response, makes it clear that submission was the most important consideration.[12]

Individuals, of course, respond differently to coercion, reflecting by their response different levels of readiness to submit, based on different cultural understandings of themselves and their predicament. Not only, that is, did acts of submission require different degrees of coercion, but they held different meanings for different individuals, and multiple and even contradictory meanings for most.[13] To one degree or another, however, "outlandish new Negroes" in the colonial South as elsewhere in the Americas had to be conditioned to respond when ordered to do so, to turn around when called by their new names, and by so doing to accept the only terms by which they could survive. The need for conditioning of course presupposed resistance, and thus the question of what was to be done if a slave resisted was ever present in the minds of slave owners and those they employed to season their "new Negroes." Thus violence, as indicated earlier, was inherent in the logic of the enslavement process, even when it was unnecessary and did not occur.

For that reason, how often "cuffing" or other forms of physically abusive encouragement were needed to condition the responsiveness of slaves is less relevant to this discussion than whether the use of violence was extensive enough to create an undercurrent of terror that pervaded the experience of enslavement for all slaves. In absolute terms, neither question can be answered with any certainty, but ads for runaway and taken-up "new Negroes" offer a basis for a reasonably conclusive answer to the latter.

In most ads, whether those seeking the capture and return of runaways, or notices reporting their capture, the amount of time they had been in a colony is suggested (stated or implied) as the factor determining their ability to respond to their own name or to give the name of their master. The longer they had been in the colony, and thus the longer they had managed to survive the conditioning process, the more likely it was that they would be able to communicate effectively with their captors. This was as it should be, the ads seem to argue, thereby casting prolonged resistance to change as aberrant and exceptional behavior and thus truly outlandish in every conceivable sense rather than allowing for the possibility that ongoing resistance to change might have been intrinsic to the captive experience itself. Ultimate submission by survivors symbolized and was an acknowledgment that change was not only necessary and inevitable but desirable. Persistent resistance by contrast was not merely pre-enlightened but primitive, and thus savage in its implications, a sign of outlandishness. We sense from the ads that slave owners understood that resistance was a normal response to enslavement but not that they recognized or were willing to admit that it formed a logic that was essential to enslavement's objectives. To enslave was to estrange and alienate; to enslave by means of forced acculturation was to make estrangement and alienation a necessary requirement of survival.

The following ad is typical of many others in its reflection of the slave owner's perspective, and its tendency to reduce conditioning to a function of time. "THREE NEW NEGROES," according to the planter who placed the ad, had either run away "or rather [were] supposed to have been seduced off from the subscriber's plantation below town [Savannah, Georgia]." Two of the fugitives were distinguished from the third, who spoke "a little English," by their inability to do so.[14] The English-speaking slave had been purchased a few months before the other two, an observation indicating for the slave-owning community the essential difference between them.

Like Polydore and many other "new Negroes," all three runaways identified in this ad were given Roman names. Caesar was the name given the one who could speak "a little English"; the other two were named Brutus and Gracchus. Where this ad differs from the norm for such notices is in the slave owner's certainty that the three runaways will respond when ordered to. Certainty regarding a "new Negro's" ability to respond is generally qualified in some form and to some extent. The term "cannot," for instance, is frequently used in this qualified way.[15] Most ads use language that implies rather than states the following: "Given the degree of the captive's acculturation, he or she probably cannot give his or her name or respond to other questions, and thus should not be expected to." Indeed, "will not" instead of some other more tentative term is so rarely utilized in this context that it virtually echoes when encountered in the ads.[16]

Often combined with qualified declarations of certainty relative to a fugitive's ability or willingness to respond appropriately when called or questioned are equivocal explanations or phrasing that further indicate uncertainty. Even though his "new Negro Fellow named SANDY" has been "in the Country better than a Year," according to a "Subscriber, living in *Frederick* County [Maryland]," and even though Sandy can "talk pretty plain," the subscriber remains unsure "whether he can tell my Name."[17] And again: "Run Away from the Governor's plantation at Ogeechee about three weeks ago, A NEW NEGROE MAN named Boson, of the Corromantee country . . . [who] speaks little or no English, but its thought sufficient to tell his name."[18] Or: "two new Negro Men, of the Ibo Country, named CHARLES and FRANK, who have been in the Province about twelve Months, and it is supposed cannot tell their Master's Name."[19]

Against this pattern of equivocation are ads like the one reporting the flight of Caesar, Brutus, and Gracchus. Caesar, in that ad, according to the advertiser whose surname was Jackson, "*will* acknowledge his master's name" [emphasis added] if questioned, which presumably means that he would also respond to Caesar if called by that name, for, according to most other ads, learning one's new name generally preceded learning a master's name. That sequence is suggested in this particular ad because the other two fugitives, although they speak no English, "*will* know their names on being called by them."[20]

Though the following ad uses "can" instead of "will," it is couched in wording that gives it the resonance of the more determinant term. The advertiser, Josiah Daly, leaves little doubt that he has experienced some difficulty in seasoning his "new Negro," but is now affirming that he has finally gotten his point across. In the ad, Daly reports that "a *Mundingo* Negro Man named TOM [owned by Daly]. . . has been in this County [Mecklenburg, Virginia] about eighteen Months; [where] he lived this Year under the Direction of Mr. *Edward Giles*, and if he should be strictly questioned can tell either Mr. *Giles's* or my Name."[21] The slave had been forced to learn new names but his owners were still uncertain if he would voluntarily respond when "hailed."

Such ads, however, are few, and none gives any indication why the advertiser could speak so confidently about a captive's "readiness" to give his or her new name or that of his or her owner, when virtually all others either equivocate or assume an inability to do so on the part of recently arrived or unacculturated captives.

In "taken up" or "committed" ads, jailers often use the phrase "cannot or will not" to explain the lack of such information, but more often the names are given without further comment. Once the ability of a slave to speak and understand English was no longer in question, or could be presumed from other behavior, such as the acquisition of a trade, captors then had to determine whether the name given was correct. Being "sensible" and "artful," fugitives, according to most advertisers, were likely to change their names or even "deny" their owner's name. Uncertainty regarding the responsiveness of "outlandish new Negroes" became uncertainty regarding the veracity of "sensible" ones, further raising questions about the source of the confidence expressed by Jackson and Daly. Here perhaps we have one important beginning of the verbal masking that literary and other historians have long identified as a distinguishing characteristic of African American folk culture.

Although eccentric in some of its details, the following ad is illustrative of the general sense of the ads regarding recently arrived fugitive "new Negroes." It makes Daly's and Jackson's, as well as a handful of others, stand out by comparison. Written by Daniel Ravenel the ad explains that three "new Negroes" have run away from him. "As they are all new negroes," according to the ad, "[they] *may not* be able to tell their own or their master's names" (emphasis added). Ravenel explains that they have only "been about three months in the province." He surmises, however, that there is a possibility that they would be able to give their overseer's and their driver's names, "which they *may* know" (emphasis added). Accordingly, Ravenel supplies the names of both. He earlier mentioned in the same ad that "[e]ach of them [meaning his three slaves, Adam, London, and York] had a piece of lead tied to their necks, on which is engraved their names."[22]

Henry Laurens, meanwhile, in an ad he placed for "a tall well-made new negro man (of the *Mindinga* country)," who "Strolled away from [his house]," captures a related concern, expressed in a scattering of similar advertisements, further illustrating and underscoring the undercurrent of unease and uncertainty that resonates faintly even in less descriptive ads. On the one hand, he writes, his fugitive slave can "speak no *English*," but on the other, he notes that "His name is John, but he will more readily answer to the name FOOTBEA, which he went by in his own country."[23]

Although representing only a small percentage of the ads, advertisements like those by Ravenel and Laurens help amplify those by Jackson and Daly, identifying a tension whose structure is clear but whose depth and particularity are not. When slave owners state unequivocally in runaway ads for "new Negroes" that a fugitive "cant speak English, but *will* answer to the Name of York very readily" (emphasis added), it is difficult not to wonder how the overseer could know for certain that a runaway slave would respond to his or her name if asked. What, for instance, made Caleb Lloyd so certain that "a new negro fellow," belonging to him, even though he understood "no other English" would "answer readily to the name Achillus"?[24] Did he and others know, as Equiano's new master came to learn, that their new slave had finally "submitted" after being repeatedly and routinely "cuffed"?

Given the suspicions raised by the ads just quoted and the patterns of reference in them implying the violent nature of the seasoning process, what significance are we to attach to the large number of missing bodily appendages reported in the ads? We know from many of the ads, both for "country born" and "new Negroes," that their absence was often the result of frostbite or burns or work-related accidents, yet we also know that in 1710 Robert "King" Carter disciplined two of his slaves, Bambara and Dinah, by amputating their toes, explaining in his petition seeking permission from the Lancaster (Virginia) County Court to do so that they were "incorrigible" and that other punishments were not adequate to control them.[25]

We also have the anecdotal testimony of Equiano, who notes in his narrative that "[o]ne Mr. D____, told me he had sold 41,000 negroes, and he once cut off a negro-man's leg for running away." Moreover, according to Equiano, who "was often witness to cruelties of every kind on my unhappy fellow slaves" and "used to have different cargoes of new negroes in my care for sale," when Mr. D. was asked how, as a Christian, he could have justified "before God" the slave's death if he had perished from the operation, Mr. D. responded matter-of-factly that "his scheme had the desired effect—it cured that man and some others from running away."[26]

And there is even one explicit admission of an amputation in the ads themselves, although not involving a "new Negro." According to his owner, "John Walton," "AARON" had run away before and tried to pass as a free man, using the alias Phil Jackson, for which "he has by his villainy lost his right great toe."[27] Otherwise the ads are strikingly silent on this subject. They unfailingly identify the missing toe or toes, but, with the one exception just quoted, when explanations are offered, they are in every case explanations of accidental injuries and deformities. The usefulness of such explanations is difficult to appreciate. Deformities from burns and frostbite would have been in most cases distinctive and thus required explanations, but accidential injuries that involved severance of an appendage—from a blow from an ax, for instance—could not have differed from deliberate amputations. In that case what purpose was served by explaining them?

Questions of this sort would cause us to be less suspicious if so many of the ads identifying missing appendages had not left their absence unexplained. Among those ads, missing appendages are simply identified as either missing or "cut off." A large number of these, moreover, make reference to a portion of a finger or toe, the tip or first joint or two, and among these a large percentage involve the little toe or finger.[28] If a captive was to be punished by means of amputation, these certainly would have been the logical places to start. The pain would have been excruciating, and the mark would have been indelible, but the impact on the slave's productivity would have been minimal.

Unlike amputated appendages cropped ears and whip marks (or marks from leg and neck irons), are often acknowledged as punishments. No doubt this was because cropped ears and whip marks were the most frequently employed punishments in the seasoning process, and because they were more self-explanatory than missing appendages. Without further explanation a missing toe or finger could be attributed to any number of causes whereas a cropped ear and marks from a whipping were generally understood as badges of criminality. As such perhaps they were more widely accepted forms of punishment.[29]

One practical reason why whippings and ear-cropping would have been preferred methods of physical coercion during the seasoning process is that they punished without in most cases incapacitating slaves. The same would have been true of brands, or other marks such as burns on the hand, which were used in the courts as a means of marking convicted thieves and punishing other anti-social behavior.

Whatever the explanation for the greater willingness by advertisers to acknowledge certain forms of punishment than others, gradations in disfigurement and dismemberment that resulted from it reflect a crude calculation measuring the limits beyond which physical correction involved a diminishing return on investment. Using this calculus, we might ask, for instance, at what point did the sexual exploitation of women become counterproductive? One measure of the logic that would have been used in making such judgments was that employed to justify castration of slaves convicted of certain felonies as a substitute for capital punishment.[30]

With the exception of castration, women were brutalized in all the ways men were. Their unique burden was the threat and actuality of sexual exploitation, which could be used not only against them but also to drive home to black men an essential reality of their own enslavement, just as every act of castration served to impress upon all blacks their essential impotence.[31]

To implicate black women in the emasculation of black men, and to force black men to acquiesce in the sexual violation of black women, was to obscure yet also increase the burden for the immediate victims, and by extension for all blacks. The redemptive nature of the victim's unmerited suffering, and their sacrifice for (and of) each other, were diminished or counteracted by the suffering itself. That is, in order to ensure the survival of all, the victim's violation and emasculation had to be endured, but to endure was to sanction slavery's original sin. Those who were directly assaulted, in that sense, were victimized by their own victimization. It would have been difficult for black people in the colonial South to avoid the implication that they were exploited, raped and castrated in this case, because they were exploitable. The victims' value within and to their communities was enhanced because by enduring they symbolized its strength (its durability), yet at the same time their endurance embodied its weakness. Without victims and their sufferance, the community would not exist, but neither would slavery itself. More than any other act, enduring and surviving sexual assault embodied the "savage paradox" of enslavement for blacks in colonial and antebellum America. Embedded in the triumph of survival was the burden of having survived.

A captive's or a survivor's violation, when used against the larger community (and it always in some sense served that purpose), resounded in the captive as an amplification of the soul-searing assault on his or her very being. Such violation, in that sense, embodied all of the self-destroying force of the enslavement process, distilling the essence of enslavement's physical and psychic brutality, as well as of its objectives and all of its radiating consequences for every survivor. The violation, moreover, did not end with the act, reverberating diffusely throughout the lives of the individuals who were violated but also throughout the experiences of blacks more generally. Its effect, for instance, lived on and was perpetuated in the public silence about the subject and in the issues of identity and the questions of illegitimacy fostered by that silence. Forced to become accomplices in the denial of the crime, thus reinforcing the psychological objectives of the violation, the victims (meaning in this case all survivors) went down on their knees, as Equiano reports in a related context, and thanked their owners, and prayed, or rather said, "God bless you."[32]

In that context, what did it mean for the slave population in the colonial South to reproduce itself by natural means, a phenomenon unprecedented in other New World slave societies? Did it mean that the alienation experienced by black women early in the history of slavery in the Southern colonies began to decline as conditions improved? Or was black family life born out of the experience of surviving, the best defense available to black women against the unbridled threat that sexual exploitation, even as an undercurrent of possibility, posed to their lives and sanity? Certainly it did not end sexual exploitation, but it did establish a basis for the possibility of its avoidance. Black families and communities were much more profitable to slave owners than were emasculated men and victimized women.

One of the lessons to be learned from the sexual exploitation of black women is that the psychic effect of an act of violence cannot be measured by its prevalence alone. This was a very real consequence that slave owners, however unintentionally, counted on, and one that was behind much of the violence done to individual blacks. Unlike castration, the extent of which there is some quantifiable basis for speculating about, sexual violations of black women by slave owners, their sons, or overseers cannot be estimated. It is reasonable to assume, however, that just as it would be hard to underestimate the sexual abuses visited on black women, some indeterminate but significant percentage of the unexplained missing toes and fingers were the results of punishments and more particularly were involved in the seasoning process. In the ads this would appear to be most reasonable in those cases where other signs of punishment are indicated. For instance, when a fugitive bore whip marks or a slit ear, or both, or a speech impediment that is described as being activated when the slave in question was closely interrogated, or harshly addressed, or suddenly confronted with an accusation, the added, and generally unrelated and unexplained, reference to a missing toe is especially suspicious.[33]

This inference is heightened when the missing appendage is a single joint of a finger or toe, especially of a little toe or finger, or a "great" toe, and especially when the phrasing used is "was cut off." The majority of references to missing appendages, however, are not contextualized or in other ways modified by such references, or by comments relative to a fugitive's character or prior behavior.

Missing teeth, which were almost exclusively "foreteeth," upper or lower, are also mentioned in a very large percentage of these ads, even more than toes or cropped ears.[34] As with missing toes or fingers, there are a large number of possible explanations for their absence, but very few are offered relative to those provided for missing appendages, and, as suggested earlier, such explanations for the latter are few in comparison with those that go unexplained. And thus again we are left with a silence that reverberates. Such silence becomes even more suspicious when we recall Cugoano's recollection of having seen his "miserable companions" in Grenada "cruelly lashed, or struck over the face to knock their teeth out" for eating a piece of sugarcane. How many "new Negroes" saw their "miserable companions" cuffed for not responding when "hailed," and how often was it necessary to see such "cruelty" before the terror of enslavement became embedded in one's consciousness?

CHAPTER 7

IMPUDENCE

In a society in which any action committed by a black person against any white person could be interpreted as defiance and thereby lead to swift and certain retribution, survivors of enslavement had to become keenly aware of the limit beyond which their behavior would be seen as defiant. Determining how far was too far was seldom easy, for the line between rebellion and effrontery could be a fine one. On one side of that line, a slave's behavior, although disapproved, would be considered less threatening or insulting than it would be on the other, and therefore it would be punishable in less severe ways. The safest course for blacks was to stay well clear of the line and to err on the side of caution rather than push the limits of acceptable behavior. But life on the edge or near the boundary also offered the greatest possibility of self-proclamation and affirmation.

Defiance breached the boundary entirely, but what specifically constituted defiance was not always clear. Jack, in "A Short Story" discussed in the introduction, apparently, had finally reached his owner's breaking point, but few owners would have been as tolerant as his. The laws of each colony specified a handful of capital offenses for which slaves could be executed, including rebellion, conspiracy to rebel, and any violent act against any white person, especially the rape of a white woman. Short of punishing such acts, slave owners, and the courts they controlled, could exercise a good deal of discretion in setting boundaries for their slaves.[1]

No doubt one of the reasons slaveowners considered "new Negroes" outlandish was their proclivity not only to defy any effort to enslave them but also to defy the terms of reference used to effect that objective.[2] Defiance by "sensible Negroes" more often expressed an inward reaction to the burden of surviving within the terms of enslavement. Survival for "sensible Negroes" *was* defiance. Behavior that was recognizable as being defiant would have almost certainly ended in execution. Such self-destructive behavior most often occurred as a result of efforts to push the limits of resistance that slave society sought to impose on them as slaves, or to live, as it were, on the edge of those limits. In order to remain resistant to their enslavement, which was necessary for their psychic survival, survivors had to redefine defiance so that it could encompass what others saw as accommodation.[3]

The term most often used by slave owners to demarcate the boundary beyond which actions by blacks became defiance was "impudence." A brief notice in the *Maryland Gazette* records a slave acting near but not beyond that very real but not always clearly defined boundary marker: "The Week before last," the editor writes, in one of that paper's earliest issues, "a Negroe-Man, belonging to William Robinson, of Patapsco, had the Impudence to [push?] and strike Mr. John Smith, the Carpenter on [in?] some slight Provocation about their Dogs fighting; On which he was carried before Mr. Vachel Denton, one of the City Magistrates, who caus'd one of his Ears to be cropp'd, pursuant to the Law in such Cases."[4]

Neither the incident described in the *Gazette* nor the punishment meted out to the slave whose ears were cropped was newsworthy in and of itself. Such behavior, as well as the punishment used as a public sanction against it, was not new to the colonies. The editor brought the case to the public's attention for only two reasons. First the incident represented "the first Instance we have heard of executing that Law."[5] The law to which the editor refers was one of many that began to appear in surviving records in the late seventeenth century, laws articulating a transformation in the practice of slavery—its institutionalization—in Maryland and Virginia.[6] Their enactment thus coincided with an important moment in the demographic history of slavery. As previously indicated, in the 1720s, in both colonies, the black population began to reproduce itself by natural means (as it would later in low country colonies).[7]

The ad just quoted was from one of the earliest surviving editions of one of the first newspapers published in a Southern colony. Normally, attacks on whites by blacks—usually involving an attack by a slave against his or her master or overseer—did not appear in local newspapers unless the attack resulted in the death of the person who had been attacked. For instance, when reporting the death of a slave owner in Baltimore County, Maryland, "by one of his Negroes," the editor of the newspaper notes, "It seems this was not the first Time this Villain had attempted his Master's Life, having before struck at him with an Ax, which cut him over the Eyebrow, and had certainly split his Skull, if he had not suddenly mov'd his Head."[8] The previous attack was not reported, as was the case with most other attacks of that nature, because the owner corrected his slave, who was legally his property, without recourse to the law, a virtually unrestricted right that the law recognized to one degree or another in every Southern colony.[9] Unless murder was involved (or an owner was incapable of controlling his or her slave and sought help from authorities), there was no need for prosecution or recourse to the law, because for all practical purposes the owner *was* the law when it came to disciplining his or her slave.

It was also customary for whites to privately discipline blacks who were not their slaves. The following newspaper account, for example, involves a dispute between a black man and a white man who was not his owner. The report shows how customary it was. According to the account, "One Donald Macpherson Skipper of a James River Craft, lying with his Vessel at Warwick, about a Fortnight ago, had her robbed of some Articles by a Negro, whom he afterwards had the Opportunity of correcting for it." Later, the newspaper reports, "the Fellow came upon the Bank and gave Macpherson scurrilous Language, who thereupon jumped ashore to lay Hold of the Negro; and he, to avoid him, ran into the Water. Macpherson followed him; and closing with him, both perished together."[10] Had "Macpherson" lived, captured "the Negro," and corrected him without help or authorization by the law, as he had previously done, the incident no doubt would not have been reported. As one essayist writing in a North Carolina newspaper puts it, "there is no danger of a mans being hurt by the law for killing a negro."[11]

Virtually anything a black person might do in public could be interpreted as improper or defiant by individual whites. In most references to behavior by blacks that was considered criminal or socially unacceptable by authorities and reported as such in colonial newspapers, the distinction between what blacks could get away with and what they could not was invariably marked by an accusation of impudence. Recall that the editor of the *Maryland Gazette* quoted earlier uses the term "Impudence" when describing the offense with which the "Negroe-Man, belonging to William Robinson," was charged, and for which his ears were cropped. In that case the term "impudence" identifies the outer limit of self-assertion deemed tolerable for blacks by law and custom in colonial Maryland. Very often it appears that the meaning slave owners attributed to that term served as a yardstick for gauging the fitness of captured Africans for enslavement. Although not consciously conceived as such, the word apparently operated as a coded point of reference identifying a standard of submissiveness used to judge the behavior of blacks more generally. It seems to have also functioned as an early warning of the threat posed by slaves and free blacks who had for whatever reason begun to act irrationally, gauged, that is, by the standard implied by the accusation. Whereas resistance had once meant defiance on the part of blacks who were considered by slave owners to be "outlandish," it had come to mean impudence as applied to behavior by survivors that was deemed intolerable by the slave-owning community. What it meant to survivors themselves is harder to gauge, but survival required that they develop a highly sensitive understanding of the terms of reference by which they were judged. It also demanded that they learn to respond accordingly, which often meant extemporaneously. Uncertainty regarding a slave owner's understanding of what constituted impudence could quite literally cost a slave his or her life. In that context the term for blacks marked a point beyond which the logic of survival no longer served its purpose, giving way to other frames of self-reference and awareness, including desperation and despondency.

🖋

Blacks were not the only ones in colonial society who were accused of "impudence" or expected to adhere to the boundary it represented. Most other nonelite groups, and women in general, were held to similar standards. Within the social hierarchy of a patriarchal slave society, impudence was not just objectionable; it was as threatening to the health of the society as was poisoning to an intended victim's life, or as arson was to an entire community's material well-being. It was not merely behaviorally deviant and thus morally and socially offensive, but treasonable and insurrectionary in its underlying implications.

Individuals who defied the behavioral limits ascribed to them by the sort of slave society that developed in the colonial South threatened in a fundamental way the entire social structure. The indentured servant who spoke disparagingly of his or her master, the landless tenant who ridiculed his or her social superior or economic benefactor, the middling farmer who scoffed at colonial officials or the British crown itself, the woman who slandered another or claimed her independence, refusing to stay in the place assigned to her by society and thereby conform to the norms of behavior and expression expected of her; all such individuals threatened the social order. By acting impudently they threatened the harmony and stability of their communities and thereby risked becoming social outcasts, a danger that the law confronted them with by shaming or threatening to shame them publicly. Blacks, of course, could not be cast out in the same sense as could other nonelites. They could, and were, banished from a colony, or threatened with banishment, for some crimes, and they were often sold away (as Carter threatened to do to Nassau), but they could not become outcasts within it.

The use of corporal punishment, including public whippings or nailing the culprit's ears to a pillory, was considered necessary to punish nonelite whites for antisocial behavior. But as slavery was being institutionalized, and increasingly thereafter, these forms of punishment were most often used on black slaves. Also, impudent behavior by nonelites was generally punished in ways designed to shame and dishonor them. By making their punishment a public spectacle, society delivered an object lesson to others, which was an especially important objective when blacks were disciplined or executed in public. However, punishments designed to shame or dishonor individuals accused of antisocial or immoral behavior (women accused of infidelity or outspokenness, for instance)[12] were rarely if ever used against blacks.[13]

Thus, for instance, the public ducking of a black woman for outspoken-ness or the tarring and feathering of a black slave for theft never occurred (or was never reported), apparently because it would have been point-less.[14] Since enslavement and racial subordination systematically de-meaned and dishonored blacks, the instruments of social control and the logic behind their use had to be modified significantly. The dilemma fac-ing colonial lawmakers and the society more generally was that, no mat-ter how morally offensive or socially deviant the behavior of black slaves became in the eyes of others, shaming could not be an effective means of either deterring or reforming it. Whippings or physical mutilations like ear cropping or in extreme cases castration offered an acceptable and nec-essary deterrent, a solution, moreover, that slaveholders could use, at their own discretion, to discipline and correct troublesome slaves.

By these methods the slave's impudence (defiance) was punished with-out at the same time substantially affecting his or her labor value. The use of castration does not contradict this point, as indicated in an earlier sec-tion, even though it would obviously have eliminated the reproductive potential of a slave owner's property. The necessary alternative of capital punishment, however, would have involved even greater loss.[15] In either case, efforts were made to limit the liability to the owner by providing market-value compensation for slaveholders who owned slaves convicted of crimes requiring execution or castration. Even if the market value was granted as compensation for executed or castrated slaves, the added value of a slave's labor, estimated over his full lifetime, not to mention his re-productive value, was lost. Of course there came a point at which the logic of profit and loss had to be abandoned in the name of security. However, considering that enslavement's boundaries were as much created by the survival of "sensible Negroes" as they were imposed by the will of slave owners, it is not altogether clear who determined when that point was reached.

On occasion blacks seems to have crossed that boundary unwittingly. Yet many times they deliberately stepped across and beyond its invisible bar-rier. As dramatic as this always was, it becomes even more so when viewed in light of an essential requirement of survival. Above all else "sensible Negroes" had to be keenly and constantly aware, not only of the existence of such limits and boundaries, but of their proximity to them in every conceivable context in which they may have found themselves. Lacking that awareness, they simply would not have survived.

The incident of the "Negroe-man" who had his ear cropped for having the impudence to strike a carpenter over what was considered a minor provocation only hints at the nature of that necessity. Other more dramatic instances are easily located. But this one, as suggested earlier, helped mark in a small way a significant change in slavery that would make such impudence increasingly threatening to slave owning interests.

In the midst of developments of this scope and nature it is not surprising that an editor of a colonial newspaper would consider such a case newsworthy, especially if, as he indicates, "we thought it not improper to publish it, as an Example to those kind of Gentry, many of whom have of late been guilty of very great Misdemeaners."[16] The account that immediately follows illustrates the concerns: "The Negroe *Stephen*," the account begins, "belonging to *Charles Carroll*, Esq., who was lately advertis'd in this Paper, for a Run-away, was brought to Town [Annapolis] last night, and carried before the Hon. *B.* [Benjamin] *Tasker*, Esq., who committed him to Prison." Stephen, the report says, confessed to "several Villainies," after which he was "harbour'd at the Plantation of the Hon. *Charles Calvert*, Esq., in *Prince George's* County by the Negroes there, and the Overseer (who is Negroe)." The latter, the report concludes, "was also brought to Town, and has been punished with a severe Whipping."[17]

Apparently the impudence represented by Stephen's crimes (directed as they were against the property of prominent slave owners rather than against a white mechanic) was much more severe than that committed by the "Negroe-Man" whose ear was cropped, and Stephen was later sentenced to death. That was also the fate of "Two Negros [who] were hang'd . . . In Charles City County [Virginia], for Robbing Mr. Harris's Store" or again of "two Negro Men, *Bob* and *Dick*, both of them born in this Country and notorious Rogues, [who] were executed at Port Tobacco [Maryland] pursuant to their sentence for robbing the Store of Mr. Mitchell."[18]

We can be fairly certain in most cases, even cases where the point is not specifically made, that a slave like Stephen (or Bob and Dick or the "Two Negros in . . . Charles City County") was executed not so much for the "several Villainies" he confessed to as for the "impudence" and effrontery that his behavior represented. This assumption derives in part from the logic governing the criminal law contained within the slave codes that were enacted in each Southern colony, a logic that made the execution of slaves for any other reason than impudence illogical or counterproductive from a slave-owning perspective. Reinforcing the idea that insolent rather than criminal behavior often determined the punishment received by slaves is the frequency with which executed slaves are described as having been particularly impudent, obstinate, or unrepentant (as well as the effort exerted by authorities to allow them to recant).

"A negro named Frank," according to one newspaper account, "was apprehended some time since for committing a robbery at St. Marys [Georgia]; he has since been tried and found guilty, and was executed the 4th inst. on the public square; after which his head was severed from his body and stuck upon a pole over his grave." Apparently, however, Frank's crime, like Stephen's, had more to do with impudence than with theft. For the newspaper account also notes that he "died obstinately, and acknowledged that he was concerned in robbing a store under the Bluff in this place [Savannah]."[19]

The price for obstinacy was often death, as slave owners frequently indicated in ads for runaway slaves by informing readers that a fugitive had been "outlawed."[20] "Run away from the subscriber, a Negro man named MANN, about 5 feet 6 inches high," runs one such ad. "He has a slit in one of his ears [a mark of former correction], gives very sensible answers, and is about 50 years old. He is outlawed from his threatening to burn my houses." "If any person will deliver me his head, severed from his body, they shall receive 10-lbs. current money: If taken alive and delivered, 40 s. besides what the law allows."[21] In a number of instances, and perhaps most often, the practice of outlawry was used as a threat, encouraging runaways to return rather than risk being formally and unreservedly outlawed, as for instance when one owner indicates that his runaway slave would be outlawed "and may be shot, unless they return to me in ten days."[22] In a few cases a greater reward was offered for the slave's return than for his or her head, thereby encouraging restraint on the part of anyone who might capture the fugitive. Such ads reflect the owner's desire to protect his or her investment if at all possible.

Complaining slave owners frequently explain the outlawing of a slave with the claim that the runaway lurked about committing various felonies.[23] More often, however, no specific explanation is offered. In most instances where details are provided, the "outlawed" fugitive is described as being unusually deceitful, treacherous, cunning, and "deceptious," strongly suggesting that it was this repeated pattern of behavior that caused an owner reluctantly to give up hope of ever reforming the slave in question. Repetitions of normally forgivable behavior could betray an unacceptable residue of "outlandishness" or an excess of "sensibility" that expressed an incorrigible impudence. In the most egregious cases forgiveness was unthinkable.

"Bristol" is almost a caricature of the incorrigibly impudent type. Described as being "likely, about forty years of age, five feet ten inches or six feet high," he was "of black complexion, and rather down look, except when pleased, in which case he shews much cunning and artifice both by his language and smiles." Bristol had run away from another owner (a member of one of North Carolina's most important political and slave-owning families) "some years ago and after weeks of persuasion and many fair promises prevailed on the subscriber to purchase him upon an expressly stipulated condition that having been used to his plantation and management for the time he was in treaty with Mr. Blount [his former owner], and being satisfied to submit to any kind of work or discipline of the other Negroes, if he ran away after drawing me into a loss by inducing me to purchase and then absconding, he would be satisfied to forfeit his head—he was solemnly assured that a reward for his head would be offered in such case." Not only did Bristol run away, he did so "without the smallest provocation" and after "committing some and been accused of many thefts, and under peculiar circumstances of treachery and provocation." His treachery apparently was unlimited, for having assured the subscriber that he would use his considerable persuasive skills to convince another slave to return from an extended absence and to reform his behavior, Bristol instead persuaded the fugitive in question "to accompany him, his brother-in-law."[24]

Death was the penalty for slaves in virtually all murder cases (as well as in cases involving the rape of a white woman, or arson or poisoning, even when those acts did not involve fatalities). When a slave was charged with other crimes such as theft, crimes for which punishments could vary, impudence (or obstinacy as an expression of it) was unquestionably a factor (and often the deciding factor) weighing heavily in favor of the death penalty for those who were convicted. Although the fact of their execution identifies an intolerable degree of impudence, most slaves were invariably described as penitent at death. So, for example, Dolly "made a free confession, acknowledged the justice of her punishment, and died a penitent." She, like her accomplice in the murder of her master's child and the attempted murder of her master, was burnt to death on the "Workhouse Green," though her accomplice, Liverpoole, made no such admission. Most penitents were Christian converts, like those slave narrators who were said to have been "very much concerned with explaining away their picaresque pasts." Unlike those narrators, however, penitents rarely attempted to "foist off their culpability onto slavery."[25] Caesar was "executed at the usual Place [in Charleston], and afterwards hung in Chains at *Hang-man's Point* opposite to this Town, in sight of all Negroes passing and repassing by Water," but "[b]efore he was turned off he made a very Sensible Speech to those of his own Colour, exhorting them to be just, honest and virtuous, and to take warning by his unhappy Example; after which he begged the Prayers of all Christian People, himself repeating the Lord's Prayer and several others in a fervent and devout Manner."[26]

The extent of Caesar's repentance, however, was unusual, and not infrequently the sincerity of the repentance offered could be debatable. A "negro wench" who was executed for setting fire to a house in Charleston declared before "being turned off" that "no other person was concerned in the nefarious act . . . and desired her master to beg pardon for her of the wench whom she had falsely accused, on her trial, being an accessory."[27] There is no indication in this report, however, that she recanted her crime or regretted having done it. Some slaves gained pardons for their role in similar crimes by naming the others responsible.[28] For instance, Kate confessed her guilt for having set fire to a house in Charleston with the "Intent of burning down the remaining Part of the town." Yet her accomplice, Boatswain, who confessed and implicated a number of others who were later proven innocent, "would make no Confession [at the stake?], but died like an impudent hardened Wretch as he was."[29]

One consistent theme in virtually all of the reports of capital offenses committed by slaves is the imputation that the crimes were senseless and unprovoked assaults. The writers impute to the slave offenders an all-consuming vengefulness stemming from very minor and entirely justified actions by the victims against the offenders. The "monstrous" behavior of those accused of such crimes was in that sense symbolic of the moral depravity to which "Negroes," sensible or otherwise, were especially prone, an innate propensity that justified, in the minds of those who benefited from the slave system, disciplining and restraining blacks, and that warranted their enslavement.

This is the obvious conclusion to be drawn, for instance, from Abram's "confession" to having murdered his master. He confessed "at the time he was apprehended [and] repeated immediately after his trial and condemnation, and on the morning of his execution." The first sentence of his "confession" confirms the understanding reflected in reports by whites of other similar cases, thereby strongly indicating why the report was published and perhaps why so few other "confessions" exist: "In consequence of some punishment inflicted on me by my master for some misdemeanor of which I was guilty, a considerable time prior to the fatal catastrophe, I ever after meditated his destruction." The remainder of the "confession" consists of a coldhearted description of the crime, concluding matter-of-factly with "and then I went home." Given the nature of the "confession," the decision to strike his head off after hanging him and to exhibit it "on a pole about 14 feet high, in view of the warehouse, where he was usually employed" seems by comparison lenient and even in a perverse sense humane.[30]

Yet another as-told-to "confession" (as differentiated from reports of preexecution confessionals discussed earlier) was given by a woman named Chloe. She was accused, tried, and convicted of killing a child of her master's and attempting to kill him. Her "confession," not surprisingly, is in its basic thrust very similar to Abram's, but she concludes with a double-edged plea for forgiveness: "I humbly ask forgiveness of every person whom I have injured, particularly my master and mistress; I ask it for Christ's sake; as I from my heart do forgive every person who has injured me. To God I commit myself, hoping that he will receive my spirit."[31]

Very few exceptions to the coldblooded wantonness conveyed in

Abram's "confession" or the self-critical and repentant reflections in Chloe's can be found in colonial newspapers or surviving court records. However, the following very unusual exception to that rule helps enlarge on Chloe's reference to those who had injured her and the provocations that were dismissed in most other reports. The incident took place the month before George Washington left on his Southern tour in 1791, and was reported in a newspaper that he often read, his hometown paper, as it were.

. Several reports about the trial of a slave accused of murdering his overseer appeared in February of that year in the *Virginia Gazette and Alexandria Advertiser*. In late January, according to this newspaper's account, "NEGRO MOSES . . . charged with the murder of Hezekiah Williams, his Overseer," was acquitted in a split decision of the county court, held in Alexandria. The decision apparently acknowledged the argument of the defense that "a Master's authority over the Slave was limited—That, even by the laws of this country, he had no right to deprive his slave of life or members—That a slave, notwithstanding his degraded station, still retained some natural rights, particularly that of self-preservation."[32]

Subsequent issues of the paper contain a debate over the verdict by individuals who sign their responses "A Bye Stander" and "Many Bye-Standers." The debate shares much in common with the one Washington was having with himself at that time. The issue for him was more practical than moral, not that ethical principles were of limited interest to him, but that the rightness or wrongness of an issue generally expressed itself as a practical concern. In the best of all possible worlds slavery would not have been a problem for him or the nation. There would be no need for slaves and no need to discipline them as Moses and his brother Bob had been disciplined by Williams. Such a requirement created a devilish dilemma for owners. (Recall that Jack's owner saw himself as a victim.) In Washington's mind, if it was possible for a man to build for himself the type of life he enjoyed at Mount Vernon without black slaves, who would chose to have them?[33]

"A Bye Stander," though "most heartily . . . wishing that this trial may produce the most happy consequences to that unhappy class of men, by impressing upon the minds and hearts of their masters and overlookers, sentiments of benevolence towards them," thought the verdict was more likely to have the opposite effect. It would have dire consequences for "the defenseless individuals of this area," if "it should encourage disobedience in those who must submit, so long as they continue slaves; if they are taught to believe that they have a right to defend themselves . . . and even to kill the man who shall offer to control them." The lengthy essay, comprising nearly three full columns in small print of a four-column format, ends with the following statement: "That they [black slaves] feel a constant struggle to get free, cannot be doubted: That they have power to effect much, is equally true. They only require encouragement."[34] The opposing letter writers do not significantly dispute the facts of the case, either during the trial or subsequently. A stronger case for self-defense is hard to imagine, Moses having been brutalized to the point of losing his own life when in desperation he shot Williams, apparently as a last resort.

A week after a "Bye Stander's" letter, "Many Bye-Standers" responded. They use language and arguments more typical of their antislavery neighbors in nearby Pennsylvania than of sympathetic northern Virginians. They reason, "The serious and awful consequences to the defenseless individuals of this State, which the Bye-Stander fears, are more likely to be produced by injustice, cruelty, and inhumanity to our slaves, than by a mild, equitable, and humane treatment of them."[35]

"Bye Stander" notes that the court might easily have made a different judgment, as the report of the trial indicated that the verdict had not been unanimous, four magistrates having considered Moses guilty of murder. Nevertheless, according to the "Bye Stander," "a numerous audience of both freeman and slaves" attended the trial, and the verdict was "applauded by the audience, by the most lively expressions of joy." Indeed, Moses' case would not have become a focus for local debate at an earlier or later period in that area's history. Nor would it at the time it occurred had Moses not been presented (and presumably had he not presented himself) as a reluctant killer acting purely out of an instinct for self-preservation. He had not struck against slavery or tried defiantly to assert his independence, as had Washington and his fellow patriots. Instead, at his wits' end he struck back to preserve his life.

Although both Chloe and Abram cast themselves in a very different

light, Chloe, Abram, and Moses are all linked by the structure of contain-
ment and repression in which they acted. As in all of the other examples
cited above, their actions also took place in a survivalist context. Whether
their intent was retributive or self-preserving, they all seem to have defined their actions using the same terms of reference. What slave owners
called impudence was an expression of that logic, whereas rebellion was a
challenge to it, and thus a self-defining act. Impudence as defiance came
out of desperation and frustration—a pushed-to-the-limits response.

The debate over Moses' acquittal is striking because it takes seriously
the possibility that resistance by an individual black person could be justified, even in a slave society, on the basis of self-preservation (as long as
the self being preserved was self-effacing). But the debate does not break
with or in any way contradict the dominant slave-owning definition of
impudence. Moses was acquitted because he literally had no other choice
but to kill his overseer, and because by all indications he regretted having
done so. Had he at any point in his trial suggested otherwise, he would
have undoubtedly been executed.

Thus even though Moses would have been fully and painfully aware of
what was required of him in order to be acquitted, he would have also
been aware, as all survivors needed to be, that survival was the opposite
of submission. Of course he need not have been consciously aware of the
distinction his survival represented. In order to be effective, the assumption that accommodation was a form of resistance would have had to be
internalized. Moses not only defended himself but lived to tell about it.
Having learned to survive, in many cases outrageously, survivors in-
vented new meanings for fighting back. Survival had not lessened their
capacity for anger or their desire for confrontation, but direct engagement
with the slave-owning community was only one option and rarely the
most realistic. Though confrontation might make sense for "outlandish
Negroes," it did not make sense in the survivalist context that the slaves
had created in response to the self-destroying challenge that enslavement
posed for them. In that context, rebellious, as opposed to subversive, behavior was most often understood as being impractical and thus self-
defeating, whereas the activity of surviving had become, survival by survival, self-validating as an action and as a tradition. To build a life for
themselves in the narrow margins between total submission and open defiance was their only realistic option. The price of survival, no one knew

better than they, was usurious in the extreme, but survival also had to be (and was in fact) subversive of enslavement's objectives. Slavery could not survive and maintain itself as a profitable institution in the long term unless they survived as other-than-Negro, but it would not, and could not, allow them to survive without being Negroes.

PART 3

THE CREOLE
DILEMMA

CHAPTER 8

THE DIVIDED SELF

The turn in self-reference that marked the transformation of "outlandish" blacks into survivors did not, and could not have been expected to, occur seamlessly. Resolving or successfully counteracting enslavement's assault on the slave's sense of self created for survivors a dilemma of self-awareness and identity. How survivors experienced that dilemma obviously varied from individual to individual. It also seems logical that the dilemma would manifest itself differently at different times throughout the history of slavery in America. Ironically, in some ways, it is easier to see during the earliest period of the region's colonial history (that is, before the enslavement of blacks was institutionalized) than afterward.

Although historians in recent decades have learned much more than was once thought possible about the black presence in the Chesapeake and low country colonies during the earliest periods of settlement, we still know relatively little about the lives of individual blacks. Fortunately, we have pictures of some of them. Historian Douglas Deal has compiled biographical sketches of more than a dozen blacks, who lived on Virginia's Eastern Shore during the earliest settlement by English colonists beginning in the 1640s. The sketches drawn from surviving court records are admittedly minimalist portraits, few of which provide more than a bare outline of information about litigants. Also, the biographies that have been compiled are only of those few blacks who managed somehow to gain their freedom, and thereby managed (albeit in only a very fragmentary way) to find their way into the records. Yet despite the impersonal and matter-of-fact nature of the records and the scarcity of detail, a sense of the individuality of the subjects described in Deal's biographies comes through. All appear as petitioners in the records, claimants defending themselves against others or claiming rights, including their freedom, that they believed to be their due. Therefore even though the records allow for only the sketchiest insights into their lives, they appear as a more self-reflective presence than do shadowy figures like Billie Lee in the Trumbull and Savage paintings.[1]

No visual record has survived of the blacks who lived in the colonial South during the early decades of its colonization. There are, however, a few portraits of captive Africans who were taken to Europe during the early history of the Atlantic slave trade. Albrecht Dürer sketched two of them during the first decade of the sixteenth century, *Portrait of the Moorish Woman Katharina* and *Study of a Head of a Black Man*. Ironically, these drawings and others like them portray the same sort of self-expressive faces we saw in the portraits or portrait studies by Copley and Reynolds, Benoist and Géricault at the end of the eighteenth or early in the nineteenth century, just as the colonial era was ending.

Images of blacks had been appearing in Western art since the late fourteenth century, but did not appear in Flemish and Dutch painting until the fifteenth century. Until the seventeenth century, when the tradition of ornamental depictions of blacks as servants became pronounced, the images were generally positive and humanizing, even "sweetening" in their effect. Allison Blakely has observed that "these works exude a vitality that demands recognition of their originality and sensitive regard for the subjects treated." Be that as it may, the portraits raise the question of "why Dutch artists [as well as others but especially the Dutch] during these centuries chose to personify Africa in such a favorable light." The answer Blakely gives largely parallels that given by historians of slavery in America to questions relating to the apparent differences in the perceptions of blacks by whites in the colonial South during much of the seventeenth century as compared with subsequent periods. After noting that blacks did not become "fairly commonplace as slaves, servants, and seamen in Dutch port cities" until the seventeenth century, Blakely, who has studied the presence of blacks and the evolution of racial imagery in the Dutch world, observes, "The Dutch perception of blacks, earlier based largely on imagination, could now be tempered by direct experience . . . The religious themes so pronounced in art of the previous centuries gave way in the seventeenth and eighteenth to those related to business and science."[2]

In the colonial Chesapeake (primarily Virginia and Maryland), which was the extent of the colonial South until the settlement that would become colonial South Carolina was established in 1670, white indentured labor used in the tobacco industry gave way, in the late seventeenth century, to labor provided by captive Africans who began arriving in large numbers directly from Africa during that period. Earlier, blacks at times appeared in surviving records not only as other-than-slaves but also as other-than-Negro. Interestingly, during the period we know the least about, the blacks we know most about are those who appear in the public records declaring or defending their servant or free status. A number of these black immigrants came not from Africa but from England, Portugal, or the West Indies. Some, such as John Baptista, a "Moore of Barbary," and Sebastian Cane, from Dorchester in New England, even came voluntarily.[3]

Ira Berlin has deepened our understanding of how different the "charter generation" of blacks in America was from subsequent ones, how different their experiences were from those of the blacks who would follow them, and thus, by implication, how different their perceptions of themselves were from those of subsequent generations. They were, he tells us, a liminal people "drawn or propelled to marginal societies." And in the seventeenth century "few New World slave societies were more marginal than those of mainland North America." Indeed, Britain's Southern colonies in North America would not become slave societies in a meaningful sense until captive Africans from beyond the creolized littoral of West Africa replaced Atlantic Creoles as laborers.[4] Unlike most blacks who were forcibly brought to colonial America during later periods of its history, most of whom became creolized in the colonies, the charter generation of blacks referred to as Atlantic Creoles by Berlin were precreolized, coming as they did from areas in West Africa, or other parts of the Atlantic world of which the West African coast was an increasingly important part, that had already been significantly transformed by contact with Europeans. Along the West African littoral and scattered throughout Europe and the Americas, the Africans who came into close contact with

European traders, explorers, sailors, and missionaries during the first century of sustained contact became "part of the three [Atlantic-connected] worlds" their society reflected. "Familiar with the commerce of the Atlantic, fluent in its new languages, and intimate with its trade and cultures, they were cosmopolitan in the fullest sense," according to Berlin.[5]

By virtue of their "experience, knowledge, and attitude," Atlantic Creoles, Berlin has explained, were better able than were those who would follow them to take advantage of the marginal societies they encountered during the middle third of the seventeenth century. In these societies, "exclusion or otherness—not subordination—posed the greatest dangers."[6]

During the latter decades of the seventeenth century and the early decades of the eighteenth, the Southern colonies were transformed from colonies with slaves into slave societies—that is, into colonies dependent on labor provided by black slaves rather than by white indentured servants. "New Negroes," who were arriving in ever increasing numbers from noncreolized parts of West Africa, began to dominate the records, along with increasing numbers of blacks born in the colonies themselves, many of whom were the children and grandchildren of the "charter generation."

However interesting the experience of the charter generation in colonial America may be, it was relatively fleeting. Much more long lasting were the questions of identity that creolization raised for its members—questions most poignantly symbolized by the name Angola that one of the earliest members of that generation gave to his land. These or related questions, as Berlin shows, persisted into the national era for all survivors.[7]

Following the American Revolution, according to Berlin, "when divisions within the planter class gave black people fresh opportunities to strike for liberty and equality, long-suppressed memories of the origins of African life on the mainland bubbled to the surface, often in lawsuits in which slaves claimed freedom as a result of descent from a free ancestor sometimes white, sometimes Indian, sometimes free black, more commonly from some mixture of these elements."[8] Between the period of the American Revolution and the world the Atlantic Creoles represented, a new generation arrived in the colonies, composed of large numbers of captive

Africans directly imported from Africa. Atlantic Creoles continued to be brought into the colonies but were no longer representative of the larger group. The dilemma posed for Atlantic Creoles by their creolization, however, continued. What changed was the locus of the creolization process. Whereas it had been in Africa itself throughout much of the seventeenth century, in the eighteenth century it shifted to the colonies.[9]

The contrast between the first "charter generation" and successive ones is vividly illustrated in the following series of ads from relatively late in the colonial era. The ads appeared in the *South Carolina Gazette* on the eve of the American Revolution and announce the arrival and sale of newly imported captives from Africa. The colony's second effort to prohibit the external slave trade, begun in 1764, had recently expired, and such ads were once again common in local newspapers. Their appearance and content usually follow predictable patterns, but they are in most cases visually striking, with bold lettering identifying the objects for sale—SLAVES or NEGROES—and drawings emblematic of the composition of advertised cargoes. For example, the predominance of women and children is symbolized by the image of a woman with one child in her arms and another holding her hand, while a third figure, suggesting an older male child, stands nearby. The ads generally provide scant information. Most offer only essential details about the arrival of the cargo and when and where it would be sold. An ad with more than one or two lines of very small print generally indicates something unusual or abnormal about the cargo or the journey, for instance, a report that there had been smallpox on board, and the efforts taken to guard against the spread of that dreaded disease.

The first ad, appearing on June 22, 1769, just as a restrictive regulation on the trade had expired, announces that "Twenty Valuable NEGROES, (Lately imported in the ship *Jenny*, Richard Webster, Master, from Africa)" were "To Be Sold at auction, at the usual place in Charles-Town, on Thursday the 13th July next, at eleven o'clock, for ready money." The slaves belonged "to the estate of Thomas Fowler, deceased" and most could speak English, "having been the property of the said Thomas Fowler, for some years past, on the Rice or Grain Coast, viz. two men, five women, twelve boys, from 12 to 18 years of age, and one girl." The previous month, on May 19, two ads in the *Gazette* explained that the *Jenny* had just arrived (that is, on the fifteenth of May) with two hundred healthy prime Negroes on board, the majority of whom were available through John Edwards and Company, while eleven others from the same ship were offered for sale by Nath. Russell. In other words, Fowler's former slaves represented a minority of the cargo that was presumably dominated by unacculturated captives.

More than three years later an ad similar to those just described announced the recent arrival of "A CARGO of Two Hundred and Thirty CHOICE NEGROES, Of whom One Hundred and Seventy-Two are Men." These slaves had just arrived in the ship *Two-Brothers* and were all reportedly in perfect health, having been inoculated for the smallpox before they left Africa. "Among them," the ad explains, "are Twenty young Men and Women, with their Children, in Families, late Servants to a Person leaving Gambia-River, most of whom can talk English, and have been used to attend a House and go in Craft." Apparently because of their unusual background, they were to "be kept separate in the Yard."[10]

We have no way of knowing whether the creolized Africans mentioned in this ad appreciated being segregated from the other Africans (or vice versa). But we do know that levels of acculturation continued to operate as important divisions among black survivors, and that those divisions served the interests of the slave-owning, rather than the slave, community. Creolization in the abstract was a process of cultural change, but for blacks living in a slave society it was experienced in the concrete as forced acculturation that worked as a process of subjection and marginalization. To survive was to become creolized and thus to choose adaptation as a means of surviving, but forced acculturation fused adaptation to subjection as an expression of self-denial. The requirements of acculturation thus acted to generate divisions within black communities reflective of degrees of perceived marginality. The more highly acculturated a slave became, the more he or she was inclined to identify with those who were by comparison less fully or effectively creolized. Thus declarations of identity, whether spoken or acted out, increasingly became negative affirmations.

In theory at least the term Creole could represent (that is, from a survivor's perspective) both an alternate, survivalist, identity and a cultural strategy for survival.[11] Creole status, that is, promised an alternate identity—the possibility of being other-than-Negro in a world where Negro symbolized a wretchedness that could only be survived. Creole status therefore offered an escape from the stigma of wretchedness, in the same sense that acculturation promised, if not freedom, then acceptance and a life less wretched than that of Negro slaves. The limit of each promise was the realization that neither could ever be realized. Being Negro was an indelible stigma because it symbolized an innate characteristic, thereby keeping alive for each survivor the possibility that the creolized African was the slave, not the "outlandish" captive, that to survive was to endure, not to overcome.

The following, taken from an early issue of the *South Carolina Gazette*, was written by Benjamin Franklin under the pseudonym "Blackamore." Drawing on what he characterizes as the dilemma of the mulatto in order to illustrate the dilemma of "our half Gentry," Franklin notes that,

> It is observed, concerning the Generation of Mulattos, that they are seldom well belov'd either by the Whites or the Blacks. Their Approach towards Whiteness, makes them look back with some kind of Scorn upon the Colour they seem to have left, while the Negroes, who do not think them better than themselves, return their Contempt with Interest: And the Whites, who respect them no Whit the more for the nearer Affinity in Colour, are apt to regard their Behaviour as too bold and assuming, and bordering upon Impudence. As they are next to Negroes, and but just above 'em, they are terribly afraid of being thought Negroes, and therefore avoid as much as possible their Company or Commerce: and Whitefolks are as little fond of the Company of Molattoes.[12]

Traditionally, the dilemma ascribed to free blacks and mulattos by contemporaries like "Blackamore," as well as by later writers and historians, has been viewed, at least implicitly, as a consequence of enslavement, as a condition produced by it rather than as a precondition for its success—the paradigmatic dilemma of identity and self-awareness that was necessary for captive Africans to be successfully enslaved, and that was required by slavery for its long-term stability.

The fictional embodiment of the mulatto dilemma "Blackamore" describes is the "noble Negro."[13] A prototype of the character is Orinooko, the protagonist in Aphra Behn's late-seventeenth-century short novel. Indeed, according to Wylie Sypher, Orinooko was "the forefather of those Negroes used by antislavery writers to convince their readers that the Negro is not really negroid." Further on in another but related context, he comments that "the noble Negress, like the noble Negro, became all things to all poets," providing antislavery writers with a ready symbol for their purposes, that is, "the African who united the traits of the white man, so that he might not be repulsive; the traits of the Indian, so that he might not seem base; and the traits of the Negro so that he might rouse pity." This character or mode of characterization had been developed to such an extent by the early 1770s that poets, according to Sypher, no longer needed to "invent but simply to adopt this hero, the Negro who is not a Negro, a creature who lives, moves, and has his being in the arcadia of primitivism."[14]

As "Blackamore" suggests, "the Negro who is not a Negro" (or who identified herself as other-than-Negro) was not entirely a fiction. Indeed, "the noble Negro," if not a real person in the sense that Behn and others imagined, represented a very real dilemma for blacks throughout the history of slavery in America and elsewhere in the Atlantic world.[15] For very different reasons, it was as important to blacks as it was to antislavery writers to convince others and to affirm for themselves that they were not really "Negro" in the sense in which the term was used to describe them during the course of their enslavement, and thus not as "ignoble" as slavery required them to be as a rationalization for their enslavement, while at the same time insisting that they were by nature incapable of nobility.

Sypher's point is that as a literary device the "noble Negro" was inherently flawed because the character could not "be a meaningful symbol of the misery that he is supposed to represent. Consequently, the downtrodden, ordinary African must be used to signify the wretchedness of the slave. . . . The princely Negro stands in sharp opposition to his miserable fellow slave."[16]

Extending Sypher's description of the "noble Negro" to encompass the dilemma that survival represented for blacks in the colonial South, would require very little modification. In seeking to proclaim their nobility or identify themselves as other-than-Negro by means of their creolization, survivors were continually confronted by the inherent contradiction in such an effort. For, in Sypher's view, "Whenever the truly noble Negro is reduced to slavery, he cannot exact a purely humanitarian pity because he cannot submit to the ignominy of slavery; he must rebel, speak the fiery language of revolt, and die operatically, evoking not pity but astonishment."[17]

Paraphrased to reflect the line of argument running throughout this part of the study, Sypher's concluding remark would read: Whenever the truly outlandish Negro is reduced to slavery, he or she cannot capitulate because he or she cannot submit to the ignominy of slavery without renouncing the identity without which he or she could not sustain a positive sense of self; such slaves must either kill themselves or rebel, speaking the fiery language of revolt, and die operatically, evoking not anger or resentment from slave owners but fear and astonishment. But what of the "sensible Negro" who survived enslavement? She shared the dilemma of the "noble Negro" and the reality of the "ignoble Negro" but not the perspective of those who created the character.

For survivors the price of survival was the Creole dilemma. Their sense of themselves at any point in its reorientation was divided against itself in much the same manner that the captives on the *Two-Brothers* were separated, each side positioned in a negative relationship to the other. Creole identities, even though they varied greatly, were structured unavoidably in that way, appearing as negative affirmations of others or as "an identity of passions."[18]

Just as the "ordinary African," according to Sypher, was used by antislavery writers to "signify the wretchedness of the slave," the "princely Negro" stood "in sharp opposition to his miserable fellow-slave."[19] Similarly, the "outlandish Negro" stood in opposition to the "sensible Negro," in the same sense as Polydore's former self stood in relation to his survivor self, not necessarily antagonistic but estranged and increasingly divergent and incommensurate.

One need not have looked upon one's fellow slaves with scorn and contempt, or condescension, in order to feel the tension of identity embedded within the fact of survival, a tension that was intuitively apparent to all survivors but felt and experienced in very different ways, reflective of the particular nature of each slave's experience of being enslaved.

❦

Perhaps nowhere else in the extant sources is the dilemma being suggested here expressed as clearly as it is in the following relatively unusual newspaper account. The brief item begins with a short introduction, noting that the "following letter" came "(well recommended) from a Gentleman in Somerset County [Maryland]." The subject of the letter is "a Negro Man, who has been a Slave, but is now free." The letter writer is uncertain about where the "Negro man" was born but speculates that he was probably a native of "the Country [the colonies]." There is no indication either, according to the author, how he was able to obtain "so good an Education, as to learn Reading and Writing, which he impro'd at all Opportunities, and of which he has made a good Use." Also, and certainly not incidentally, the letter notes that "he was and is remarkable for his Fidelity, Sobriety, and Honesty, and has been for many Years a Communicant in the Parish where he lives; and has liv'd a regular, Christian, blameless Life."[20]

In the letter that follows it is explained that the free black man, whose character was testified to in the introduction, is well known in Somerset County for his medical knowledge and healing skills. According to the author, who signed him or herself "A. B.," the man "has had Physical Secrets communicated to him by an old, skilful, experienced *Guinea* Doctor, his Predecessor." Of special note in that regard, according to "A. B.," is "a Cure for the Stone and Gravel, the Bite of a Snake, Dry Gripes, and Fluxes of both Kinds, more especially the Bloody Flux." The value of these cures, the author insists, is not based on hearsay or idle rumors. The doctor, we are told, "has had so remarkable success, that none have died of that Distemper under his Care, and he has attended Numbers for near thirty Years past." Moreover, many people in the area could and would gladly attest to these statements.[21]

The unsigned introduction, interestingly, was concerned to authenticate the source of the letter and attest to the subject's sobriety and honesty by emphasizing the level and quality of his acculturation, manifested by his hard-won literacy and religious conversion. The letter itself, however, is concerned to promote the miraculous nature and effectiveness of the subject's medical skills (and cures) by tying them to an African past. Enslavement of course embodied many levels of paradox, so it should not be surprising to find expressed in this description of an anonymous "guinea doctor" two contradictory concerns. On the one hand was the demand that captives be culturally assimilated as fully and as quickly as possible; on the other hand was the need not break "their hearts" to such a degree that their will to survive would be diminished or eliminated. The irony of course is that something of their former selves, the selves from which enslavement was to save them, had to survive in order for captives to become what owners wished and needed them to become.

The newspaper account took for granted, as slave society in general did, that acculturation ideally moved in one direction, toward a detachment from Africa and all things African, rather than oscillating within its movement, and that therefore whatever former cultural attribute survived either reflected the failure of the process, which meant most often that the slave had proven incorrigible, or was made useful by means of his and her cultural transformation.

Though premised on the innate moral and intellectual incapacity of those forced to submit to its assault, forced acculturation, as examined in part 2, depended on the ability of slaves to maintain and preserve (so as to build upon) those culturally imprinted resources of mind and spirit that made their survival possible and that made them valuable as slaves. Yet the portrait we are given of the anonymous former slave described above is of a man whose life and personality contained and drew upon equal portions of folk wisdom and literacy, African and European cultural influences, Christian and non-Christian belief systems. This mix of elements was drawn from diverse sources; it represented a transatlantic history, and had been forged, as a distinctive experience, in a relatively remote but also relatively typical part of plantation America, by a resilient and creatively adaptive individual.

Rather than vying with one another, the multiple dichotomies appearing in the portrait are presented in a way that suggests that they not only coexisted comfortably with one another but were also in some sense complementary. Instead of competing for supremacy within the portrait's subject, and thereby for dominance of the subject's identity, the various influences and cultural survivals coexisted, no one of them appearing to have been more or less essential than were others to his well-being. Yet there is also a distinct sense of incompatibility in the striking juxtaposition of two such fundamentally antagonistic references. The portrait, however, offers little if any basis for understanding how the two juxtaposed parts of its subject's life interrelated or interacted, converged or conflicted with one another.

As a cultural dilemma, the Creole dilemma was subsumed within the experience of being and becoming Negro and transformed by it. At some point during their transition from "outlandish" to "sensible Negroes" Africa, for survivors, became a variable of their Negroness, something to be identified with or denied, not something to be or become. Africa was and remained a central part of each survivor's experience, of the survival experience for all blacks, even as the relation of most survivors to Africa grew faint, even when they no longer recognized its influence on the ways in which they expressed themselves. More and more it came to distinguish, rather than define or determine, the forms of expression they relied on. As it faded and dissolved as a remembered presence, Africa remained vital to each survivor's identity as a point of departure, even for those who tried their best to distance themselves from it. For survivors it was ever the thing rejected and denied or longed for and cherished. Being and becoming Negro involved a negation of Africa but survival also renamed it. The distinctiveness of survivors' expressive culture gave its creolized embodiment definition as a self-proclaimed identity, an identity that was prior-to-Negro rather than other-than-Negro. However much Africa remained important to survivors in their efforts to deal with the dilemma of their survival, it also remained embedded in it.

When Jack in "A Short Story" became an obedient servant under the terms set by his owner, he became a Negro. When he decided to survive rather than resist his owner's ultimatum, he accepted the necessity of playing the part of a Negro, which meant that no matter what or who he thought or felt he was in his heart of hearts, he had to pretend to be someone else in order to survive. Although he undoubtedly understood the pretense as a form of resistance, from a slave owning perspective his acceptance of the part was what a "sensible Negro" would do.

"A Short Story" begins with an effort by Jack to determine the role he will play but ends with his agreeing to take on the part assigned to him by his owner. The story does not go on to describe how he played that role, other than to say he became an obedient servant, but we know from the ads for runaway slaves and from many other sources that survivors inter-preted their roles, through their performances, in many different ways. One of the more extreme ways a few survivors attempted to meet the challenge was by playing the part of being a Negro in ways that were so exaggerated that their performance bordered on parody. If intended as parody, however, the performance, like defiant behavior, could not be ob-vious as such. Acquiescing to forced acculturation without at the same time fully accepting its expectations or its assumptions meant that sur-vivors were required to play the roles assigned, or rather ascribed, to them convincingly. Playing the part, no matter how skillfully (no matter how cleverly and subversively), was (and was intended to be) the clearest sign of the actor's subjection. To preserve a sense of self, survivors had to play a self-denying role. For those who survived enslavement in the colo-nial South, the drama of their enslavement meant playing the part of a racially subordinate slave and thus acting like a Negro.

The challenge to survivors was to perform their ascribed roles so well that the performance never betrayed insincerity, at least not blatantly, but not so well that the performer was taken over by the part. Faced with this difficult assignment, some blacks responded by overacting, or throwing themselves into the part with such enthusiasm that it was hard to judge their sincerity. Old Stepney apparently took this tack. In a classic scene of its type, his greet-ing of Henry Laurens, Stepney's owner, when he returned from England in 1774 borders on the burlesque. Even Laurens, who expected to be "loved" by his slaves in return for his protection, support, and kindness, could hardly believe it. Recalling the incident, he says, "my Knees were Clasped, my hands kissed my very feet embraced & nothing less than a very, I can't say fair but full Buss of my Lips would satisfy the old Man [meaning Step-ney] weeping and Sobbing in my Face." They (Stepney and the two other "old Domestics" who greeted him) wanted to know how "Master Jacky Master Harry Master Jemmy" were, and they all "encircled" Laurens, squeezing him so tightly that he says he "could scarcely get from them—Ah said the old Man I never thought to see you again, now I am happy."[22] Philip Morgan notes of Laurens's description of the scene, "Laurens, as much as he tried to make a joke about the 'fair' kiss on his lips, was obviously moved." He also makes the point that "Stepney seems to have served quite faithfully thereafter" and that a number of planters like Laurens, Landon Carter for in-stance, "adopted a respectful attitude toward [their] more elderly slaves."[23]

A number of other planters in the colonial and early national South left accounts of similar greetings.[24] Laurens's fellow South Carolinian, General William Moulton, experienced the same sort of elated welcome in 1782 that Laurens says he was given in 1774. Stopping at his plantation on his way to Charleston to see the British end their occupation of that city, Moulton says he was greeted warmly by a few of his slaves. "On entering the place, as soon as the negroes discovered that I was of their party, there was immediately a general alarm and an outcry through the plantation that, 'Massa was come! Massa was come!'" So enthusiastic were they, Moulton felt compelled to stand "in the piazza to receive them. They gazed at me with astonishment . . . and every now and then some one or other would come out with a 'Ky!' and the old Africans joined in a war-song in their own language of 'Welcome the war home.'"[25]

There is certainly ample evidence to support the idea that, "[a]s masters relied on slaves, so slaves returned the favor." It is also undoubtedly true that in at least some cases, the welcome-home scene was a ritualized event. Indeed, "some receptions seem too effusive to be explained away as a set of cynical maneuvers."[26] We know with greater certainty that in some cases mutual respect between a master and a slave, both male and female, did exist. The certainty in these cases, however, is based on indications that it was earned and on both sides of the relationship. But even in those cases there was a limit to the affection that accompanied the respect, because the relationship was always an unequal one. Ironically what makes the behavior of slaves like Stepney seem so suspicious to us (and to Laurens as well) is not that there were no reasons beyond self-interest for him to be glad to see Laurens again. Rather it was the exaggerated way he chose to show his delight that makes us suspicious.

The runaway ads help put Stepney's greeting in broader perspective. The part of the ads of interest here is where the writer describes the fugitive's response "when spoken to." Some of these we have already discussed, the ones for instance that describe how a runaway would stutter when questioned harshly, or those that indicate that the escaped slave was bold or brazen or full of self-confidence. A large number of others comment on the smiling countenance of the individual being sought. And of these a substantial majority express some doubt as to the sincerity of that gesture.

One example is the ad for Will. He is remarkable, the ad claims, for "shewing his teeth [in a] clonish grin when spoke with." The ad also notes that "his dress [is] uncertain," meaning he would, like his name, probably change it to avoid recapture.[27]

Another, in the same vein, advertises for the return of a slave who is said to have "a smiling submissive countenance when spoken to, but is a desperate, blood-thirsty fellow." Similarly, another runaway slave is said to smile when spoken to "and appears as if he was very obliging." Other ads use descriptions such as "generally smiles when spoken to but is naturally surly," or has "an expressive countenance and when spoken to assumes a smiling and good natured aspect."[28]

A unique variation on this general theme is the ad that says of Ned: "He is an agreeable fellow in his address, and will attempt, with an assumed name, to pass as a free man; but when arrested will probably use the words 'my dear master' very frequently." Another advertiser says that the man who ran away from him was very "sensible" and of "a submissive behavior," yet he is also described as a very good actor, who would likely change his clothes and pretend to be a sailor.[29]

Occasionally an ad will capture in its tone and with the specificity of its description what is vague in many others, or implied more than stated, or said in such an awkward way that its meaning is obscured. The ad for Jacob is of that sort. Jacob, who ran away nearly four years before the ad was placed, the ad tells us, is about twenty-four or five, "about five feet 10 inches high, very strait and well made." One of his distinguishing features is his "somewhat . . . Indian colour . . . [and] fine white teeth." "He is very chatty," the ad continues, "affects to talk politely, and seems very ready, obliging and complaisant." Next, after having described for readers the fugitive's observed appearance and behavioral characteristics, the woman who placed the ad offers the following information about his activities since his departure. "Shortly after he went away," she reports, "he enlisted with Capt. Bradford, in Col. Voce's regiment of the Pennsylvania line, while laying at the Head of Elk, on their way to Virginia, and when in Virginia he played some prank for which he was confined, and afterwards made his escape." This apparently is in line with and confirmation of her observation that he "*affects* to talk politely, and *seems* very ready, obliging and complaisant."[30]

A few advertisers were more trusting, almost defiantly so, insisting (as

George and Martha Washington did regarding Olney Judge) that their slave could not have, or would not have, run away unless motivated by some other cause than disaffection from his or her owner. One of those ads describes a waiting man who is smiling and complaisant and honest. The advertiser has convinced himself that the only reason the slave ran off is that he had quarreled with his wife. Perhaps, but if so, why offer to pay ten dollars "to any Person that will deliver him to me." He adds the stipulation "let him be well used,"[31] but what did "well used" mean, or, rather, how would readers looking to earn a quick ten dollars interpret the phrase. No visible bruises or other marks? No broken limbs? Well fed? And of course if the slave ran away because he had had a fight with his wife, and was so content and honest, why advertise for him at all? Was not such a person bound to return of his own accord?

In contrast to the doubts we may have, few advertisers express any doubt that their fleeing slaves are sincere in what they say or do, and warn the public to beware of their devious ways. One owner even thought his runaway slave, who had a habit of "repeating his words when he speaks," was pretending to stammer. John repeats his words, the ad explains, "with a kind of stammering that appears rather affected than natural."[32]

Repeatedly ads express doubt about the way that a slave presented him or herself. Jacob, one ad observes, is "very chatty, affects to talk politely, and seems very ready, obliging and complaisant." In another ad, Sambo, one of ten slaves to run away from the subscriber, is said to "affect valour." According to another ad, one of several fugitives sometimes pretended to be in deep "consumption." Cuffee, who was being sought because he had broken out of jail, was accused of affecting much innocence and honesty. Frank, commonly called Frank Mutton, is described by his owner as having "a smiling submissive countenance when spoken to, but is a desparate, blood-thirsty fellow." In the same vein Toney is described in another ad as having "a cheerful countenance," but as being in reality extremely deceitful. Sarah, for her part, according to yet another ad, "universally [greets] every person she meets, black or white, with a hypocritical smile, by which means she appears to have obtained many friends."[33]

As would be expected given the nature of the ads, advertisers rarely express confidence in the sincerity of blacks who appear good-natured, happy, and content. Instead, their confidence is generally placed in those fugitives who appeared to be "blood-thirsty" without any pretense of "submissiveness" in their appearance, those with "sullen, ill-natured countenance[s]" or who were "very bold" and appeared self-assured.[34]

Whether or not Stepney identified with the role of Laurens's fawning and adoring slave, his behavior offered an interesting counterpoint to the ideal expected of him, and one that obviously made Laurens uncomfortable, as it did most other slave owners who left a record of their experience with similar displays. Sensible, ideally, meant judicious not obsequious. Obsequiousness subverted the recognitive relationship that resulted from objectification, turning it rather forcefully and unexpectedly on its source. It so exaggerated the logic and presumptions of the process that the relationship momentarily became uncomfortable and embarrassing for the one who had sought most to objectify the actor. Masters were made uneasy not because they were nonplussed by flattery of that nature. Their discomfort stemmed instead from how the behavior trivialized the master/slave relationship and reduced it to a farce. Where is the honor in such a relationship? Whereas the slave's subjection by means of objectification elevated and illuminated the slave owners' self-image, obsequious behavior by blacks ridiculed it. If only briefly, it turned the spotlight into a floodlight, a blinding light that caused the nearest shadows to recede, exposing rather than flattering those toward whom it was directed.

In most cases we cannot know whether a particular slave or a group of slaves identified with the role they were playing (whether they had become the part they played so often), but we do know how important masking was to the survival of slaves more generally, whether in Athens or Rome, Egypt or Brazil, or the American South. And of course, given the possible consequences, doing it well was critical. Making the audience believe in the performance was essential if its objective, whatever that may have been, was to be achieved. The whole point is that we are not, any more than slave owners were, supposed to know.

CHAPTER 9

BEING AND BECOMING CREOLE

Pretending to be happy and content, loyal and trustworthy, grateful and truly fond of one's master or mistress might have been a relatively low-risk way of having some fun at his or her expense. As an indulgence it was extremely dangerous, however, because it could easily become its own objective rather than a means to transform an inherently demeaning role into one that was more positive and self-affirming. But for many blacks (runaway slaves, for instance, and in some sense for all blacks) the need to deceive an owner, or others who threatened their survival, was not a matter of personal indulgence. For runaway slaves, who were invariably described by advertisers as capable of great deception and likely to pretend to be anything other than themselves in order to avoid recapture, a certain degree of pretense was necessary to have any chance of gaining their freedom. However, for its own sake, or purely as a self-indulgence, self-denial could easily become a habit, and in the most negative and addicting sense.

In surviving records the risk appears clearest in accounts of the most highly acculturated slaves and free blacks. Most of them no doubt would have been offended by Stepney's behavior. The whole point of becoming highly acculturated was to distance oneself from such roles and the performance style associated with them. Yet, no less than Stepney, they sought the acceptance or approval of slave owners. The logic of survival for at least some of the most highly acculturated blacks in the colonial

South impelled them to strive for freedom by becoming more and more literate. They believed, or wanted to believe, that they deserved being free by virtue of having become more completely acculturated than other slaves or free blacks (or for that matter nonelite whites). At its most extreme, the acculturated self thought of freedom as a natural right shared by all those who were recognized as being other-than-Negro, either because they were born so or because they had demonstrated their humanity. Those survivors, who saw themselves as being anything but stereotypical Negroes, came to identify themselves, and expected to be identified by others, as something other-than-Negro. Stepney is striking by contrast because he sought to present himself as the quintessential Negro. At its most highly acculturated extreme, the compulsion to be other-than-Negro could, and often did, manifest itself as a refined version of the obsequious behavior examined in the previous chapter. For assimilated or assimilating blacks, however, appearing highly acculturated was not a pretense. What is fascinating about their performance, as it appears in surviving records, is that they seem to have fully identified with their role, offering no hint that they were acting at all even when the performance seemed tragically self-denying.

In the ads for runaway slaves, fugitives described as being highly acculturated and also having a high regard for themselves were seen by advertisers as pretending to be something they were not and could never become. Respect for blacks, whether slave or free, was reserved for those who accepted who and what they were with dignity, meaning by being judicious, deferential, and decorous at all times (and perhaps also for those rebellious and defiant slaves who died operatically).

The case most often cited, perhaps because it is one of the most obvious examples of its type, is that of Christopher McPherson. Before losing much of what he had managed to acquire as a free black, he had climbed so high that it would have been surprising if he had not begun to think of himself as other-than-Negro. He "owned a fine home" in Richmond and his own carriage and horses in which "his wife and two daughters were driven about the town." But of course this was not appropriate behavior for blacks in Richmond (or anywhere else in the early national South), even for free and well-connected blacks. Thus, McPherson was required to come up with an acceptable explanation for the anomaly his behavior represented. The reason he offered was that his age and job required that mode of transportation. But of course the need to explain, however true or convincing the explanation, was a recognition that the practice was against the law and customs of the area, thus a recognition that he had lost his social bearings. However, he thought of it as a gesture that would allow the city fathers to make an exception in his case. When they did not, prominent whites sent letters of reference to the city council on his behalf, "but the ultimate suggestion of these men," according to the account being relied on here, "was that it would be best for McPherson and his family to live elsewhere than in the state of Virginia."[1]

At some point McPherson sent to the legislature a careful, chronological itemization of his rise to prominence, as a testimony to his claim that an exception should be made in his case. Clearly he was not like other Negroes. He was not sure, like many other blacks, when he was born or even if his birth had taken place in Louisa County, Virginia, although to the best of his recollection that was his place of birth. Thereafter the chronology is very specific: "1770 I went to school in Goochland, near the Courthouse. . . . Remained 1-3/4 years." From there in 1772 he went "behind the counter at the Elk Horn Store, at Petersburg." Then for the period between 1776 and 1777 there is simply this brief comment: "Schooling[,] children, etc." McPherson must have been a gifted student because from 1778 to 1781 he served as "Clerk for the Commercial Agent for the State; during this time and at the siege of Yorktown [he] was clerk for one of the Commisaries Genl. And otherwise rendered essential service for the Continental Army." After the war he served for many years as clerk for David Ross, Esquire, who is not otherwise identified by McPherson, becoming by 1788 his "principal clerk . . . Whilst 2 to 6 gentlemen were under my direction (I mustered in this time . . . Which I disliked)."

For the period 1788 to 1799, during which he served as Ross' principal clerk, there is only one reference in his chronology, but it is as remarkable and bizarre as everything else in his extraordinary life. "Twas I think 1797 that a riot was passing in the road by my door near Columbia, of a number of slaves. . . . I turned out with my sword, to suppress it, without expecting any help. Major John Quarle's certificate goes to prove that with my help mischief was prevented." In contrast, but in the same vein and to the same intended effect, is a note for 1802, mentioning that he had been a "witness for a man of colour . . . . When my oath was taken by the jury in the District Court, in preference to the opposite oaths of two white witnesses." Two years later he "Enrolled for Congress . . . Till Spring 1800," the year in which "Mr. Jefferson by letter introduced me to Mr. Madison . . . . I sat at table noon and evening with Mrs. Madison, his lady, and company, and enjoyed a full share of the conversation." Summing up the last few years of his life, up to the date of his petition, McPherson writes, "Throughout the whole course of my life I have been considered by numerous white acquaintances as one of their number . . . And they have uniformly treated me as such." In closing he made this final plea: "(Color is nothing . . . Worth is all with liberal minds) I can prove all the above by very many substantial witnesses."

One of the first scholars to examine McPherson's life closely suggested that it "affords an illustration of the fact that free Negroes occasionally attained a position high in the respect of the white citizens of the state [Virginia]."[2] A more recent examination concludes that "McPherson's career illustrates [that] even those who combined exceptional skill with unusual luck could not escape the bonds of race." The saga of McPherson's extraordinary rise and tragic decline, in this reading, demonstrates the "common use of patron-client relations for limited goals" that is reflected in "McPherson's failure to win recognition of his claim to special equality." That failure in turn underscores "the way in which people of African descent living in early Richmond forged their identities in spaces produced through their simultaneous inclusion in and exclusion from the state's and the city's dominant culture."[3]

In a more limited context, another scholar remarks relative to McPherson's effort to open a night school for blacks in Richmond that the attempt taught McPherson a very clear lesson: "any black man who would attempt to found a school was 'crazy.'"[4] All these readings seem reasonable, as does yet another analysis of McPherson's personal life. In this reading McPherson is seen as a champion of his people brought down by the racism of his time: "A kind master, an education, the courage to publicize unpopular ideas, and years of hard labor," the study concludes, "raised him temporarily from the mass of his fellows, but the realities of Virginia Negro life soon returned him to obscurity."[5]

His life when elaborated, in addition to raising questions about his mental state throughout its many dramatic moments, is filled with events and behavior that suggest not that he was undone by taking on and internalizing the role of other-than-Negro but that he became lost in a confusion of roles. What leaps out from this telling of his story, though it is buried and offered without comment, is his relationship to his wife and two of his children mentioned in his will. At a critical point in the litigation growing out of his effort to found a school for free black children in 1811, he was brought into court "on charges of disturbing the peace which grew out of an argument with his wife over the carriage and coachman." He died in 1817, she in 1816, so there is no mention of her in his will, just as there is no mention of her after he was taken to court in 1811. In his will he left money for three grandchildren, the children of one of his daughters, presumably by his wife. He also left money to purchase the freedom of "his two children by different slave mothers."[6] Ironically, the fact that he fathered two children by slave mothers replicates in part the circumstances of his own birth. His mother, apparently, was a slave and his father "a Scots merchant named Charles McPherson," who persuaded the woman who owned McPherson's mother to sell McPherson to the merchant for whom he would eventually clerk.[7]

To add to the issues that these aspects of his life raise, on Christmas day of 1798, Christopher had "the first glimmering" of a religious experience that would play a central role in the remainder of his life. Later, he says, his mission became clear to him. It had become his duty "to warn the world of the impending doom described by St. John." Although his behavior thereafter frequently borders on (or even transcends) the bizarre, there is also consistently running through it what might best be termed a very rational approach to the bizarre. He is careful, even meticulous, in documenting his experiences, as when he led a procession through Norfolk at high noon on July 4, 1799, in order to inform as many people as possible of his revelation. Beforehand he had sought and received permission from the mayor of Norfolk to lead the procession. After baptizing himself at the conclusion of another procession led through nearby Portsmouth on that same day, he received certificates from the Norfolk mayor, from a man named William King in Portsmouth, "and from other citizens about his performances." These documents were to be used "as evidence of his 'Baptism' and the seriousness of his work." Moreover, while still in Norfolk, he wrote former president George Washington to obtain an introduction to the current president, John Adams, because, McPherson said, he was planning to travel to the North. He did travel north, but apparently without Washington's endorsement. Nonetheless, once in Philadelphia he wrote directly to Adams and requested an audience in order to make the president aware of his revelation, and to warn him about the coming calamity he had foreseen in a vision earlier that year, 1799. He wanted to tell him, as Adams's biographer has explained, that he was convinced that he was "the person described in the 11th and 16th chapter of the Revelation of St. John the Divine."[8]

Whereas neither Washington nor Adams responded, McPherson says that he was able to meet, and subsequently dine with James Madison, because of a letter of introduction written for him by Thomas Jefferson. Indeed, he was never shy about requesting references. He obtained one from William Waller Hening, for whom he clerked in Charlottesville, and another from George Wythe. Though Hening proved to be very helpful, his recommendation could be read in different ways. Wythe's recommendation amounted to a negative endorsement, stating in effect that he had not heard anything bad about him. McPherson, apparently, had decided to take any letter written for him by a prominent person that could not be interpreted as a criticism as an endorsement. He seemed to have understood that association with prominent men, no matter how incidental, was its own endorsement. And he was right.

However, he does not seem to have recognized how counterproductive his public promotion of his vision was to his career and even his personal well-being. Clearly he was also nothing if not ambitious. Thus, in his letter to Adams, along with the certificates he received from the mayor of Norfolk, he provides a description of his baptism. With a black friend, he says, he "went into the Water, waist high—and the whole body of the said Chris. McPherson was backwards immersed in Water for some time, he arose and went to a post . . . and kneeled down by it, for about the Space of half an hour—praying, and singing as before-mentioned. . . . Many people were Witnesses to this Ceremony."[9]

He was apparently never daunted or deterred when people rebuffed him. Virtually all of the prominent individuals he mentions in his various writings ignored him, yet he was able to solicit from some of them a written acknowledgment of his existence. Whites seemed to take serious note of him only when he acted to quell black rioters and when he tried to open a school for free blacks in Richmond. Indeed, the attention of many whites became suddenly intense when he placed an advertisement in a local newspaper to announce that the school had opened and to recommend that "people of colour throughout the United States" should do the same "in their neighborhoods." The larger public, he quickly added, would also benefit "from a wide expansion of light and knowledge among this class of people founded upon the pure principles of Morality and Religion." If that meant he expected whites in Richmond to support his efforts, he was wrong, which is not as surprising as the fact that he thought they would, or might.[10]

Perhaps he was insane, even though the board of directors of the Williamsburg asylum said he was not. He was sent there after having been thwarted in the courts and then taking his cause(s) to the streets of Richmond. His behavior, based on his own descriptions of it, was erratic, but his explanation for it was not. He thought he had something important to tell the world, and he wanted people to listen, to pay attention. Perhaps whites in Richmond thought he was insane because he acted so unlike the ways Negroes were expected and required to. Indeed, perhaps it was insane, even if McPherson was not, for a black man, no matter how exceptional he considered himself to be, to want to save the world in a Christian sense and at the same time to help his nation by helping other free blacks.

Be that as it may, many questions remain. What were he and his wife arguing about? About the carriage, or something to do with the two other women he had children with? Who brought charges? Was it just an excuse by authorities to harass him at a time when important people in the city were outraged by his plans for opening a school for free blacks? Was it a combination of both? And which of the many personas (or variations of the same one) was McPherson's? The one who wrote that "color was nothing"? Or the one who wrote after his court appearance for disturbing the peace that "a man of colour . . . had but a slender chance of success, in going to law with weighty officers of the land"? And how crazy was he, if he was at all? Crazy like Nat Turner, who would be called to revolt by his own apocalyptic vision? Was he a free black version of Turner? And who did he really think he was? Other-than-Negro, or the Negro as prophet? A Negro for whom race as color had become "nothing," a messenger of "impending doom," or its embodiment as the inevitable consequence of forcing a people to survive by living a life of self-denial?

Of the many hard-to-explain aspects of McPherson's life, his relationship to other blacks is not least among them. He seems consistent in his effort to identify with whites, but on closer examination it is clear he did not mean all whites. Apparently he came to believe that his attainment of such a high level of acculturation had separated him from other blacks, but had not made him white. He had become an exception to the generally held slave-owning view of blacks, and he sought recognition by prominent whites. As an exception he sought to identify with other exceptional people.

The few glimpses of his behavior toward blacks, and his conduct among them, all seem to be based on an assumption by him that he had a right by virtue of his exceptional attainments to speak for and to lead them. Thus he sought to establish a school for blacks and to control their riotous behavior. No one had asked him to intercede in the latter; and when he did, it surprised the leader of the militia unit assigned to restore order. That officer would write, following McPherson's sudden appearance with a drawn sword: "He being a Negro . . . I did not know . . . but he might be concerned in the riot. I rode instantly towards him, and as soon as I could distinctly hear what he said, I heard him declare that he would cut off the arm of the first negro who should strike a blow; and endeavoring by every means in his power to suppress the riot, which, with his assistance, was shortly done, and the principals punished."

Here McPherson seems to be demonstrating his loyalty to his employer, near whose office the riot took place, and to the interest his employer represented, thereby reinforcing his identification with both. But he was also clearly asserting a presumed authority over the black rioters. This was not, he seems to be saying, the way he expected them to behave. It was not in their best interest and it did not reflect well on him. He even seems to have been upset that they were acting so decisively without first gaining his consent.

Often free blacks like McPherson seem to have had a sense of having risen above other blacks rather than of having become in some sense white. Obviously that can be a very fine distinction, but it does point up how potentially destabilizing an exchange of roles could be or become.

Certainly the color-caste bias against other blacks that developed among many free blacks (as well as among many slaves) would suggest how self-destructive it could become. But again, as with Stepney, it is often (indeed, most often) hard to tell when the part is being performed and when it is being lived.

Less ambiguous than McPherson in that respect was John Chavis. His exact date and place of birth, as for many blacks of his time, whether slave or free, are uncertain. But the most informed speculation assumes that he was born in the early 1760s in Oxford, North Carolina. He mentioned late in his life that he was a freeborn American and that he had fought in the American Revolution, an assertion for which there is documentation.[11]

The most fully documented portion of his life, however, has to do with his efforts to become ordained as a minister in the Presbyterian church. The scrutiny he received from church authorities was perhaps no less rigorous than that received by other aspiring ministers. Yet in addition to his general fitness for the position, examiners were clearly concerned whether he could be trusted to serve as a missionary among his people. For missionary service was always assumed to be his only calling. His ordination was recognized by the General Assembly of the Presbyterian Church of the United States in 1801, following a process of close examination begun by the Presbytery of Lexington, Virginia, in 1799. His recognition by the national body echoed concerns of the local when it identified Chavis as "a black man of prudence and piety," qualities that had encouraged the Lexington Presbytery to license him to preach and to be "employed as a missionary among people of his own colour."[12]

The examination process that Chavis underwent is important because it parallels so closely that experienced by most blacks who sought to express themselves publicly, whether from the pulpit or in print. Chavis' scrutiny identifies an important frame in which literate blacks struggled to find a means for self-expression and definition. Yet another test, among an endless number of them, served to determine how "sensible" blacks were.

Chavis first appeared before the Lexington Presbytery at its meeting held between October 15 and 19, 1799. According to the minutes of the meeting, he was "personally known to most members of the Pres. & of unquestionably good fame, & a communicant in the Presn. Church." At that meeting, he was required to articulate formally his desire to a minister and explain why he thought himself deserving of the opportunity to seek ordination. The minutes state that the Presbytery "being satisfied with his narrative, agreed, notwithstanding his colour, to take him under their care, for further trials in the usual form." His first trial was to write "an Exegesis in latin on the theme 'In quo consistat salvatio ab precatto,' and a homily on the decree of Election."[13]

Chavis, for unexplained reasons, did not show up at the meeting at which he was to present his efforts to meet that requirement. The minutes of that meeting refer to a letter he sent to explain his absence and his failure to complete the trial assignments. But the minutes do not tell us what his explanation was. The minutes, however, do note that in addition to his explanation, he also requested that he be allowed to undergo other trials, implying that he had asked to be exempted from the first one.

Before his inquisitors Chavis presented himself as a trustworthy servant to his people, a person who could be trusted to serve responsibly in that calling. He would do much the same later when he announced in a local newspaper the opening of a school that would teach separated groups of white and black students. The former would come in the mornings or afternoons, whereas the latter would be allowed to attend in the evenings. Many years later, Chavis would again do the same in his private correspondence with a few of his former white students, some of whom had become important figures in state and local government. Relying on their regard for him, he took liberties in addressing them that few other blacks could or would have attempted. He offered his unsolicited opinion on important issues of the day and even criticized their conduct on some occasions.

Regarding blacks, Chavis, like McPherson, had no hesitancy in speaking for them, leaving little doubt that he knew what was best for them. Referring to blacks once as his "brethren," he declared that they were not prepared to be freed. By contrast, it was not necessary for him to point out that he was exceptional and deserved, as McPherson continually insisted, to be recognized as such. Chavis appears to have more consistently played the role that reflected his sentiments relative to his "brethren" than did McPherson. Yet he had little more success with his school than McPherson had. Chavis, however, was less confused by the role he wound up playing, and was apparently better able to handle the disappointment of failing in his efforts to display his exceptional qualities by educating other blacks. From the tone of his letters to his former students, he appears to have maintained a positive outlook despite those failures. Yet it is hard to imagine that he was not aware, at some level of his consciousness, that he was being indulged by his former students, albeit respectfully. Surely, he must have sensed that no matter how hard he tried to prove otherwise, to his most sympathetic white patrons he was merely an exceptionally "sensible Negro" and not an exceptional human being. Similarly the blacks he presumed to speak for and educate could not have missed his view of them.

Both Chavis and McPherson lived most of their lives as free blacks. Chavis, in fact, claimed to have been born free. The role-playing dilemmas they faced, however, were not restricted to the free. Most large slave owners developed close relations with some of those slaves they had regular contact with. Some of these attained the same degree of exceptional acculturation as McPherson and Chavis. The few that can be followed to any extent in surviving records seem to have experienced similar sorts of difficulty with the parts they were expected to play by virtue of their acculturation.

Jefferson, for instance, owned an entire family that he privileged above his other slaves. Some of the members of that family, the Hemings family, matched or exceeded the levels of acculturation achieved by Chavis or McPherson. This was true of one of them in particular.

It would not be too much of an exaggeration to suggest that James Hemings was one of the most highly acculturated black men in late colonial or early national America, and certainly so in the South. Yet, although he was literate, little of what he wrote has survived. That may be because he wrote very little. His talent was not as a writer, and he appears not to have had much reason to write. Unlike McPherson, he was not interested in self-promotion. The impression is that he had much too high an opinion of himself to consider self-promotion necessary.

One of the things he wrote that did survive was an inventory of the kitchen he had been in charge of when he left Jefferson's service after gaining his freedom. He also apparently left a letter or two written to Jefferson and others, which gave some indication of the motives behind his eventual suicide. From what Jefferson tells us about him, including the letters he received from him, and from the bits of information that Jefferson received from others, Hemings seems to have been estranged from his family. He lived and died alone.

As will become clear below, the quest for freedom by slaves did not of necessity have to lead to an estranged relationship with family and friends, and blacks more generally. It did, however, for the sort of freedom James sought. James's story as it emerges from meager sources that have survived centers on issues that were at the heart of the Creole dilemma, especially for highly acculturated, literate, and otherwise privileged blacks.

His story, as we are given to know it, begins with his arrival in Paris with Jefferson, where he learned to speak French and was trained, far beyond the expectations of his owner, to become Jefferson's chief chef. It continues from this extraordinary accomplishment, and the self-confidence and arrogance that it reflected, with his reluctance to return to America with Jefferson when he was recalled by his government. Back in Virginia James was unable to adjust to life as a slave in a society that denied or rejected every quality that had come to define him. Jefferson eventually relented and granted him freedom but in the end, Hemings was disillusioned by life as a free black, unable to adjust to a world in which his understanding of himself could not be recognized or honored.

McPherson, Chavis, and Hemings all thought of themselves as being exceptional and tried to identify themselves as such by reference to other exceptional men. None of them was successful in that effort, nor could they have been. Nonetheless, it seemed logical to them that they, like other exceptional men, should aspire to be recognized for their hard-won attainments.

Things of course were much different for women, but not because there were no exceptional and highly acculturated black women in the colonial South. James Hemings's sister, Sally, was probably as capable as he was to master the trade he was given the opportunity to learn. By all accounts she was just as acculturated. But like their white counterparts, exceptional and highly acculturated black women could not expect to be recognized as such, except as the wives of exceptional men like Chavis and Hemings and McPherson. In other words, in order for most black women to aspire to be recognized as being exceptional or, more often, to seek to become other-than-Negro, they needed to attain the elevated dependency that distinguished the wives of important white men. However, unlike their white counterparts, black women had to look other-than-Negro in order to marry men like McPherson. For black men driven by the same or similar aspirations, achieving a high level of acculturation was the objective necessary to make the impossible seem somehow plausible. For black women, however, acculturation was not enough. Color, rather than literacy, was the only measure by which they could expect to be or become other-than-Negro. That is, they had to look the part more than their husbands did in order to aspire to it. The relation between physical appearance and identity was much more determinate for women than for men.

At the core of this painful drama was a heightened sense of color consciousness by which the quest to become other-than-Negro was turned destructively against the larger black community, as well as against its purveyors. Its most vicious and lasting impact was on black women, on whose physical appearance it was primarily based. Yet what we know about its impact and how it was used by blacks against other blacks dates from a much later period. It becomes most recognizable in towns and cities as they gained substantial free black populations, in Charleston, for instance, in the latter part of the eighteenth century, when the Brown Fellowship Society was founded "by free Afro-Americans who belonged to the white St. Philip's Episcopal Church, where they worshipped, were baptized and married but could not be interred in its burial ground." But it also existed in rural communities.[14]

For most blacks attaining high levels of acculturation was not generally possible, and for at least some of them probably not desirable. Yet survival required some level of acculturation of all blacks. The dilemma that requirement created for survivors is easy to see in extreme cases like

McPherson's, but is less obvious for the vast majority of survivors whose degree of acculturation made other-than-Negro aspirations impractical. For the majority of survivors the dilemma can often seem remote, the peculiar burden of relatively privileged blacks. However, if we examine the runaway ads in order to learn more about how the dilemma was experienced by blacks representing a wide range of acculturation, it becomes clear that the experience could vary considerably, even among the most highly acculturated slaves and free blacks. In the ads, the spectrum along which Stepney and highly acculturated blacks like McPherson are so conspicuous is marked by extremes at either end but also by a blurring of opposites. The blurring occurs, moreover, not only between the opposite ends but also at each position. Thematically, the extremes manifest themselves as motivations for flight, drives toward objectives that very often reflect a fugitive's level of acculturation but are rarely fully explained by it. By far the two most dominant themes running throughout the ads are the quest for freedom and the quest for community.

However, one of the first impressions that emerges when the ads are read thematically is the absence of either of the two principal motivations in notices for unseasoned or incompletely seasoned "new Negroes." Newly imported captive Africans, as we saw in an earlier chapter, sometimes (and probably much more often than surviving documents suggest) ran away hoping to find their way back to their homes in Africa, even though they lacked any understanding of the local geography or presumably how to man a seaworthy vessel and navigate tricky and dangerous wind and sea currents back to Africa.

For "new Negroes" freedom and community, as motivations for flight, were not divisible. Instead, both objectives were embodied in their desire to return home. Once these "new Negroes" were seasoned, however, freedom and community were no longer contained within a single objective or represented by a single destination. They not only were bifurcated as impulses but had a complicated relation to each other.

Slaves who were born in the colonies, and who thus inherited the world that seasoned slaves made for them, ran away (as did "sensible new Negroes") for a great variety of reasons: to protest their treatment, or to avoid punishments, or because of a quarrel between a husband and a wife, or because the fugitive had been enticed away by other slaves or "evil disposed" persons. But by far the majority ran to visit friends or family or to avoid being separated from one another. A sale of slaves or a division of an estate was invariably followed by the flight of at least some of those left behind or taken away. Polydore, perhaps, was held fast by a wife and family, as were many other "sensible new Negroes," including women who felt bound to a spouse and children.[15]

The following case is extreme in one sense but typical in its broader symbolism. A man at "Flower-de-Hundred" on the south side of the James River in Virginia advertised for the capture and return of his slave Dick in November of 1763. He describes him as being "24 years of age, 5 feet 7 or 8 inches high, slender made, of a yellow complexion, and much addicted to liquor." He goes on, as was customary for such ads, to detail what Dick was wearing when "he went away" and what he "carried with him." Thereafter he tries to indicate where he thinks Dick might try to go: "I believe he is gone to North-Carolina, and from thence may proceed to South-Carolina, he having relations at both places." All of this is typical to the point of being formulaic. What is distinctive is that "[h]e was bought of one Mathew Davis, in Brunswick, about 12 years ago." Typically when fugitives ran away with the idea of returning to friends or relatives, their separation had occurred relatively recently, a matter of months or a few years at the most. Other slaves remained persistent over long periods of time, and even those for whom there is no record generally demonstrated their determination and persistence in other ways. Most, unlike Dick, ran to relatively nearby places, although there is little in the ads suggesting that runaways, spurred on by love of family, were deterred by long distances.

Instead, we see all manner of men and women and children fleeing alone or together in search of other family members or to keep those together with whom they had run away. Men ran to be with their wives, women to be with their husbands. Children ran in search of their parents, which usually meant in search of their mothers but also other family members, including their fathers. Mothers running away with their children or to be with them appear in the ads more frequently than fathers. But women also ran for many other reasons. Men, more than any other group (old or young, male or female), ran most often.[16] The elderly for obvious reasons rarely ran. Families at times ran together, as did friends and various other combinations of friends and family and others. Some groups took the where-with-all to remain at large for long periods of time or to start their own communities in swampy inaccessible places. There simply was no end to the variety of individuals who ran away or the particular objectives of their quest for community.[17]

The ads are highly formulaic, as might be expected, and are most often terse in terms of the information they provide. Terseness, however, does not always mean sparsity. Indeed, the ads are as full of useful data for historians as they were for potential captors, and they are very frequently laced with illuminating asides about the fugitives' perceived character, attitudes, inclinations, and idiosyncrasies. One impression that recurs in the course of reading through the thousands of such ads that have survived is that the genre served as an outlet for observations, concerns, and curiosity that slave owners were constrained from expressing in other written mediums. Later this urge to give voice to their thoughts about blacks would find an additional outlet in anecdotes that employed caricatures of blacks, using an exaggerated form of what slave owners called "Negro dialect."

The tone of many ads is businesslike, betraying no obvious assumptions about the fugitives' character or capabilities. Some, as we have seen, laud fugitives for their skills or honesty, but more often they are sarcastic in that regard, or condescending, clearly implying the widely shared assumption that blacks lacked the capacity for genuine human feeling unless it was expressed in some demonic or self-destructive way. In some ads, however, the depth of a fugitive's feelings for loved ones could not be avoided, having been imposed on the advertiser by the fugitives themselves. This ad for Dinah is one of those. She was suspected of having run away to be with her husband. Her husband, the ad explains, was the "negro Hews . . . , Who is well known in Edenton [North Carolina], as a river pilot," an occupation that allowed blacks virtual freedom, defined as mobility and little if any direct supervision. Hews, according to the ad, had informed Dinah's presumptive owner that he "would keep his wife out eternally." For that reason caution was urged on those who might "take her up," because "Hews will, at the risque of his life, rescue her, should it come to his knowledge." The ad a few sentences further on then concludes: "I have been informed that said wench is lurking in and about Edenton, for the purpose, I suppose, of better effecting her escape, together with her husband, who has threatened to march off, and take her with him."[18]

A similar story is told by an advertiser in South Carolina, who explains that one of the "Out-houses, at his Plantation, on James-Island, was broke open, and one of his Negro Wenches, named Tena . . . was carried off by a Negro Fellow, named Toby." Later, the ad continues, "The Wench was found . . . in the Possession of the Fellow, and in Consequence of a War-rant, he absconded, and came armed to his Place on Thursday, with In-tention (from exceeding good Grounds) to take away the Life of the Sub-scriber." Regardless of whether Toby's "Grounds" were good, "a reward of Fifty Pounds currency" was offered for his capture and return, and "Twenty Pounds like Money for Delivery of the Wench."[19]

Hews and Toby were not alone in their determination to rescue their wives and to live permanently with them. Most such ads, however, are less dramatic and describe the efforts of slave spouses in less detail. Such is the case, for instance, with a slave named Tom, whose master says he has "reason to believe, from what [Tom] told my overseer a little before he went off, that he intends for South-Carolina, as his wife was sold to a gen-tleman there a few months ago; and my refusing to sell him is the only oc-casion of his run-ing away." Similarly, as is true of a large number of ads, Cuffee's owner says he has run away because his wife and child were "sold from him."

Other ads tell of a wide variety of other family-related reasons for run-ning away. For instance, sisters Lucy and Tyra, aged twelve and ten re-spectively, were suspected of having run to their mother, Moll, and/or to their father, Peter, both of whom were owned by different people; or "Came to my plantation . . . Phillis and four of her children, the property of the heirs of Ralph Willow, deceased," fleeing potential separation in a dispute over their dead master's will.[20] A similar case occurred when one of Jefferson's most valued and trusted slaves ran away unexpectedly to be with his future wife. Jefferson, like most other slave owners, was well aware of the risk of separating such couples, but in this case he inexplica-bly allowed the separation to occur.[21]

Often fugitives ran toward familiar places to which they had become at-tached, where, for instance, they had been born or grown up or lived for a long time, and where, of course, friends and families would welcome them and thus where they could expect to be harbored. The ads show awareness of the emotional ties: "expect them to go towards Norfolk or the lower parts of Carolina, as they were brought from there a few years ago." Again, "supposed he will run to Hampton, where he was raised." Or "maybe in Pasquotank where his mother and other relatives are." Or, mysteriously, "Dick [a new Negro] .... Three toes on his right foot cut-off ... Believed to have gone below Newbern because he had run there three previous times."[22]

Many ads point to a familiar place as a likely destination without offering (probably because advertisers in most cases did not know) any indication of what or who awaited the runaways there. Moreover, many of these point toward destinations that were either quite far away or difficult to reach. The latter must have been the case for the two unnamed fugitives living in Brunswick County, Virginia, who were expected "to go down country" and cross the bay in order to return to the Eastern Shore, where "they were lately brought." Similarly, Cudjo ran away from a plantation on the Santee River in South Carolina, in order to return to Georgia, from where he had been brought a year earlier. Like these other slaves, Jack ran away to return to the place he had recently come from, but the distance he had to travel was unusual. He ran from Charleston and was expected to "head for Rhode Island, where he came from, by ship," having tried to do so two months earlier, "but being taken sick, and the vessel detained rather longer than was expected, he was set ashore."[23] Likewise a number of others sought to return to the West Indies.

Community, in other words, was first and foremost where friends and family were, but it was also very often a specific place, strongly suggesting a close identification with, or affinity for, a particular social and natural environment, a point in time and space that served as a source of a runaway's sense of self. Often it is difficult to distinguish the pull of family from that of community. Sall, for instance, is described as being "of a numerous Family of Mulattoes, formerly belonging to a Gentleman of the Name Howard, in York County, from whence I purchased her a few Years ago, and where probably she may attempt to go again, perhaps to Cumberland, or Amelia, where I am informed many of her Kindred live."[24]

Slaves with a "numerous family," as in Sall's case, or a wide acquaintance in one or more places, as was true of a very large percentage of those who ran away, could be easily identified because of those connections but were at the same time often difficult to locate for the same reason. This perhaps is most graphically illustrated in Landon Carter's diary beginning in early March of 1766, when he began to make entries regarding two

of his slaves, Bart and Simon, who, according to "old Tom," had been harbored by "Johnny my gardener . . . All the while they were out, sometimes in his inner room and sometimes in my kitchen vault."[25]

For those seeking freedom, the help of friends and family was often essential, or at a minimum very useful, but ties to particular places in the
end were expendable. In most cases the desire to be free, or even to improve one's situation, made it necessary that connections with family or
friends, or both, be broken. Strongly suggestive of that requirement is the
following comment that was one of the most frequently employed ways
of indicating that a fugitive's design was freedom: "as the man is a sensible ar[c]h fellow, he will probably attempt to make his escape from off the
continent."[26] A large percentage of that group, according to the ads, would
change their names and their clothes, as we will see later, or even in some
cases disguise their gender, in an effort to pass for free.[27]

These ads, as have many of the others that we have examined, make clear
how difficult it is analytically to separate community from freedom as
motivations driving the flight of fugitive slaves, and how tortuous it must
have been for those who felt compelled to flee, as well as for those who
could not or for various reasons chose not to. They also strongly suggest
the dual nature of the physical presence of blacks throughout the colonial
era, representing both rootedness and transiency. Though many slaves
were sold and resold, inherited and transferred by other means from
place to place and owner to owner, many others, as well as many of those
whose familial or communal lives were frequently disrupted, remained
for many years, and not infrequently for many generations, in particular
places, coming to define those places by their presence.

One example of how rooted to particular places many survivors became can be observed in a scattering of obituaries for slaves that were
printed in colonial newspapers. Most of these were of very elderly slaves
and contained a brief description of their lives. All of them identify the deceased slave as a long time resident of the communities in which they
died.

"*Old Davy*, an *African* negro," for example, died on Christmas day, 1818,
at "upwards of a 120 years." That, at least, was the age that had been sug-

gested to the obituary writer. He died at the residence of George Chapman and "was purchased by Nathaniel Chapman sometime early in the 18th century. The latter," it was explained, "died about the year 1763, and Davy was then considered to be middle aged." Neighbors, apparently, marvelled at his longevity "and he became much noticed [as in the case of Yarrow Mamout] in consequence thereof." Unlike Jack Lubbar, however, he had been "emancipated many years before his death." Like Lubbar, however, he continued to "plant crops," as he had before he was freed. The profits from that effort were "bestowed on his children until a few days before his death." Lubbar, by contrast, felt estranged from his offspring.[28]

Bristol was described as "a Negro Man, who had lived here [Annapolis] an old Man a great many Years [although as "a Man-Boy" he had served a master in Barbados], and who, "By his own Account . . . must have lived at least 125 Years." The brief account of his passing agreed with Bristol's estimation of his age because Bristol had recalled that while in Barbados, "waiting Dinner, behind his Master's Chair . . . they receiv'd News of King *Charles's* being Beheaded."[29] Both of these very old slaves were characterized in their obituaries in ways that strongly inferred that these men embodied, for many residents of the communities they had lived and died in, a living memory of those places. This point, however, is made more graphically by reports of a severe flood in the Richmond area in 1771, which included a reference to "Old Joe," as quoted earlier, and in which Joe was referred to as "an honest and well known negro Fellow at the Falls of James River, who is intimately acquainted with the Remains of an Indian Nation that has resided there for Ages." Joe had been in the area longer than any other living local resident and strongly indicated that through his contact with "their old Men" he was linked with the land's original inhabitants.[30]

However, it was the death of "Boot Harry, an African, aged one hundred and twenty six years" that best exemplified the rootedness of some blacks in particular places. The writer of his obituary explained that, "We have often listened to the marvelous tales of this old man, with wonder and amaze [sic], hearing him recount the many skirmishes he assisted the whites in against the Indians, when the settlement of this part of the country was first attempted by the whites." Sometimes, the account continued, "he would point to a memorable spot, where savage barbarity appalled his youthful heart; then he would direct the eye to the place whence they fled for safety; and how they returned with force and vigour, more terrible than before."[31]

No matter how long a black slave, or community of slaves, remained in a particular place, including those who were shifted about from quarter to quarter on a single estate spanning a large area, they were in the first instance placed there by owners. Decisions that determined their placement, in addition to geographic and related economic considerations, included purchase patterns (reflecting sex ratios that to a large extent determined reproductive patterns) and other demographic factors, as well as the stability of ownership reflected in inheritance patterns.[32]

Even, however, where all of these factors were optimal, over the long term families were invariably broken to one degree or another. But most individuals in the colonial South, whether white or black or native American, did not live over the long term, notwithstanding the examples just described. And the long term for others included many generations; even those who had experienced separation from their families, which for many occurred at a very early age, or separation from a home community, such separation did not always place them beyond the reach of local networks of friends, family, and acquaintances.

The story of the Butler family in Maryland which, after a century of enslavement, achieved its freedom in a court case based on the claim that they were descended from an Irish mother named Nell, who was a seventeenth-century servant, was not only unusual because of the legal victory it represented but because that victory had been achieved so long after the family had originated. Though the family had been scattered throughout Maryland during all those years, it had retained a strong sense of itself right up to the court's final ruling in 1784.[33] After the Butler ruling, a family named Shorter, made a similar case for its freedom in a Maryland court, but failed because, in the court's opinion, there was a lack of sufficient or convincing proof.[34]

Mixed-race blacks of various kinds had been petitioning for their freedom virtually from the beginning of a permanent black presence in colonial America.[35] For slave families for whom the Butler case does not serve as a realistic model, continuity in a given area is powerfully reflected in the testimony provided in the ads, and in other ways, such as the naming patterns documented for blacks on the Good Hope plantation in colonial and antebellum South Carolina, and in the following less well-documented but similar example from colonial North Carolina.[36] The first reference to a black couple appearing in surviving records from colonial North Carolina was to Manuel and Frank in 1695, a very early moment, compared to Virginia, South Carolina, and Maryland, in the development of that colony's slave society. The couple had five children, a number of whom were given to members of their owner's family, who took them with them to other plantations, but not so far away as to disconnect them entirely. A list of the owner's slaves compiled by his heirs seventy-five years later identifies a long line of slaves named for Manuel and Frank.[37]

The runaway ads, however, make clear that for large numbers of survivors freedom from enslavement required a severance of family or communal ties, a decisive uprooting. It is also clear that a desire for freedom involved a degree of cultural divisiveness that could be a spur to creativity but also an alienating and distancing force. For whatever strategy a fugitive may have used in quest of freedom it was assumed by advertisers that fugitives would have been greatly aided in their effort if they did not speak in a "negro dialect" or did not dress as "Negroes usually do." Again, valued skills were assumed to help fugitives to find employment and support. Similarly if they were clever or ingenious, it was assumed they would obtain a forged pass or the assistance of "evil disposed" persons. The following, for example, is fairly typical in that regard: "JOHN, sometimes called Johnson, at times calling himself John Hill, at other times John Howe . . . [Was] sensible and shrewd, civil in his manners and plausible in conversation; he served his time with a cabinet maker, and has worked as a journeyman with a Windsor-chair maker; he is very ingenious, and well acquainted with the use of joiners tools. John reads and I believe can write a little." Being sensible, as other ads invariably point out, John was expected to make for "one of the Northern ports or perhaps Charleston."[38]

Any of the characteristics attributed to John in this ad, or any combinations of similar ones, would have greatly enhanced the possibility of a fugitive's avoiding recapture or achieving his and her freedom. At least that was the general assumption shared by most advertisers. This was especially so, according to the ads, if in addition to any or all of those distinguishing signs, they were also literate; if, that is, they could read a little or even better if they could write well enough to forge their own pass. Jefferson, like other slave owners, was keenly aware of strategies of this sort, and is reported to have told Lafayette, while he was visiting Monticello, that whereas it might be useful at some future time to teach slaves to read, it would not be advisable ever to teach them to write. Jefferson feared that such a skill would make it too easy for them to forge passes.

Thus, success in running away, according to an overwhelming majority of advertisers, depended on the slave's level of acculturation, broadly defined. A field hand, that is, with limited commercial skills, who spoke a dialect that tended to identify him and her as such, and who dressed in "Negro clothes" had little if any chance of passing for free or avoiding recapture without the help of others. Blacks knew, as did slave owners, however, that low levels of acculturation did not place black slaves beyond any realistic expectation of freedom. Many relatively unacculturated runaways were able to compensate for the lack of characteristics that aided others in their quest for freedom, but the odds were clearly against them.

Escape was possible, according to the ads, if a fugitive, even one bearing the markings of a slave, "could tell a plausible" story or had sufficient local knowledge of both the geography and the social landscape to take advantage of the opportunities available in the area of their confinement as well as the spaces for maneuver within it. Such slaves, as we have seen, as well as those fugitives who bore clear signs of relatively high degrees of acculturation, were invariably and insistently accused of being cunning and devious, capable of thinking quickly and cleverly in difficult or dangerous situations.

No amount of compensatory cleverness, however, could have adequately substituted for the ability to read and write (or to present oneself in a way that suggested that ability) as a signification of freedom for blacks. Nothing else could put in question, if only tentatively, the presumption that all people identified as Negroes in any Southern colony were slaves. Nothing else, in other words, could cause whites to hesitate to make an assumption about any black person of whom they did not have personal knowledge. In that sense it would have been extremely difficult for any person of African origin living in the colonial South not to have made the connection between literacy and freedom.

But few blacks in that place and time had the opportunity to achieve even low levels of literacy, if we define literacy exclusively as the ability to read and write. If on the other hand literacy is conceived more broadly—to include, for instance, those who spoke "very good" or "excellent" English or those who were sufficiently acculturated to move easily and with confidence in the free world beyond the area in which they were known as slaves—the number of literate blacks was much larger.

Moreover, to the extent that survival required a substantial amount of the sort of cleverness that slave owners so often lamented or decried, few slaves could be described as unacculturated. Thus, acculturation was a gesture no matter how reluctant toward literacy and all that it represented. But the experiential nature of survival for most blacks, its urgency and its required spontaneity, its play-it-by-ear-and-by-eye quality, as Ralph Ellison has characterized it, was rooted in a vernacular reality.

The quest for freedom, like the quest for community, was necessarily echoed with a different resonance in the lives of individual blacks, as well as in those of different groups of blacks, according to the varied circumstances leading to and surrounding their enslavement or freedom and their experience of racial subordination.[39] Judged by the behavior we have seen described in the ads the choice between family and freedom was rarely clear cut. Many of those who were suspected of trying to pass for free, as we have seen, were also believed to have been in search of friends and family, or aided by them in their quest for freedom. Similarly, many relatively unacculturated fugitives, who were thought to be primarily interested in locating friends and family, were also seeking their freedom.

This in turn was reflected in what historians of slavery in America have long acknowledged, and what slaves and slave owners alike well knew, that the slave's life was lived to one extent or another in two worlds. "It was often said [during slavery]," according to one historian, "that a slave was two persons, the one who worked in his master's field by day and the other who 'pleasured' himself at night."[40] Family and community were not simply motivations, they were also the sites of "the hidden world" beyond slavery in which the vernacular was most often rooted and had its freest reign. By contrast, the more literary or acculturated self was generally expressed outside of those sites or where they intersected, and in that sense they were most often associated with free blacks and favored slaves. For that reason the quest for community often projects a collectivizing sensibility or ethos, whereas the quest for freedom as literacy seems much more individuating. Similarly, the literary traditions often appear to be at odds with the vernacular, mirroring in that sense color-caste and other divisions among and between blacks on plantations as well as those living outside of that world, whether free or slave.

Most blacks in the colonial South, however, were in touch with both worlds to one degree or another. Many were owned for instance by small to middling farmers and few were wholly detached from the lives of non-elite whites. Also, throughout the period, as the large numbers of ads for runaway 'mustees' attests, a significant number had various levels of contact with native populations in the areas in which they lived and traveled.

A significant number of blacks, meanwhile, were extremely mobile. Those included slaves who were forcibly moved from one to another of their owners' plantations, or left to relatives of owners who moved far from their original homes, or were sold to people in another part of a colony or in another colony entirely, or were brought from other north American colonies or various parts of the Caribbean.

Mobility was built into the lives of many black slaves throughout most of the colonial era. Such slaves included boat and watermen, message carriers, wagoners, slaves who drove hogs and cattle long distances to market, or rolled tobacco hogsheads over equally long distances, male body servants and female maids to a lesser extent, market women, carriage drivers or postillions. Moreover, it was frequently alleged by slave owners that slaves traveled at night to socialize and not infrequently over long distances. The "Stranger" for instance noted the large number of blacks who had come to Charleston on the weekends, as had early laws in most colonies that prohibited such gatherings.

Other indications of significant mobility within the slave communities of the colonial South include the large number of fugitives who were described as having a wide circle of acquaintances, in some instances throughout a very expansive area. Another important source of outside contact and communication was black sailors, who like Equiano, docked at various ports and visited among local blacks. Sailors, like most of the other groups mentioned, served as an uncoordinated communication system with great reach, either potentially or in point of fact.

However much freedom and family may have pulled fugitives and other blacks in different directions, and were in tension with one other, more often they were intertwined. Neither freedom nor community, in the survivalist sense that most survivors experienced one or the other of them, or as reflected in other ways, was sufficient unto itself as an objective or motivation for flight, or as a source for the survival of blacks in the colonial South more generally.

Of necessity, freedom had many meanings for fugitives, as for all other blacks. It meant, among many other things, the freedom to visit, to create and maintain a family, to be with friends, to establish or determine the terms of their enslavement, if only minimally, to celebrate and mourn with each other, to fight and love one another, to complain about enslavement, or about any and everything, to argue amongst themselves, to commune and pray together, to discuss their dilemmas, or to plan with others the group's liberation by means of rebellion. And each of these meanings in turn relates to or was premised on the need for community.

At the same time however freedom also involved a compulsion by many favored slaves and free blacks to estrange themselves from any identification with the lives of most slaves, or of necessity to escape from the communities that had served as points of self-reference and nurture for most of the runaways. A consequence of this need at times was to leave behind the familiar places to which they had become attached and in which their sense of self had been developed. It also meant in many cases leaving behind friends and parts or all of one's family.

In other words, survival was never without its costs for blacks in the colonial South, and those costs had to be deeply embedded in both freedom and community. The aspiration for freedom could be energizing and inspiring, but the experience of becoming free, of passing for free and thus acting the part, was at best a bitter-sweet one and more often painful and traumatic, just as freedom as community was self-affirming yet confining of freedom. Survival for blacks in the colonial South, it seems fair to suggest, was a self-creating process but also a self-defining problematic.

NOTE ON SOURCES

$\mathbf{A}$s indicated in the preface, this book, though intended to stand alone, is in a number of important yet silent ways connected to a prior and continuing project. One of those ways (those connections) has to do with its relation to the sources in which it is grounded. The other project was (and continues to be) premised on the assumption that if there is anything useful to be said (anything left to be said) about the lived experience of blacks in the colonial South it is not likely to be found in newly discovered or even unused or underutilized sources. The core of what was to be learned, according to that logic, would have to come from asking existing sources new questions and combing them carefully and systematically from the perspective that those questions reflect. That expectation, based less on a substantive experience with available primary sources than on a deepening engagement with the relevant secondary literature, assumed that clues to the lived experiences of blacks have not so much been absent from the records as they have, like the experience itself, been "secreted" in them. The more you learned about what was said in the records, the better able you would understand what they left unsaid or only superficially acknowledged. The logic, not unlike that informing archeological research or methodologies based on statistical analysis, was that accumulated fragments would make more sense when systematically collected and analyzed. It was clear that a full picture of the puzzle could not be found, but perhaps enough pieces could be located and related to one another to give us a sense of what the completed puzzle pictured. The problem for the originating study was on the one hand practical (whether it is humanly possible in a single lifetime to exhaust the sources in that way) and on the other conceptual (how to make compatible a research objective that was in many ways at odds with its methodology—how to do a cultural history using the tools and adapting the perspective of social history).

The present book has in the main not shared in those problems, but it is nonetheless a product of them. In some significant ways it has diverged from the originating study in terms of its research requirements and thus to some extent in terms of its approach to the sources. This is partly explained by why and how the two studies diverged, ultimately becoming incompatible as a single study. The originating study, although rooted in a number of long-standing and preexisting concerns, was initially conceived in very broad terms and was not, in relative terms (at least not self-consciously), issue or argument driven. Its approach both to its subject and to available sources began and has remained largely exploratory. At some relatively advanced point in that exploration, the question that has engaged the present book emerged. It emerged, however, as a two-sided question. Asked in one way it was the question that the originating study had begun to answer. That is, it was a reflection of the understanding that the original study's exploration had begun to take (its recognizable and interpretive form). Framed in the way the present book has framed it the question has elicited a response that has taken the shape of an argument much more than has the study from which it originated.

Thus, though ultimately the two studies grew apart, becoming in the end incompatible as a single project, in terms of the research that informs both they have a common origin and process of development. Consequently, most of the sources cited in the present study do not fully reflect the context in which they were read. For example the original study began, without necessarily intending to do so, by reading colonial newspapers, issue by issue, front to back, rather than only the ads for runaway slaves (or for other material of explicit relevance to an interest in black life that could be found in them). The newspapers, meanwhile, were being read alternately with court and legislative records and private manuscript collections.

Each ad was collected, along with all other items of interest identified in the newspapers, and catalogued by reference to the various aspects of their content that were considered of relevance to the project, categories of data and comment topically or thematically ordered. Generally the cataloguing occurred after an extended period of collecting. The first time this occurred the previous ads were reread as the newly read ones were added to the various files, a process that proved startlingly revelatory. Not only, as would be expected, were specific items of information invariably overlooked or went unrecognized new questions about previously identified material occurred and new understandings of others developed. Thereafter, each time that the cataloguing process was undertaken a rereading of all the ads took place and each time a small but significant amount of overlooked material was discovered, new questions were raised, and new understandings were developed. This was partly a function of having read more ads but it was also the result of having read more newspapers in the context of reading more court and legislative records, more private papers and an increasingly rich body of secondary literature, both within the field and beyond.

The ads for runaway slaves (and related items) were always an important focus of the originating study's research strategy (even when it didn't really have one) but they never became as central to the original study as they have been for the present one. This reflects the narrower focus of the present study and its tendency to make a case rather than explore a broadly defined experience. Indeed, one of the realizations that marked the present study as a separate project was its recognition that the ads offer the clearest and most comprehensive surviving narrative of the assault of interest to it, even though they do not reflect a cross section of the enslaved population (or even necessarily of the fugitive population). They do not tell us how or to what extent the average black person (slave or free) experienced the assault but they do convey, better than any other single source, a reality that all blacks shared.

NOTES

Preface

1. A few studies of slavery in America have made reference to the dilemma that is my central concern. The most extensive description and analysis is Eugene Genovese, *Roll, Jordan, Roll: The World the Slaves Made* (New York: Pantheon, 1972). A more recent study is Michael A. Gomez, *Exchanging Our Country Marks: The Transformation of African Identities in the Colonial and Antebellum South* (Chapel Hill: University of North Carolina Press, 1998).

2. For purposes of analysis, I define *self* in phenomenological terms as an orienting process: "Self is neither substance nor entity, but an indeterminate capacity to engage or become oriented in the world, characterized by effort and reflexivity." Thomas J. Csordas, *The Sacred Self: A Cultural Phenomenology of Charismatic Healing* (Berkeley: University of California Press, 1994), 5.

The period and region on which I focus will frequently be referred to as the colonial and early national South, a phrase that merely refers to plantation America (i.e., that part of British North America that would become the United States of America) prior to its large-scale expansion into the trans-Appalachian South and Southwest. I use the term "colonial" more often than "early national" because even though many sources that date from the latter period are used their use is always in terms of their relevance to the earlier one.

3. I do not explicity address the cultural response of survivors to their enslavement; that is, the survival of blacks as reflected in the way of life they created (see "Note on Sources").

Introduction: Seeing the Subject

1. *Virginia Gazette*, October 6, 1774, p. 3, col. 1. The first emphasis is mine.

2. The quotation is from an anonymous reader who read a draft manuscript for Cornell University Press and offered the following interpretation: "The disobedient Virginia colony (Jack) is brought into line by the caring but frustrated master (England), when 'A Person who had lived with Jack in his own Country, and who knew his Temper perfectly' (an American moderate or loyalist) counsels firm discipline and harsh warnings which, when applied, bring about 'the most desirable Success.' In the end of this hoped scenario,

Jack (Virginia) broke off his Connections with bad company (New England radicals), did his work faithfully, found his Master (England) to be a good Man, and in a little While became the best Servant (colony) in the Province (empire)." The reader noted that the story "does indeed draw on slave colony imagery, and it underscores better than almost anything how thoroughly the Virginia planters entangled ideas of their peculiar financial and political enslavement with their own actual enslavement of Africans." Woody Holton discussed this linkage in *Forced Founders: Indians, Debtors, Slaves, and the Making of the American Revolution in Virginia* (Chapel Hill: University of North Carolina Press for Omohundro Institute of Early American History and Culture, Williamsburg, Va., 1999). See also Holton, *Forced Founders*, 46n. 8.

3. Jack's story was not presented as unusual because it was not intended as a discussion about slavery. Apparently, both writer and editor were so absorbed by political issues that neither registered that the story's subject had rarely been discussed in the *Gazette*. The "outer" story makes assumptions about what prospective readers would already know about not only the evolving political crisis but slaves and slavery. For instance, literate "new Negroes" would not have been impossible for local residents to imagine. Note, for example, the following ad: "Committed to the goal of Westmoreland . . . two Negro men. . . . They are both Africans, and speak very little English, so that they are not able to tell their master's name. They had with them two muskets, and two small books." *Virginia Gazette* (Rind), October 31, 1771, p. 3, col. 2.

Similarly, slave owners made agreements with slaves. A runaway ad seeks the return of an outlawed fugitive: "[Bristol] ran away from [his former owner] John G. Blount, Esquire, some years ago, and after weeks of persuasion and many fair promises prevailed on the subscriber to purchase him upon an expressly stipulated condition that having been used to his plantation and management for the time he was in treaty with Mr. Blount, and being satisfied to submit to any kind of work or discipline of the other Negroes, if he ran away after drawing me into a loss by inducing me to purchase and then absconding, he would be satisfied to forfeit his head." *Wilmington Gazette* (North Carolina), May 5, 1803, p. 3, col. 5.

4. Thus, what Rhys Isaac has observed about the sources on colonial life in general is especially true for the study of black life in colonial America. To overcome the problems such sources pose for scholars, he notes that "the social historian can everywhere find traces—occasionally vivid glimpses—of *people doing things*. The searching out of the meanings that such actions contained and conveyed for the participants lies at the heart of the enterprise of ethnographic history. Actions must be viewed as statements. . . . The 'sources,' with the purposes and meanings of their authors, always stand between historical ethnographers and the worlds they seek to know. Yet with patient attention to the processes of reporting it is possible to collect action-statements and to set about interpreting them." Isaac, *The Transformation of Virginia 1740–1790* (Chapel Hill: University of North Carolina Press for the Institute of Early American History and Culture, Williamsburg, 1982), 324.

5. Wylie Sypher, in his *Guinea's Captive Kings: British Anti-Slavery Literature of the XVIIIth Century* (Chapel Hill: University of North Carolina Press, 1942), 1, refers to "[t]he British movement against the slave-trade" as not "merely the earliest instance of modern propaganda; it is a phase of the enlightenment." The phrase "the capacity to create beauty and to be beautiful" is a paraphrase of Henry Louis Gates Jr., "The History and Theory of Afro-American Literary Criticism, 1773–1831: The Arts, Aesthetic Theory, and the Nature of the African" (Ph.D. diss., Clare College, University of Cambridge, 1978), 117.

6. Though my emphasis is on the colonial South, the same was true of the discourse in the northern colonies, including that of antislavery advocates eager to prove the humanity of enslaved blacks. This myopia reflects a class perspective as much as a racial one, encompassing poor whites as well as blacks.

7. See David Brion Davis's comparison of Jefferson's views on slavery with those of "two foreign contemporaries [Edwards and Moreau de Saint-Méry] who shared many of

NOTES TO PAGES 3–11 **187**

his interests, prejudices, and opportunities," in *The Problem of Slavery in the Age of Revolution, 1770–1823* (Ithaca, N.Y.: Cornell University Press, 1975), 184–95.

It is important to note that the difference between Southern planters and their West Indian counterparts was often marginal. I emphasize small variations to illustrate an absence that was so striking in the colonial South.

For a survey of planter and colonialist views, see Anthony J. Barker, *The African Link: British Attitudes to the Negro in the Era of the Atlantic Slave Trade, 1550–1807* (London: Frank Cass, 1978). On the myopia of West Indian planters who questioned the humanity of their slaves because of their presumed incapacity for resistance, see Michel-Rolph Trouillot, *Silencing the Past: Power and Production of History* (Boston: Beacon Press, 1995), 83–95.

8. The first installment in the five-part serialization of the speech appeared in the November 29, 1788, edition of the *Charleston Gazette* and was introduced to readers as follows: "*A late Jamaica paper contains a speech made by Mr. Shirley, on the prospect of the slave trade, in the house of representatives of that island, as the arguments apply with considerable force in this state, a few extracts will therefore be given.*" Subsequent extracts appear in the December 1, 4, 17, and 19 editions of the *Gazette*.

9. Scholarly discussions of Jefferson's views on race and on blacks in particular, although once extremely rare, are now prolific. Winthrop Jordan's discussion in *White over Black* established the standard by which the literature still measures itself. John Chester Miller's *The Wolf by the Ears: Thomas Jefferson and Slavery* (1971; Charlottesville: University Press of Virginia, 1991) also remains essential. For a more recent study, see Anthony F. C. Wallace, *Jefferson and the Indians: The Tragic Fate of the First Americans* (Cambridge: Belknap Press of Harvard University Press, 1999).

10. *Charleston Gazette*, December 19, 1788, p. 2, col. 2.

11. On the history of proslavery thought, see Larry E. Tise, *Proslavery: A History of the Defense of Slavery in America, 1701–1840* (Athens: University of Georgia Press, 1987); the introduction by Drew Faust, ed., *The Ideology of Slavery: Proslavery Thought in the Antebellum South, 1830–1860* (Baton Rouge: Louisiana State University Press, 1981); and George M. Fredrickson, *The Black Image in the White Mind: The Debate on Afro-American Character and Destiny, 1817–1914* (New York: Harper & Row, 1971).

12. *Charleston Gazette*, December 19, 1788, p. 2, cols., 1–3.

13. For a recent study that provides a very striking view of this tradition, see Woody Holton, *Forced Founders*, chap. 5.

14. On *The Old Plantation*, see Rhys Isaac's speculation about its provenance and meaning in his *Transformation of Virginia*, 419: "This painting was found in South Carolina without any records or even clear internal evidence to establish its provenance." He then speculates that it was painted about 1800 and that "[t]he scene depicted could be located anywhere from the Susquehanna to the Caribbean." See also the brief caption discussion of the watercolor in Cynthia Adams Hoover, "Music and Theater in the Lives of Eighteenth-Century Americans" in *Of Consuming Interests: The Style of Life in the Eighteenth Century*, ed. Cary Carson, Ronald Hoffman, and Peter J. Albert (Charlottesville: University Press of Virginia for the United States Capitol Historical Society, 1994), 333. Hoover notes that the painting was "[f]ound in Columbia, South Carolina," and that it "is thought to have been painted on a plantation between Charleston and Orangeburg. It was "executed on paper with a watermark used by English papermaker James Whatman Jr., between 1777 and 1794." A similar, less elaborate and finished drawing is owned by the Mint Museum in Charlotte, N.C. The Abby Aldrich Rockefeller Folk Art Center in Williamsburg, Virginia, holds *The Old Plantation*.

The visual image of blacks in a wide variety of illustrative mediums is surveyed by Barbara E. Lacey, "Visual Images of Blacks in Early American Imprints," *William and Mary Quarterly* 53 (January 1996):137–80.

Wylie Sypher in his brief discussion of "picturesque writers" in *Guinea's Captive Kings*, 144–49, notes the influence paintings had on their writing. William Beckford Jr., especially, is singled out as possessing "[t]he most elegantly picturesque eye." According to Sypher,

Beckford's effort to describe "Negro village" life in his *Descriptive Account of Jamaica* (1790) was inspired by his admiration of the "picturesque beauties in which the Dutch painters, have so much excelled." On the black image in art by Dutch painters see Allison Blakely, *Blacks in the Dutch World: The Evolution of Racial Imagery in a Modern Society* (Bloomington: Indiana University Press, 1993). For a parallel discussion of the black image in England, see Kim F. Hall, *Things of Darkness: Economies of Race and Gender in Early Modern England* (Ithaca, N.Y.: Cornell University Press, 1995). Two studies of the French colonial experience with blacks are informative: William B. Cohen, *The French Encounter with Africans: White Response to Blacks, 1530–1880* (Bloomington: Indiana University Press, 1980), and Christopher L. Miller, *Blank Darkness: Africanist Discourse in French* (Chicago: University of Chicago Press, 1985).

15. Albert Boime, *The Art of Exclusion: Representing Blacks in the Nineteenth Century* (Washington, D.C.: Smithsonian Institution Press, 1990), 15, 19–30; Guy C. McElroy, *Facing History: The Black Image in American Art 1710–1940* (Washington, D.C.: Bedford Arts, Publishers, in association with the Corcoran Gallery of Art, 1990), 5.

16. The discussion of the Benoist painting relies on Hugh Honour, *The Image of the Black in Western Art*, vol. 4, pt. 2 (Cambridge: Harvard University Press, 1989), 7–8. A full-color photograph of the painting is on page 9.

17. Philip Morgan, "Three Planters and Their Slaves: Perspectives on Slavery in Virginia, South Carolina, and Jamaica, 1750–1790," in *Race and Family in the Colonial South*, ed. Winthrop Jordan and Sheila Skemp (Jackson: University of Mississippi Press, 1987), 57–58; see also Robert Olwell, "'A Reckoning of Accounts': Patriarchy, Market Relations, and Control on Henry Laurens Lowcountry Plantation, 1762–1785," in *Working Toward Freedom: Slave Society and the Domestic Economy in the American South*, ed. Larry E. Hudson Jr. (Rochester, N.Y.: University of Rochester Press, 1994), 41. U. B. Phillips makes reference to Stepney for other purposes in his *American Negro Slavery: A Survey of the Supply, Employment and Control of Negro Labor as Determined by the Plantation Regime* (1918; Baton Rouge: Louisiana State University Press, 1969 [1918]), 324. He in turn cites David D. Wallace's biography of Laurens, *The Life of Henry Laurens* (New York: G. P. Putnam's Sons, 1915), 436. Laurens's relations with Stepney can be traced in Philip Hamer, George C. Rogers, David Chestnut, et al., eds., *The Papers of Henry Laurens*, 10 vols. to date (Columbia, University of South Carolina Press, 1965–85), 7:566; 8:67–68, 96; 10:2–3,17, 203, 205.

18. See, for instance, the photograph of "An unidentified African-American" in *Before Freedom Came: African-American Life In The Antebellum South* (Charlottesville: Museum of the Confederacy and the University Press of Virginia, 1991), 7. The caption explains that the picture "is included in an album of formal portraits taken of Robert E. Lee's slaves." In "The Hidden History of Mestizo America," *Journal of American History* (December 1995), Gary Nash discusses a "genre of paintings, known as 'Las Castas,' [which] marked the first time that Mexican artists chose to represent their own surroundings rather than using European models." This series of family portraits produced in Mexico in the eighteenth century "provides a fascinating grafting of racial backgrounds onto the Enlightenment passion for classification as well as its keen interest in the human condition." Some, he also notes, "consider this body of paintings a self-portrait of Mexican society." No such pictures, however, existed in the British American colonies. Indeed, "artists and publishers of such caste paintings would probably have been expelled from colonial towns (while going broke). The reason is not that racial intermingling was emotionally or sensuously unacceptable; rather it was ideologically repugnant." Ibid., 951, 954.

19. Hugh T. Taggart, "Old Georgetown," *Records of the Columbia Historical Society* 11 (1908):221–23; Charles Sellers, "Charles Willson Peale and Yarrow Mout," *Pennsylvania Magazine of History and Biography* 71 (April 1947), 99–102; Lillian B. Miller, ed., *The Selected Papers of Charles Willson Peale and His Family* (New Haven, Conn.: Yale University Press, 1991), 3, 617, 650–53. A black-and-white photograph of Simpson's portrait of Yarrow (juxtaposed with a similarly proportioned one of Peale's painting) appears in Kathleen M. Lesko, Valerie Babb, and Carroll R. Gibbs, *Black Georgetown Remembered: A History of Its*

Black Community from the Founding of "The Town of George" in 1751 to the Present Day (1991; Washington, D.C.: Georgetown University Press, 1999), 11.

Chapter 1: The Missing Subject

1. *The Times; and District of Columbia Daily Advertiser*, April 22, 1801, p. 3, col. 4; *Maryland Gazette*, November 2, 1769, p. 2, col. 3; *Georgia Gazette*, October 22, 1795, p. 2, col. 2. I use these illustrations as representative examples of the aspect of the ads being discussed, and that except where specified they could be expanded considerably. For studies that make extensive use of runaway ads, including those that have analyzed them statistically, see: Lathan A. Windley, "Profile of Runaway of Runaway Slaves in Virginia and South Carolina from 1730 through 1787" (Ph.D. diss., University of Iowa, 1974); Philip D. Morgan, *Slave Counterpoint: Black Culture in the Eighteenth-Century & Lowcountry* (Chapel Hill: University of North Carolina Press for Omohundro Institute of Early American History and Culture, Williamsburg, Va., 1998), "The Development of Slave Culture in Eighteenth-Century Plantation America" (Ph.d. diss., University College of London, 1977), and "Colonial South Carolina Runaways: Their Significance for Slave Culture," *Slavery and Abolition* 6 (December 1985), 57–78; Peter H. Wood, *Black Majority: Negroes in Colonial South Carolina from 1670 through the Stono Rebellion* (New York: W. W. Norton, 1974); John Donald Duncan, "Servitude and Slavery in Colonial South Carolina 1670–1776" (Ph.D. diss., Emory University, 1971); Daniel C. Littlefield, *Rice and Slaves: Ethnicity and the Slave Trade in Colonial South Carolina* (Baton Rouge: Louisiana State University Press, 1981); Shane White, "Black Fugitives in Colonial South Carolina," *Australasian Journal of American Studies* 1 (July 1980), 25–40; Betty Wood, *Slavery in Colonial Georgia, 1730–1775* (Athens: University of Georgia Press, 1984); Marvin L. Michael Kay and Lorin Lee Cary, "Slave Runaways in Colonial North Carolina, 1748–1775," *North Carolina Historical Review* 63 (January 1986), 1–40, and their *Slavery in North Carolina, 1748–1775* (Chapel Hill: University of North Carolina Press, 1995); Michael A. Gomez, *Exchanging our Country Marks: The Transformation of African American Identities in the Colonial and Antebellum South* (Chapel Hill: University of North Carolina Press, 1998); John Hope Franklin and Loren Schweninger, *Runaway Slaves: Rebels on the Plantation* (New York: Oxford University Press, 1999); Freddie L. Parker, *Running for Freedom: Slave Runaways in North Carolina, 1775–1840* (New York: Garland Publishing, 1993); Robert L. Hall, "Slave Resistance in Baltimore City and County, 1747–1790," *Maryland Historical Magazine* 84 (Winter 1989), 305–18; Gerald Mullin, *Flight and Rebellion: Slave Resistance in Eighteenth-Century Virginia* (New York: Oxford University Press, 1972); Michael Mullin, *Africa in America: Slave Acculturation and Resistance in the American South and the British Caribbean, 1736–1831* (Urbana: University of Illinois Press, 1992). For an invaluable analysis that places the ads, and the sort of resistance they reflect, in a broader context see James C. Scott, *Domination and the Arts of Resistance: Hidden Transcripts* (New Haven: Yale University Press, 1990).

2. *Georgia Gazette*, December 31, 1801, p. 3, col. 3; *Maryland Gazette*, July 7, 1796, p.3, col. 3; ibid., September 22, 1796, p. 3, col. 3; *Charleston Gazette*, December 15, 1797, p. 3, col. 3; *Raleigh Register, And North-Carolina State Gazette*, July 19, 1811, p. 3, col. 2.

3. *The State Gazette of North-Carolina* (Edenton), July 9, 1790, p. 3, col. 3; *Maryland Gazette*, December 6, 1764; ibid., December 2, 1756, p. 4, col. 2; ibid., August 12, 1762, p. 3, col. 2; *D. C. Times*, December 18, 1800, p. 4, col. 3; *Virginia Journal*, March 24, 1785, p. 3, col. 3; *Maryland Gazette*, June 6, 1793, p. 4, col. 1; *Royal Gazette* (South Carolina), January 26–30, 1782, p. 2, col. 3; *Maryland Gazette*, June 21, 1770, p. 3, col. 1.

4. Note Sterling Brown's comment about how blacks were depicted in the prose fiction produced in late-eighteenth and early-nineteenth-century America. In that extremely modest body of work, Brown wrote, the Negro "was a shadowy figure in the background, an element of romantic side interest." Sterling Brown, *The Negro in American Fiction* (Washington, D.C.: Associates in Negro Folk Education, 1937), 5–6. All of the

works by Boime, Honour, Hall, Blakely, and McElroy cited in the introduction are relevant here.

5. The paintings by Savage and Trumbull are reproduced, as are a wide variety of other drawings, sketches, and paintings of Washington, his friends, associates, and family, along with visual representations of the material world they shared, in the various volumes of *The Diaries of George Washington*, eds., Donald Jackson and Dorothy Twohig, 6 vol. (Charlottesville: University of Virginia Press, 1976–79). The painting by Savage is in 6:253; that by Trumbull, 2:279. The painting *A Family Group* is reproduced in Mechal Sobel, *The World They Made Together: Black and White Values in Eighteenth-Century Virginia* (Princeton, N.J.: Princeton University Press, 1987), 140. On the portrait of Byrd's daughter, see Maude H. Woodfin, ed., *Another Secret Diary of William Byrd of Westover, 1739–1741: With Letters & Literary Exercises 1696–1726* (Richmond, Va.: Dietz Press, 1942), 9 (ft. 1). The Soest portrait of Cecilius is reproduced and briefly described in Kim Hall, *Things of Darkness*, 332–33, and in Anne Elizabeth Yentsch, *A Chesapeake Family and Their Slaves: A Study in Historical Archaeology* (New York: Cambridge University Press, 1994), 15. The paintings of the Calvert children in Maryland can also be seen in Yentsch, 251, 287. The drawing of Spotswood's grandchildren is reproduced in Sobel, *World They Made Together*, 137.

6. Winthrop Jordan, for instance, has noted that there was "more logic than has commonly been supposed" in the decision by the framers of the Constitution "to count three-fifths of a state's slaves for apportionment of representation and taxes." "This famous compromise," he explains, "for which there were precedents in the Confederation period, was a practical resolution of political interests," but it was also a realistic expression of how black slaves were defined socially: "the three-fifths rule," he adds, "treated . . . [black slaves] accordingly, adding only a ludicrous fractional exactitude." Jordan, *White over Black: American Attitudes Toward the Negro, 1550–1812* (Chapel Hill: University of North Carolina Press, 1968), 322.

7. Ibid., 322–23.

8. John Bernard, *Retrospections of America* (New York, 1887), 91, quoted in James Thomas Flexner, *George Washington: Anguish and Farewell (1793–1799)*, 124. George Washington, *The Writings of George Washington, From the Original Manuscript Sources, 1745–1799*, ed. John C. Fitzpatrick, 39 vols. (Washington, D.C., 1931–44), 32:66; also quoted in Flexner, *George Washington*, 437.

9. The quotes are of course from *Notes on the State of Virginia* reprinted in *The Life and Selected Writings of Thomas Jefferson* (New York: Modern Library Paperback Edition, 1998), 237–42. See note 11 in the introduction for sources that have examined Jefferson's views on questions of race and on blacks in particular. For the intellectual sources of Jefferson's and Washington's racial attitudes and a sense of how typical they were, in addition to Jordan, *White over Black*, Gates, "The History and Theory of Afro-American Literary Criticism," and David Brion Davis, *The Problem of Slavery in the Age of Revolution*, see Thomas F. Gossett, *Race: The History of an Idea in America* (1963: New York: Oxford University Press, 1997), David Brion Davis, *The Problem of Slavery in Western Culture* (New York: Oxford University Press, 1988), Anthony Pagden, *European Encounters with the New World: From Renaissance to Romanticism* (New Haven: Yale University Press, 1993), and George W. Stocking Jr., "French Anthropology in 1800," 13–41, in Stocking, *Race, Culture, and Evolution: Essays in the History of Anthropology* (1968; Chicago: University of Chicago Press, 1982).

10. Rhys Isaac, "The First Monticello," in *Jeffersonian Legacies*, ed. Peter S. Onuf (Charlottesville: University Press of Virginia, 1993), chap. 3. The concept of "storied worlds" refers to Isaac's "notion that we as humans, and the cultures to which we belong, are largely constructed in and knowable through, the stock of stories we possess (or that possess us?). It is in that framework that we shall look at the world of Monticello as it was being constructed by the stories that its founder and others brought to it" (78). Other quotations from pages 79–80.

11. Jefferson, *Notes on the State of Virginia*, 240.

12. Isaac, "First Monticello," 80.

13. Ibid., 88–89.
14. Ibid., 100–101.
15. Ibid., 101.
16. Ibid., 89.
17. Ibid., 101.
18. Roger D. Abrahams, "Traditions of Eloquence in Afro-American Communities," and (with John F. Szwed) "After the Myth: Studying Afro-American Cultural Patterns in the Plantation Literature," both in Abrahams's *The Man-of-Words in the West Indies: Performance and the Emergence of Creole Culture* (Baltimore: Johns Hopkins University Press, 1983). See also the introductory essay by Abrahams and John Szwed in *After Africa: Extracts from British Travel Accounts and Journals of the Seventeenth, Eighteenth, and Nineteenth Centuries concerning the Slaves, their Manners, and Customs in the British West Indies* (New Haven, Conn.: Yale University Press, 1983).

19. David Brion Davis, *The Problem of Slavery in the Age of Revolution, 1770–1823* (Ithaca, N.Y.: Cornell University Press, 1975) 195.

20. Abrahams, "Traditions of Eloquence in Afro-American Communities," 29.

21. On his role in the "Making of the Gentry Class" see Allan Kulikoff, *Tobacco and Slaves: The Development of Southern Cultures in the Chesapeake, 1680–1800* (Chapel Hill: University of North Carolina Press for the Institute of Early American History and Culture at Williamsburg, Virginia, 1986), 263–65; on the value of Carter's papers, see Lorena Walsh, "'A Place in Time' Regained: A Fuller History of Colonial Chesapeake Slavery Through Group Biography," in *Working toward Freedom: Slave Society and Domestic Economy in the American South*, ed. Larry E. Hudson Jr. (Rochester, N.Y.: University of Rochester Press, 1994). In that essay she demonstrates how valuable Carter's diaries and other personal papers are by way of answering the question of whether the lives of slaves as a group have a recoverable history, given the fact that "we are unlikely ever to be able to trace family trees or to recover much of anything of the life stories of" individual slaves (2). Also, in the same essay (29n. 48), she notes: "The Carter family papers are one of the most detailed sources that address the procedures whites used to acculturate recent African captives in the early eighteenth-century Chesapeake." The same of course is true regarding the procedures they used to purchase those African captives, as she and others have demonstrated by their efforts to describe the process. Walsh, "'Place in Time' Regained," 2.

22. Robert Carter Diary, 1722–27, MS, Alderman Library, microfilm M-113, Colonial Williamsburg Foundation Library. All subsequent references to the diary are to the microfilmed copy at the Colonial Williamsburg research library.

23. Other collections of papers surviving from the late seventeenth and early eighteenth centuries take note of blacks, but of the surviving manuscript records none is as comprehensively detailed as Carter's about as wide a variety of concerns, and Carter's papers are relatively meager compared with many of those that have survived from later in the eighteenth century. For other detailed references to blacks surviving from as early as 1712, see for example the extraordinary "List of the Negroes with a perticular Account of their Cloathing and Bedding Their Working Tooles etc. . . . belonging to Edmund Jenings Esq'" in the Francis Porteus Corbin Papers, MS, Perkins Library, Duke University, microfilm, Colonial Williamsburg Foundation Library.

24. Jackson and Twohig, *Diaries of George Washington*, 1:xvii–xviii.
25. Ibid., 1:xviii–xix.
26. See note 8 in chap. 2 for sources on Landon Carter and his diaries.
27. Ibid, 1:222.
28. Ibid., 1:211–30.
29. Ibid., "The diary of his Southern Tour March–July 1791," 6:96–169.
30. Ibid., 6:114.
31. Charles Joyner has noted in a related sense that "The American Revolution is part of the historical consciousness of the Waccamaw. When the French marquis de Lafayette and the German Baron de Kalb crossed the Atlantic on the Victor in 1777 to join the American

colonists' struggle for independence, they first came ashore, led by a black slave, in All Saints Parish." In addition, when Francis Marion "fought the British in these forests along the Waccamaw and rested his men—former black slaves as well as whites—on the Waccamaw plantations of his in-laws, the Allstons." Joyner, *Down By the River: A South Carolina Slave Community* (Urbana, Ill.: University of Illinois Press, 1984), 5.

Also when "James Monroe was a guest at Prospect Hill in April 1819, cruising the Waccamaw on down to Georgetown on one of the plantation barges, profusely decorated and adorned for the occasion with United States colors proudly floating at its head. Eight negro oarsmen dressed in livery propelled the barges" (5).

32. Ibid., 120. Hunter also visited Mount Vernon during his travels in America. See Louis B. Wright and Marion Tinling, eds., *Quebec to Carolina in 1785–1786: Being the Travel Diary and Observations of Robert Hunter Jr., a Young Merchant of London* (San Marino, Calif.: The Huntington Library, 1943), chap. 6.

Chapter 2: Shadow Casting

1. For a full and fascinating reading of *Watson and the Shark*, see Boime, *Art of Exclusion*, 20–22, 24–26, 31–36.

2. The quotes are from P. Morgan, "Three Planters and Their Slaves," 39–40. See also his more extensive discussion of the same subject in *Slave Counterpoint*, chap. 5.

3. P. Morgan, "Three Planters and Their Slaves," 39–40. For colonial Virginia, in addition to the works by Morgan that have been previously cited, see Anthony S. Parent Jr., " 'Either A Fool or a Fury': The Emergence of Paternalism in Colonial Virginia Slave Society," (Ph.D. diss., University of California, Los Angeles, 1982). Also valuable is Rhys Isaac's discussion of the transition from patriarchalism to paternalism in *The Transformation of Virginia*, a discussion that has been extended, and to some degree challenged, by Kathleen Brown, "Gender and the Genesis of a race and class system in Virginia, 1630–1750" (Ph.D. diss., University of Wisconsin, Madison, 1990), 553 and chap. 8 in which Brown takes Isaac to task for not adequately considering issues of gender related to or driving the transformation. On the whole, however, Brown's analysis builds on Isaac's rather than argues against it. *Good Wives Nasty Wenches & Anxious Patriarchs: Gender, Race, and Power in Colonial Virginia* (Chapel Hill: University of North Carolina Press for the Institute of Early American History and Culture, Williamsburg, Va., 1996) by Brown is based on her dissertation.

For a powerful argument against a meaningful transformation, but one which at the same time recognizes the value and power of Isaac's description of it, see Marvin L. Kay and Lorin Lee Cary, *Slavery in North Carolina, 1630–1750* (Chapel Hill: University of North Carolina Press, 1995), chap. 2.

What we see in the self-portraits of planters, and more broadly throughout their papers, is a process of self-fashioning not unlike that described by Stephen Greenblatt in *Renaissance Self-Fashioning: From More to Shakespeare* (Chicago: University of Chicago Press, 1980), 2, 7–8. We see, that is, "a manipulable and artful process" involving "an increased self-consciousness about the fashioning of human identity." (2)

4. The letter is reproduced and contextualized in Marion Tinling, ed., *The Correspondence of the Three William Byrds of Westover, Virginia, 1684–1776* (Charlottesville: University Press of Virginia for the Virginia Historical Society, 1977), 1:354–56.

5. Ibid., 355–6. For a discussion of this letter, and more broadly an interpretive reading of Byrd's other writings as they relate to his life as a slaveholding patriarch, see Alexander Ormond Bolton, "The Architecture of Slavery: Art, Language, and Society in Early Virginia" (Ph.D., diss., College of William and Mary, 1991), chap. 2. On Byrd and his diaries also see Michael Zuckerman, "The Family Life of William Byrd," 97–144, in his *Almost Chosen People: Oblique Biographies in the American Grain* (Berkeley: University of California Press, 1993); Brown, *Good Wives Nasty Wenches & Anxious Patriarchs*; Louis B. Wright, *The*

NOTES TO PAGES 27–47

First Gentlemen of Virginia: Intellectual Qaualities of the Early Colonial Ruling Class (San Marino, Calif.: Huntington Library, 1940); and the two studies by Kenneth A. Lockridge on Byrd: *The Diary and Life of William Byrd II of Virginia, 1674–1744* (Chapel Hill: University of North Carolina Press for the Institute of Early American History and Culture, Williamsburg, Va., 1987), and *On the Sources of Patriarchal Rage: The Commonplace Books of William Byrd and Thomas Jefferson and the Gendering of Power in the Eighteenth Century* (New York: New York University Press, 1992). Pierre Marambaud, *William Byrd of Westover, 1674–1744* (Charlottesville: University Press of Virginia, 1971) is also helpful.

6. Far away in time and space but close in shared sentiment was Frederick George Mulcaster's dream. Writing to a correspondent in 1768 from East Florida, which had only recently come under British control, the young Scottish planter sought to describe the special quality of the area by reference to a recent dream: "I stood in a Hall and beneath me was Indigo Rice Cotton etc, in great abundance [and] at my Command my slaves . . . instantly gathered the Crop and put it on Board Vessels" bound for England and when they were somehow magically transformed into "Corn Wine and Oyl." The historian who used this dream as an introduction to her study explains that "Mulcaster's dream presented (albeit unconsciously) three crucial images of the early Lower South . . . : the dizzying plenty of its agriculture and the mutability of its crops but also the dependence of these two happy phenomena on the labor of black slaves." The references to the transformed crops as "Corn Wine and Oyl," moreover, are "classical and biblical symbols of plenty. . . . (The reverie omitted only the figs of ancient tradition.) And thus Mulcaster's dream underscored how the Lower South resembled venerated societies of the past that had also relied on slavery." Joyce E. Chaplin, *An Anxious Pursuit: Agricultural Innovation and Modernity in the Lower South, 1730–1815* (Chapel Hill: University of North Carolina Press for the Institute of Early American History and Culture, Williamsburg, Va., 1993), 1–2.

At the beginning of the last decade of the eighteenth century, the recent settlement of Lake Phelps in North Carolina inspired this description by minister-planter Charles Pettigrew: "I write you from Bonarva—a name I have given my situation on the Lake. I sit under the shade of three beautiful Holleys. The surrounding Scene is truly romantic. On the one side, the prospect toward the water is very beautiful & extensive, while the gentle breezes play over the surface of the crystal fluid, and render the air grateful for respiration, now when the Sun sheds his warmest influence upon the earth—it being the meridian hour. On three angles of the improvement, yᵉ woods are luxuriantly tall, & dressed in a foliage of the deepest verdure, while the cultivated field exhibits the utmost power of vegetative nature, and arrests my eye from every other object." *The Pettigrew Papers, Vol. I: 1685–1818*, ed. Sarah McCulloh Lemmon (Raleigh, N.C.: State Department of Archives and History, 1971), 88.

7. *The Diary of Colonel Landon Carter of Sabine Hall, 1752–1778*, ed. Jack P. Greene (Charlottesville: University Press of Virginia for the Virginia Historical Society, 1965), 2:750–51.

8. The best biography of Landon Carter is contained in Jack P. Greene's introduction to the first volume of *The Diary of Colonel Landon Carter*. Isaac, *Transformation of Virginia*, is also essential for a well-grounded understanding of Carter. Also, in addition to P. Morgan, "Three Planters and Their Slaves," see Rhys Isaac, "Stories of Enslavement: A Person-Centered Ethnography from an Eighteenth-Century Virginia Plantation," in *Varieties of Southern History: New Essays on a Region and Its People*, ed. Bruce Clayton and John Salmond, (Westport, Conn.: Greenwood Press, 1996), 3–20.

9. On Sabine Hall, see Rhys Isaac, *Transformation of Virginia*, especially 350–54, but also note his other references to it elsewhere in that study.

10. *Diary of Colonel Landon Carter*, 2:750–51.

11. *Virginia Gazette*, (Rind) April 14, 1774, pp. 1 and 2, cols. 1–2.

12. G. Mullin, *Flight and Rebellion*, notes that the "patriarchal role sometimes had an insidious influence on the master's behavior. Landon Carter's paternalistic care of his slave children changed his normally embittered outlook. Carter knew himself well enough to seek out situations that brought out his generous, humane qualities. He was especially

gentle to those whom he perceived as weaker than himself, including 'my negro children,' whom he sometimes doctored." (23)

13. *Virginia Gazette* (Dixon & Hunter), June 20, 1777, p. 3, col. 1.

14. For a discussion of efforts by planters like Robert Carter to support the war effort by becoming more self-sufficient, see Louis Morton's biography, *Robert Carter of Nomini Hall: A Virginia Tobacco Planter of the Eighteenth Century* (Williamsburg, Va., 1941).

15. *Virginia Gazette* (Purdie), March 28, 1777, p. 1, cols. 1–3.

16. The ad Carter makes reference to reads as follows: "I will give g1 reward, beside reasonable traveling expenses, for apprehending and bringing to *Williamsburg JAMES ORANGE*, who deserted from my company last week. He is an *Englishman*, about 6 feet and an inch high, and was lately a grenadier of the 17th *British* regiment, from which he deserted 6 or 8 weeks ago. He has a pass signed by several gentlemen on his way from *Philadelphia* here." *Virginia Gazette* (Purdie), June 6, 1773, p. 3, col. 3.

17. The latter observation suggests, as does the ad's general tone, that Carter believed Orange was a runaway indentured or convict servant.

18. There is also this related reference, dated April 15, 1758: "I can't but take notice of the death of my little Canary bird, an old housekeeper having had it here 11 year this month and constantly fed it with bread and milk, and I wish the heat of this weather did not by Souring its food occasion its death, for it sung prodigiously all the forepart of the day. At night it was taken with a barking noise and dyed the night following, vizt, last night. I know this is a thing to be laught at but a bruit or a bird so long under my care and protection deserves a Small remembrance." *Diary of Landon Carter*, 1:216.

19. The closest and most perceptive reading of Carter's relations with Nassau is by Rhys Isaac, "Stories of Enslavement: A Person-Centered Ethnography from an Eighteenth-Century Virginia Plantation," in Bruce Clayton and John Salmond, eds., *Varieties of Southern History: New Essays on a Region and Its People* (Westport, CT: Greenwood Press, 1996), 3–20. The quote is on page 15.

20. *Diary of Colonel Landon Carter*, 2:940–41.

21. On Landon Carter as a paternalist, see Isaac, *Transformation of Virginia*, and his article "Communication and Control: Authority Metaphors and Power Contests on Colonel Landon Carter's Virginia Plantation," in *Rites of Power: Symbolism, Ritual, and Politics since the Middle Ages*, ed. Sean Wilentz (Philadelphia: University of Pennyslvania Press, 1985). On Robert Carter of Nomini Hall as an exemplary paternalist and Landon Carter as a failed patriarch, see Mullin, *Flight and Rebellion*, 70. On the inheritance they both received and what they made of it, see Greene's introduction to Carter's diary and Robert Morton's biography of Robert, both cited earlier. On Landon Carter's intellectual and political life, see Greene's introduction and Isaac, *Transformation of Virginia*.

22. Robert Carter to Sol. Nash, Nomini Hall, December 15, 1789. Robert Carter Letterbook. I have used the microfilmed version of Robert Carter's letterbooks at Baker Library, Microtext Department, Dartmouth College. The originals are owned by Perkins Library, Duke University.

23. In his study of the critical reception of Phillis Wheatley's poetry, Henry Louis Gates Jr. has noted that Washington was among the first notable Americans to formally recognize what Washington termed her "great poetical genius." In a letter dated February 10, 1776, to his former military secretary, Joseph Reed, Washington acknowledges that he has received a letter and a poem in his honor from Wheatley. Wheatley's very brief letter to Washington had almost apologized for taking "the freedom to address your Excellency" and send him "the enclosed poem" commemorating his "being appointed by the Grand Continental Congress to be Generalissimo of the Armies of North America."

Washington's reference to Wheatley in his letter to Reed begins, "I recollect nothing else worth giving you the trouble of unless you can be amused by reading a letter and poem addressed to me by Mrs. or Miss Phillis Wheatley." He then goes on to explain that he had forgotten all about the letter and the poem until recently, when "searching over a parcel of papers the other day, in order to destroy such as were useless." Finding them again in that

way reminded him that he had been so impressed by them that "I had a great mind to publish the poem; but not knowing whether it might not be considered rather as a mark of my
vanity, than as a compliment to her, I laid it aside." Subsequently Washington would write
Wheatley and invite her to visit him in Cambridge or at his headquarters, which she did in
March, "a few days before the British evacuation of Boston."

"The event is noteworthy," Gates claims, "for the honor accorded to Phillis," which according to one authority he cites was the first such visit Washington had granted to an "African"
and the first time "he ever accorded the civility of 'Mrs.' or Miss' to one of her race."

See Gates, "The History and Theory of Afro-American Literary Criticism," 292–94. He
quotes Benson J. Lossing, *The Pictorial Field-Book of the Revolution*, 2 vols. (New York:
Harper & Bros., 1851), on the timing of Wheatley's visit, and Walter H. Mazyck, *George
Washington and the Negro* (Washington, D.C.: Associated Publishers, 1932), 55, on the
unusual nature of the visit in terms of Washington's relations with blacks.

24. Flexner, *George Washington: Anguish and Farewell*, 432–33, 433–34, 435, discusses both
Hercules and Judge. A fuller account of Judge's flight can be found in Sobel, *World They
Made Together*, 139. Fritz Hirschfeld, *George Washington and Slavery: A Documentary Portrayal*
(Columbia: University of Missouri Press, 1997), provides the relevant documents and a
useful discussion of the relationships. For an informative recent look at Washington and
the blacks at Mount Vernon, see Robert F. Dalzell Jr. and Lee Baldwin Dalzell, *George Wash-
ington's Mount Vernon: At Home in Revolutionary America* (New York: Oxford University
Press, 1998).

25. Flexner, *George Washington: Anguish and Farewell*, 435–36.

26. Olwell, " 'Reckoning of Accounts,' " 34. See also Olwell's *Masters, Slaves, and Subjects:
The Culture of Power in the South Carolina Low Country 1740–1790* (Ithaca, N.Y.: Cornell University Press, 1998).

27. Olwell, "Reckoning of Accounts," 35, 34.

28. Quoted in ibid., 34.

29. Quoted in ibid., 37. See the following articles by Philip Morgan on the slave's
domestic economy: "Work and Culture: The Task System and the World of Lowcountry
Blacks, 1700 to 1880," *Williams and Mary Quarterly* 39 (October 1982):563–99, and "The
Ownership of Property by Slaves in the Mid-Nineteenth-Century Low Country," *Journal of
Southern History* 49 (August 1983):399–420. Also of interest are Betty Wood, *Women's Work,
Men's Work: The Informal Slave Economies of Lowcountry Georgia* (Athens: University of Geor-
gia Press, 1995), and the editors' introduction, "Labor and the Shaping of Slave Life in the
Americas," and relevant essays in Ira Berlin and Philip Morgan, eds., *Cultivation and Cul-
ture: Labor and the Shaping of Slave Life in the Americas* (Charlottesville: University Press of
Virginia, 1993).

Chapter 3: Ambiguity

1. For sources on Byrd see note 5, chap. 2.

2. Scholarship on the demographic transformation of the colonial Chesapeake and the
related emergence of the gentry class has since the early to mid-1970s grown rich and
abundant. A convenient, relatively recent summary of its findings can be found in John L.
McCusker and Russell R. Menard, *The Economy of British America, 1607–1789* (Chapel Hill:
University of North Carolina Press for the Institute of Early American History and Culture, Williamsburg, Va., 1985), and in Robert Fogel, *Without Consent or Contract: The Rise
and Fall of American Slavery* (New York: W. W. Norton, 1989). Important studies that have
incorporated, extended, and developed those findings in relation to particular areas
include E. Morgan, *American Slavery American Freedom*, and Kulikoff, *Tobacco and Slaves*. See
also Gloria L. Main, *Tobacco Colony: Life in Early Maryland, 1650–1720* (Princeton, N.J.:
Princeton University Press, 1982); Paul G. E. Clemens, *The Atlantic Economy and Colonial
Maryland's Eastern Shore* (Ithaca, N.Y.: Cornell University Press, 1980); Carville V. Earle,

The Evolution of a Tidewater Settlement System: All Hallow's Parish, Maryland, 1650–1783 (Chicago: Department of Georgraphy, University of Chicago, 1975); Lois Green Carr, Russell R. Menard, and Lorena S. Walsh, *Robert Cole's World: Agriculture & Society in Early Maryland* (Chapel Hill: University of North Carolina Press for the Institute of Early American History and Culture, Williamsburg, Va., 1991); and Lorena Walsh, "Charles County, Maryland, 1658–1705: A Study of Chesapeake Social and Political Structure" (Ph.D. diss., Michigan State University, 1977). For historiographical surveys of the pathbreaking literature these and many other related studies build on and reflect, see the editors' introductions to Thad W. Tate and David L. Ammerman, eds., *The Chesapeake in the Seventeenth Century: Essays on Anglo-American Society and Politics* (New York: W. W. Norton, 1979), and Lois Green Carr, Philip D. Morgan, and Jean B. Russo, eds., *Colonial Chesapeake Society* (Chapel Hill: University of North Carolina Press for the Institute of Early American History and Culture, Williamsburg, Va., 1988). Still valuable is Wesley Frank Craven, *White, Red, and Black: The Seventeenth-Century Virginian* (Charlottesville: University Press of Virginia, 1971) in combination with his *The Southern Colonies in the Seventeenth Century, 1607–1688* (1949; Baton Rouge: Louisiana State University Press, 1970).

The best brief overview of slavery in the colonial South during the seventeenth century is to be found in the prologue to P. Morgan's *Slave Counterpoint*.

3. For biographical information on Byrd see note 5, chap. 2. On Carter's diaries and his relations with his slaves see note 8, chap. 2.

4. Louis B. Wright and Marion Tingling, the editors of *The Secret Diary of William Byrd of Westover, 1709–1712* (Richmond, Va.: Dietz Press, 1941), make this point: i.e., "It is usually impossible to tell whether the servants mentioned in the diary are negro slaves or white servants" (2); as does Mechal Sobel, *World They Made Together*, 147; and Bolton, "Architecture of Slavery," 51.

5. Here is Byrd's reference to the "dark angel" he encountered in the woods: "I took a walk into the woods and called at a cottage where a dark angel surprised us with her charms. Her complexion was a deep copper, so that her fine shape and regular features made her appear like a statue *en bronze* done by a masterly hand. Shoebrush was smitten at the first glance and examined all her neat proportions with a critical exactness. She struggled just enough to make her admirer more eager, so that if I had not been there, he would have been in danger of carrying his joke a little too far." *The Prose Works of William Byrd of Westover: Narratives of a Colonial Virginian*, ed. Louis B. Wright (Cambridge: Harvard University Press, 1966), 60. Bolton and Sobel assume that the reference is to a black woman, but the description could just as easily be to an Indian. It is important to note as background to Byrd's and Beverley's comments regarding Indians how important trade with them had been to the economic development of early colonial Virginia and especially how deeply involved Byrd's father was in promoting that trade and benefiting from it.

6. For Byrd's critique, contained in a letter to Sir John Percival, earl of Egmont, see *Correspondence of the Three William Byrds*, 2:487–89. On the role played by Percival in the establishment of colonial Georgia, see Betty Wood, *Slavery in Colonial Georgia, 1730–1775* (Athens: University of Georgia Press, 1984). See also Michael Crowley, *This Sheba, Self: The Conceptualization of Economic Life in Eighteenth-Century America* (Baltimore: Johns Hopkins University Press, 1974), 119.

7. All quotes taken from Byrd's diaries are from *Secret Diary of William Byrd of Westover* and *Another Secret Diary of William Byrd of Westover*. The dates given in the text locate the quotes in the diaries.

8. See Bolton's close reading of this episode ("Architecture of Slavery," 55–60) for a broader view of Byrd's relations with his slaves and the local community in which they all lived.

9. For examples of that analysis, see the sources cited in note 2 above.

10. Brown, "Gender and the Genesis of a Race and Class System in Virginia," 176. Of course the first blacks to arrive in the English colonies came as slaves and thus as part of an exchange unlike that experienced by any whites in the colonies. Some gained their free-

dom, but most of those who did probably gained it through an incentive based process such as self-purchase. Essential for an understanding of this early moment in the history of the black presence in colonial America is J. Douglas Deal, *Race and Class in Colonial Virginia: Indians, Englishmen, and Africans on the Eastern Shore during the Seventeenth Century* (New York: Garland Publishing, 1993). On racial distinctions and attitudes in the Chesapeake colonies before they became slave societies see (in addition to Deal, Jordan, *White over Black*, Brown, *Good Wives Nasty Wenches*, and E. Morgan, *American Slavery American Freedom*) Ira Berlin, *Many Thousands Gone: The First Two Centuries of Slavery in North America* (Cambridge: Belknap Press of Harvard University Press, 1998); and T. H. Breen and Stephen Innes, *"Myne Owne Ground": Race and Freedom on Virginia's Eastern Shore, 1640–1676* (New York: Oxford University Press, 1980).

11. Inga Clendinnen, " 'Fierce and Unnatural Cruelty': Cortes and the Conquest of Mexico," in *New World Encounters*, ed. Stephen Greenblatt (Berkeley: University of California Press, 1993), 39. Clendinnen's discussion of otherization can also be found, in a more abbreviated form, in the epilogue to her study *Aztecs: An Interpretation* (New York: Cambridge University Press, 1991).

12. Morgan, *American Slavery American Freedom*, 89–90.

13. *The Correspondence of the Three William Byrds of Westover, Virginia 1684–1776*, ed. Marion Tinling (Charlottesville: University Press of Virginia for the Virginia Historical Society, 1977), 1:183.

14. This topic is discussed extensively in chap. 6 below.

15. Also, "There is plenty of evidence from Byrd's diary that deference to authority was not something automatically given . . . . Even the most basic categories of family, race, and class were subject to dispute" and "had to be constantly negotiated." His great wealth, most of which he inherited, and the privileged position it conferred upon him gave Byrd considerable personal authority, or the presumption of it, but in order to maintain it he had to be able to use it effectively as a focus for negotiation "between blacks and whites, free and slave, family and society" in the community in which he was the dominant figure by virtue of his great wealth. Thus, "Byrd's position depended on cultivating a certain degree of ambiguity," as a means of establishing "a balance between hierarchical rankings and their continual negotiation. The constantly shifting alliances between Byrd, his wife, his neighbors, his overseers, his servants and his slaves acted to cement Byrd's authority by guaranteeing that he was constantly the focus of power." Bolton, "Architecture of Slavery," 82–83.

16. Ibid., 82–83. Bolton's development of this view, as I indicated earlier, includes a fascinating description of Byrd's efforts to recapture Betty, framing it in terms of the local negotiations he makes reference to in the quotes that I have used in the text.

17. How typical Byrd was in this regard is debatable. Of his contemporaries it is probably better to think of him as one extreme on a continuum with Robert "King" Carter at the other end.

18. On the evangelical challenge, see Donald Matthews, *Religion in the Old South* (Chicago: University of Chicago Press, 1977), and Rhys Isaac, *Transformation of Virginia*. Isaac is also useful on the political challenges, as of course is Jordan, *White over Black*, and David Brion Davis, especially *The Problem of Slavery in Western Culture* and *The Problem of Slavery in the Age of Revolution*.

19. Ibid., 153–54. Good examples of how restless whites were becoming in the colonial South during the latter half of the eighteenth century and of the ways in which they were beginning to look back are offered by Rhys Isaac, in his "Preachers and Patriots: Popular Culture and the Revolution in Virginia," in Young, ed., *The American Revolution*, 127–56, and his *Transformation of Virginia*. See also, from a related but different vantage point, the expression of a class-consciousness among nongenteel whites in Marvin L. Kay and Lorin Lee Cary, "The North Carolina Regulation, 1766–1776: A Class Conflict," which is also in Young, *The American Revolution*, 72–123, and chapters 2 and 4 in their *Slavery in North Carolina, 1748–1775* (Chapel Hill: University of North Carolina Press, 1995).

20. Though the distinction between free citizens and others in Revolutionary America was considerable, according to Jack P. Greene, in Revolutionary South Carolina, "South Carolina excluded not just slaves but all blacks from citizenship, specifically confining the 'rights of *election* and *representation*' to 'free white men' of 21 or older, a limitation that makes clear that it was not just their status as dependents but their presumed disabilities, as men, that debarred slaves from citizenship." Greene, "Slavery or Independence," *South Carolina Historical Magazine* (1979), 207. The same of course was true elsewhere throughout the colonial and Revolutionary South.

21. George C. Rogers Jr., *Charleston in the Age of the Pinckneys* (Norman: University of Oklahoma Press, 1969), 108; and Rachel Klein, *Unification of a Slave State: The Rise of the Planter Class in the South Carolina Backcountry, 1760–1808* (Chapel Hill: University of North Carolina Press for the Institute of Early American History and Culture, Williamsburg, Va., 1990), 217. Winthrop Jordan, *White over Black*, noting that Ramsay was born in Pennsylvania, points out that even though Ramsay owned slaves, he "was regarded by many persons in the state as distinctly unsound on the subject of slavery" (456). For the intellectual and ideological framework and background in which Ramsay's experience took place see Greene, "'Slavery and Independence'"; on social relations between poor and working-class whites and free and enslaved blacks, see Morgan, "Black Life in Eighteenth-Century Charleston," in *Perspectives in American History, New Series* 1 (1984), 204–19. See also Robert Olwell, "'Domestick Enemies': Slavery and Political Independence in South Carolina, May 1775–March 1776," *Journal of Southern History* 55 (February 1989):21–48, for an examination of the fear among ruling class whites in South Carolina "that disunity or enmity among white inhabitants might inspire a slave uprising or that dissident whites might ally with blacks in order to gain power" (26).

22. Ibid., 153.

23. *South-Carolina Gazette And Timothy & Mason's Daily Advertiser* Nov. 10, 1796 (pp. 4, col. 1).

24. *South Carolina Gazette*, May 11, 1738, p. 3, col. 1; Charles City County, Virginia, June 3, 1659, in Deeds Wills, Orders, 1655–65, microfilm, Virginia State Library; Colonial Court Papers: Criminal Papers—General and Assize Courts, 1740–44: General Court and Assize—Criminal—1743, August 1743, North Carolina State Archives.

25. These all appear in various colonial court records surviving from throughout the eighteenth century in the North Carolina State Archives but could be located in other similar records surviving from other parts of the colonial South or occasionally in commentary in colonial newspapers. On slander see Philip J. Schwarz, *Twice Condemned: Slaves and the Criminal Laws of Virginia, 1705–1865* (Baton Rouge: Louisiana State University Press, 1988); and Brown, *Good Wives Nasty Wenches*, 94–95, 99–102, 145–49, 210–11.

26. Jack P. Greene, "Society, Ideology, and Politics: An Analysis of the Political Culture of Mid-Eighteenth-Century Virginia," in *Society, Freedom, and Conscience: The American Revolution in Virginia, Massachusetts, and New York*, ed. Richard M. Jellison (New York: W. W. Norton, 1976), 15–16. On the meanings of gentility, its modes of expression, and the challenges to it that emerged in the second half of the eighteenth century, see Isaac, *Transformation of Virginia*. See also T. H. Breen, *Tobacco Culture: The Mentality of the Great Tidewater Planters on the Eve of Revolution* (Princeton, N.J.: Princeton University Press, 1985). On the economic and demographic details of "the making of the gentry class" in the colonial Chesapeake, see Kulikoff, *Tobacco and Slaves*, chap. 7, and part 2 of the study more generally.

Governor James Glen of South Carolina in 1751 divided Carolina's white population into four distinct social classes: those (around five thousand), he said, "who have plenty of the good things of Life," those (also estimated at about five thousand) "who have some of the Conveniencys of Life," those (representing about ten thousand inhabitants) "who have the Necessarys of Life," and those (five or six thousand) "who have a bare subsistence." Quoted in Eugene Sirmans, *Colonial South Carolina: A Political History, 1663–1763* (Chapel Hill: University of North Carolina Press, 1969), 228.

27. Greene, "Society, Ideology, and Politics," 54, 34.

28. Greene, *Diary of Colonel Landon Carter*, 2:732.

29. De Graffenreid said that he voluntarily returned to the county from a visit with friends in an adjacent county when he heard of the charges against him, and that he was jailed after inquiring about the charges and being examined by a local magistrate. The summary of the case against him, which composes the bulk of his letter "To the Public," concludes with the following testimonial: "We the undersigned justices do hereby certify, that we sat on the examination of Doctor Robert De Graffenreid and that the above statement is a correct report of the substance of his case."

30. Wesley Frank Craven, *White, Red, and Black: The Seventeenth-Century Virginian* (Charlottesville: University Press of Virginia, 1971), 80.

31. On the antislavery threat posed by evangelism, see Matthews, *Religion in the Old South*, 66–80; on the cultural challenge posed by "the austere culture of the evangelicals, with their burden of guilt" see Isaac, *Transformation of Virginia*, 322, chaps. 8 and 11.

32. *Mistress of Riversdale: The Plantation Letters of Rosalie Stier Calvert, 1795–1821*, ed. Margaret Law Callcott (Baltimore: Johns Hopkins University Press, 1991). On the range and extent of intimate relations between blacks and whites, especially on large plantations in eighteenth century Virginia, see Sobel, *World They Made Together*, chap. 10, "Sharing Space inside the Big House," 127–53.

33. Peter A. Coclanis, *The Shadow of a Dream: Economic Life and Death in the South Carolina Low Country, 1670–1920* (New York: Oxford University Press, 1989), 49.

34. Quoted in Wallace, *Life of Henry Laurens*, 79n. 1.

35. An appreciation of the inhibitions restraining Laurens is offered in Wallace, *Life of Henry Laurens*, 448–49, where a portion of this letter to his son John, who had begun to vigorously advocate the raising of a black regiment both as a means of supporting the war effort and as a step toward eventual emancipation of all black slaves in his native South Carolina. His father had at first expressed qualified support for the idea, but then wrote on February 6, 1778: "The more I think of and the more I have consulted on your scheme, the less I approve of it." Clearly aware of the response the idea would and did eventually receive from South Carolina authorities and members of their class more generally, the elder Laurens added: "Your own good sense will direct you to proceed warily in opposing the opinions of whole nations, lest, *without effecting any good*, you become a bye word, and be so transmitted to your children's children." Wallace, further on in his survey of Laurens's views on slavery, offers in a note (451n. 2) a lengthy genealogy of antislavery sentiment in the Laurens family, including in addition to Henry's son and daughter and grandson, his brother, James, and stretching back to their father, John. He also mentions in the same note other members of South Carolina's ruling elite who possessed strong antislavery sentiments, including the branch of the Grimke family who went north and became abolitionists "of an extreme type," referring of course to the Grimke sisters, Sarah and Angeline. In this way, Wallace indirectly reinforces the cogency of Henry's advice to his son, for none of those he mentions was allowed to give extended expression to those sentiments or vigorously and successfully press for their implementation in South Carolina.

36. This discussion is based entirely on John Scott Strickland's description. See his dissertation, "Across Space and Time: Conversion, Community, and Cultural Change among South Carolina Slaves" (Ph.D. diss., University of North Carolina, Chapel Hill, 1985), chap. 3: "The Time of Judgment Foretold: Slave Conversion, Social Action, and Order Imperiled." His discussion of the Bryan episode begins on page 133, from which the quote in the text is taken.

An equally interesting instance of the sort represented by Bryan is the story of Christian Priber, "a fascinating and enigmatic figure who sought to erect a 'kingdom of paradise' in the southern Appalachians" while living among the Cherokees from 1736 to 1743. Not surprisingly, as Robert Weir notes, "Priber died imprisoned in Georgia." See Weir, *Colonial*

South Carolina: A History (Millwood, NY: kto press, 1983), 21. According to J. Leitch Wright, Jr., Priber welcomed runaway blacks to his kingdom. See Wright, *The Only Land They Knew: The Tragic Story of the American Indians in the Old South* (New York: Free Press, 1981), 275–76. See also Verner W. Crane, "A Lost Utopia of the First American Frontier," *Sewanee Review* 27 (1919):48–61.

The fullest recent reading of the documents relating to Priber's experience among the Cherokee is provided in John Donald Duncan's dissertation, "Servitude and Slavery in Colonial South Carolina, 1670–1776" (Ph.D. diss., Emory University, 1972), 613–20. In addition to Cherokee, Duncan explains, Priber also intended to include "Creeks & Catawbaws, French & English, all Colours and Complexions" in the utopian society he sought to establish. When captured in 1743 he was with "a few Cherokee and one Negro." Authorities, apparently, were especially concerned about the inclusion of runaway slaves in this project. Duncan quotes a 1743 report to the secretary of state in London by James Oglethorpe of Georgia to that effect. Describing Priber's scheme as an "Imitation of the Paullis in Brazil," Oglethorpe says he expects Priber's society to become "a great Resort for the Benefit of the Asylum from the number of debtors, Transport Felons, Servants, & Negroe Slaves in the two Carolinas & Virginia." The latter expectation disturbed Oglethorpe most; he states his belief that "they [Priber and his supporters] were to take particularly under Protection, the runaway negroes of the English."

Bryan was at the time—the late 1730s and early 1740s—in the process of amassing a substantial number of black slaves to work a very large and increasingly widely dispersed landed estate. See Alan Gallay, *The Formation of a Planter Elite: Jonathan Bryan and the Southern Colonial Frontier* (Athens: University of Georgia Press, 1989), 16–18, for a description of Bryan's economic activities. There Gallay speculates that Hugh had between seventy-five and one hundred slaves by the 1750s. On the Bryans and other large slave and landowners in the Port Royal region of colonial South Carolina, see Lawrence Sanders Rowland, "Eighteenth Century Beaufort: A Study of South Carolina's Southern Parishes to 1800" (Ph.D. diss., University of South Carolina, 1978), 141–45.

37. Strickland, "Across Space and Time," 138.

38. Ibid., 150–60.

Chapter 4: The View of Strangers

1. To reiterate a point made in the introduction, in order to understand or better appreciate the challenge to self-expression and awareness that such an assault posed for blacks in the colonial South (one, as will become clearer later in the book, that demanded repeated acts of self-abnegation, of being and becoming Negro), it is necessary to develop an understanding of how they met that challenge. That is an important concern of this book but beyond its more limited objective. Here, the purpose is to see the challenge as fully as possible.

2. For Fithian's journal, see *Journal and Letters of Philip Vickers Fithian, 1773–1774: A Plantation Tutor of the Old Dominion*, ed. Hunter D. Farish (1943; Williamsburg, Va., 1996). The distinction being made here can perhaps best be seen in the use historians have made of Fithian's diary to amplify the account of Robert Carter's world that Carter's surviving papers offer. See, for instance, Louis Morton's still invaluable biography, *Robert Carter of Nomini Hall, A Virginia Tobacco Planter of the Eighteenth Century* (Williamsburg: Colonial Williamsburg, Inc., 1941); and John Randolph Barden's more recent "'Flushed with Notions of Freedom': The Growth and Emancipation of a Virginia Slave Community, 1732–1812" (Ph.D. diss., Duke University, 1993).

3. *Journal and Letters of Philip Vickers Fithian*, 192.

4. Ibid., 61–67.

5. James Sidbury, *Ploughshares into Swords: Race, Rebellion, and Identity in Gabriel's Virginia, 1730–1810* (New York: Cambridge University Press, 1997), 157–58.

6. It is natural of course that visitors to someone's home would notice things that their

host had come to overlook or take for granted. Nonetheless the difference in what visitors like Fithian reported about blacks and slavery and what can be learned from their hosts remains striking. A comparison of *The Natural History of North Carolina* written by the Irish born doctor John Brickell with similar or related works written by Robert Beverley or William Byrd, or any other writer born in the colonies and intimately involved with slavery, is telling in that regard. The ethnographic information provided by Brickell about blacks is unique, whereas most of the rest of his observations are not. For Brickell's "Short account of the Negroes or Blacks" see Brickell, *The Natural History of North-Carolina* (1737; New York: Johnson Reprint Corporation, 1969), 271–76. On Brickell and the history of his *Natural History* see the introduction to the cited edition by Carol Urness, v–ix, and the introduction by Hugh Talmage Lefler to John Lawson's *A New Voyage to Carolina*, ed. Hugh Talmage Lefler,(1709; Chapel Hill: University of North Carolina,1967), lii–liii. Examples parallel to Brickell in North Carolina and Fithian in Virginia can be identified in each of the other Southern colonies. In Georgia, for instance, there is the report written by the spiritual leader of Salzburger settlers in Georgia, Johan Martin Bolzius, in response to questions from a benefactor in Augsburg: "Johan Martin Bolzius Answers a Questionaire on Carolina and Georgia," translated and edited by Klaus G. Loewald, Beverly Starika, and Paul S. Taylor, *William and Mary Quarterly* 14 (April 1957), 218–61. For South Carolina there is, in addition to the "Stranger" and many other travelers, the "Journal of Josiah Quincy, Junior, 1773," ed. Mark Antony De Wolfe Howe, *Massachusetts Historical Society Proceedings*, 49 (October 1915–June, 1916), 424–81. From Maryland a good example is the "Story of Dick the Negro" in John Davis's *Travels of Four Years and a Half in the United States of America During 1798, 1799, 1800, 1801, and 1802*, ed. A. J. Morrison (1803; New York: Henry Holt, 1909), 413–29.

As suggested by Brickell's case many longtime residents of a colony often viewed blacks and slavery through the eyes of strangers, reflecting a division of perspective within the colonies. Those colonists who were for the most part born in Europe and who maintained close ties to it (to "the metropolis"), colonists such as colonial officials, missionaries, or merchants often tended to share its views of slaves and slavery. For a discussion of these divergent perspectives see Jeffrey R. Young, *Domesticating Slavery* (Chapel Hill: University of North Carolina Press, 1999), introduction and chap. 1. For a striking illustration that parallels to some extent the distinction being drawn in the text see page 43.

7. *South Carolina Gazette*, August 27, 1772, p. 1, cols. 1 and 2. His first "letter," in which he introduces himself, appears in *South Carolina Gazette*, August 13, 1772, p. 1, col. 3, cont. p. 2, col. 1. The second, in which he explains how and why he decided to disguise himself to secretly view black life in Charleston, is in *South Carolina Gazette*, August 27, 1772, p. 1, cols. 1 and 2. The third in the series, in which he describes what he saw while "perambulating" about Charleston as an "indigent" person, follows in *South Carolina Gazette*, September 17, 1772, p. 1, col. 3, cont. p. 2, col. 1. His last letter appears in *South Carolina Gazette*, September 24, 1772, p. 1, col. 3, cont., p. 2, cols. 1 and 2. One measure of the value and distinctiveness of the "Stranger's" observations relating to blacks is the extensive use historians have made of them. Few studies of the colonial low country that have attempted to substantively exam black life in the region have failed to draw on the letters.

8. The "Stranger" follows in general outline the traditions of travel accounts that had been developing in the West since the fourteenth century, while at the same time adhering closely to the tradition of observation that had long since become distinctive of travel accounts by first-time visitors to the Carolina low country. See Joyce E. Chaplin, *An Anxious Pursuit: Agricultural Innovation and Modernity in the Lower South, 1730-1815* (Chapel Hill: University of North Carolina Press for the Institute of Early American History and Culture, Williamsburg, Va., 1993), 66–91, for a discussion of those traditions as they were manifested in the lower South during the colonial and early national periods.

Of course the "Stranger" was not the first or the last to express surprise at the large numbers of blacks in Charleston or the low country more generally. As early as 1737, according to Peter Wood, a recent Swiss immigrant expressed a similar sentiment in a letter to his mother, brothers, and friends in Switzerland. See Wood, *Black Majority*, 132. Such reactions, however, were not limited to the low country. Note, for instance, the comments of William Strickland, an English gentleman farmer, during his first visit to New York City in September of 1794. He observed the "greater number of the Blacks particularly of women and children in the streets who may be seen of all shades till the stain is entirely worne out." Quoted in Shane White, *Somewhat More Independent: The End of Slavery in New York City,1770–1810* (Athens: University of Georgia Press, 1991), 3.

9. The quote is from merchant and assistant judge Robert Pringle in his charge to the grand jury in 1769, quoted in Weir, *Colonial South Carolina*, 263.

10. See Chaplin, *Anxious Pursuit*, chap. 4, "The Local Work Ethnic," especially 93–108, for a discussion of how "[w]hites tried to control climate, wealth, and slavery in their plantation society rather than allow these factors to manipulate them and thereby transform them into the stereotypic figures that populated travelers' narratives." She writes, relative to their adjustment to the disease environment, that "[t]he idea that they [whites] could become seasoned against endemic fevers gave whites in the Lower South an exclusive definition of themselves. It provided those who lived in the swampy lowcountry, particularly, a sense of unique identity."

11. Philip Morgan, "Black Life in Eighteenth-Century Charleston," 221, 228. Note also the following from Hugh Jones's *The present state of Virginia; from whence is inferred a short view of Maryland and North Carolina*, ed. Richard L. Morton (Chapel Hill: University of North Carolina Press for the Virginia Historical Society, 1956): "In each country is a great number of disciplined and armed militia, ready in case of any sudden irruption of Indians or insurrection of Negroes, from whom they are under but small apprehension of danger" (93).

12. Weir, *Colonial South Carolina*, 190. See also Philip Morgan, "Black Life in Eighteenth-Century Charleston," 187–232. His comment regarding Charleston as a haven for runaway slaves helps illustrate some of the reality of black life in Charleston that the "Stranger" missed while serving to make a larger point of Morgan's essay: "the ability of slaves to enjoy a change of scene, visit a relative, or go underground probably siphoned off as much potential disorder as it created" (221). *South Carolina Gazette*, September 24, 1772, p. 1, col. 1.

13. *South Carolina Gazette*, September 24, 1772, p. 1, col. 1.

14. *Diary of Colonel Landon Carter of Sabine*, 1:495, 214–15. Carter's effort to obtain information about his slaves from a variety of sources recurs throughout his diaries, but the following example is illustrative. Furious once again at one of the slaves he relied on most, especially in caring for injured or ill slaves, Carter notes in his diary on Wednesday, January 18, 1770, that "Nassau," his valuable medical assistant, was "so constantly drunk that I cannot with every day's inquiry hear who pretends to be sick but there will come a warm day for the punishment of these things" (1:347).

In the writing of visitors like Fithian and the "Stranger," blacks are often sought out for purposes of observation, and almost always pointed out at times and in places where their absence would have been noticeable; and we find in their writings descriptions of blacks involved in self-proclaiming behavior, whereas with native-born writers like Robert Carter and Henry Laurens, the reverse is generally true.

15. Legal and legislative records unavoidably offer on occasion fuller and more extensive descriptions. In both cases, however, black actions force the information that is provided. However, the information that allows us to gain such a sense is scattered throughout surviving records as brief, very sketchy references that are almost always incidental to event or occurrence being discussed or described.

16. David Dabydeen, *Hogarth's Blacks: Images in Eighteenth Century English Art* (Athens: University of Georgia Press, 1987).

17. *Supplement To The South Carolina Gazette*, January 6, 1757, p. 1, col. 1.

18. *South Carolina Gazette*, October 17, 1754, p. 2, col. 1.

19. For Latrobe I have depended on the two-volume edition of his Virginia journals edited by Edward C. Carter, *The Virginia Journals of Benjamin Henry Latrobe, 1795–1797* (New Haven: Yale University Press, 1977, published for the Maryland Historical Society).

20. Ibid., I, plate 11 (preceding page 97), Fig. 58 (in vol II, p. 516), Fig. 27 (v. I, 168), plate 24 (v. I preceding page 241).

21. "Negro Head point": *Maryland Gazette*, April 4, 1776, p. 2, col., 3; "Guinea bridge": *Virginia Gazette*, November 16, 1769 (pp. 3, col. 2); "Guinea creek": Ibid., August 22, 1766, p. 2, col. 3 (also referred to in another ad as "Great Guinea Creek": Ibid., October 10, 1755, p. 4, col. 1); "Negroe-Creek": Ibid., January 2–9, 1746, p. 4, col. 2; "Guinea road": Ibid., August 1, 1777, p. 3, col. 2; "Negro Ground": *South Carolina Gazette*, March 29–April 7, 1760 (pp. 3, col. 1); "Mulatto alley": Ibid., February 2–9, 1765, p. 1, col 3; "Cuffee Town Creek": *Supplement to the South Carolina Gazette*, May 16, 1774, p. 2, col. 2; "Negro Hammocks": "A Description of Occacock Inlet," (1795) *North Carolina Historical Review* 3 (October 1926), 626.

22. *Virginia Gazette* (Purdie and Dixon), September 16, 1773, p. 2, col. 3. The report concludes: "After the Fright and Disturbance occasioned thereby were over, the Congregation, which was remarkably numerous that Day, again repaired to Church, where an excellent Discourse was delivered by the Reverend Mr. Giberne, exposing the dangerous Tenets of those Sectaries the Anabaptists, which are so very pernicious to Society, and subvdersive of almost every Christian and moral Duty."

23. *City Gazette, Or The Daily Advertiser* (Charleston), September 19, 1797, p. 3, col. 3.

24. *Maryland Gazette*, December 27, 1755, p. 2, col. 1.

25. *South Carolina Gazette*, July 16–23, 1737, p. 3, col. 1.

26. *Augusta Chronicle and Gazette of the State*, May 28, 1796, p. 2, col. 3.

27. *Virginia Gazette and Weekly Advertiser*, April 17, 1788, p. 2, col. 3.

28. *Augusta Chronicle and Gazette of the State*, June 26, 1790, p. 2, col. 3.

29. *Virginia Gazette* [Purdie and Dixon], June 6, 1771, p. 3, col. 2.

30. Dena Epstein, for instance, has written that "If the search for contemporary descriptions of black music is confined to mainland North America, an anomalous situation is revealed: the blacks arrived in the colonies in 1619, but almost nothing about their music has been found before the end of the seventeenth century, when they were already playing the fiddle." She therefore concludes "it seems reasonable to look to contemporary accounts of the West Indies for illumination on aspects of black life on the mainland that were ignored in local sources. Happily, accounts of the West Indies yield rich descriptions of African dancing, instruments, and music, far beyond expectation." Dena J. Epstein, *Sinful Tunes and Spirituals: Black Folk Music to the Civil War* (Urbana: University of Illinois Press, 1977), 21–23. The quote goes on to state that the little evidence that has survived from the seventeenth century comes from very "fragmentary accounts of music and dancing," not enough by themselves, according to Epstein, "to present a convincing case that African music and dancing continued among the Africans after their arrival in the thirteen colonies." It should be noted that Epstein was not concerned about the source of the evidence but with its sufficiency for a study of black folk music. Her extensive survey of extant sources available to make such a study offers, however, one of the clearest illustrations of the point being made in the text.

31. Elizabeth Langhorne, "Black Music and Tales from Jefferson's Monticello," *Folklore and Folklife in Virginia* I (1979), 60. Langhorne also notes by way of preface that Thomas Jefferson's grandson, Thomas Jefferson Randolph, recalled in a memoir that his "earliest recollections are of my grandfather playing on the violin, his grandchildren dancing around him" (60).

32. Langhorne, "Black Music and Tales from Jefferson's Monticello," 62. Ursula, who was "nicknamed Queen, because her husband was named George & commonly called King George," was Isaac Jefferson's mother. See "Memoirs of a Monticello Slave as dictated to Charles Cambell by Isaac," in *Jefferson at Monticello*, ed. James A. Bear Jr. (Charlottesville: University Press of Virginia, 1967), 3. Bear adds in a footnote (n. 1) that Isaac's mother was Ursula. His father was called 'Great George' as well as 'King George.' At Monticello he was a blacksmith, nail maker, and first manager of the Monticello nailery" (123).

33. Lucia Stanton, "'Those Who Labor for My Happiness': Thomas Jefferson and His Slaves," in *Jeffersonian Legacies*, 166.

34. *Norfolk Herald*, December 31, 1803, p. 3, col. 1.

Chapter 5: "He is fast, he can't go."

1. *Journal of a Tour to North Carolina by William Attmore, 1787*, ed. Lida T. Rodman, The James Sprunt Historical Publications 17, no. 2 (Chapel Hill, N.C., 1922), 44–45. All subsequent quotes are from the same two pages.

2. Compared with the writing style in the rest of his journal, the diction and grammar Attmore uses when questioning Polydore is worth nothing.

3. The remainder of Attmore's journal, except for one additional page unrelated to his conversation with Polydore, is missing. The journal is laced with vignettes of this sort, with stories told to him and observations of local customs, and with bits of conversation he had along the way—with travel companions, hosts he stayed with, or his fellow guests. His conversation with Polydore is distinctive because it is the only one he had with a black person and because it is related without further comment in question-and-answer form.

It is reasonable to assume that Attmore considered the conversation as just another curiosity, a bit of local color like his description of "musterday" in New Bern, or the bear hunt told to him by a "General" at dinner one evening. However, from the perspective of this book it is curious in other ways.

Was this, for instance, the extent of their conversation, or a condensed version based on those aspects of it that Attmore for unexplained reasons found interesting? If so, what was the basis of his interest? Did he have an antislavery objective in mind? Most of his observations about blacks or slavery reflect that concern. A few days earlier, for example, on December 22, he noted that he had "had another tête à tête Conversation . . . on the Slavery of the Negroes, [and] on Liberty." Some days prior to that he had involved himself in "an Argument" that "arose between" two dinner companions, an unnamed "Gentlemen" and a judge from Williamsboro, North Carolina, "Judge Williams."

The judge, Attmore explains, made the point that the state needed many more slaves, that he wished "that there was an immediate addition of One hundred Thousand Slaves to the State." Attmore says that he "principally endeavour'd to shew the political inexpedience of the practice of keeping Slaves by argument on the advantages a State having none but Free Citizens must have over a State encumber'd with Slaves in case of a contest for power; and by shewing the disadvantages to posterity from the practice.—With just glancing a few hints on the general rights of Mankind, such as I thought that my auditor might bear."

Also, just prior to his encounter with Polydore, he stayed at a house where he observed "playing at his [host's] door[,] five Negroe Children every one dress'd in a Shirt only—Clothes are not bestowed on these Animals with much profusion—At Johnson's one was Walking abot, the Court Yard absolutely naked, and in Newbern I saw a boy thro' the Street with only a Jacket on, and that unbuttoned."

In this as in other places in his journal where he makes reference to blacks or slavery, it is difficult to determine the nature of his antislavery sentiments, how passionate he was in his beliefs, and whether his concern was for the slave owners or their slaves, slave society or the communities of slaves on which it was based? He seems to have been comfortable in the society of slaveowners and married a daughter of a prominent New Bern family, whose wealth included the ownership of slaves.

4. For the narratives of African-born slaves who were converted to Christianity after their capture and enslavement, see *Unchained Voices: An Anthology of Black Authors in the English-Speaking World of the Eighteenth Century*, ed. Vincent Carretta (Lexington: University Press of Kentucky, 1996), and *I Was Born a Slave: An Anthology of Classic Slave Narratives, Vol. 1: 1772–1849*, ed. Yuval Taylor (Chicago: Lawrence Hill Books, 1999). See also

Pioneers of the Black Atlantic: Five Slave Narratives from the Enlightenment, William L. Andrews and Henry Louis Gates Jr. (Washington, D.C.: Civitas, 1998), and *Africa Remembered: Narratives of West Africa from the Era of the Slave Trade*, ed. Philip Curtin (Madison: University of Wisconsin Press, 1967). For Muslim narrators, in addition to those in the sources just cited, see Allan D. Austin, *African Muslims in Antebellum America: A Sourcebook* (New York: Garland Publishing, 1984), and Ronald A. Judy, *(Dis)forming the American Canon: African-Arabic Slave Narratives and the Vernacular* (Minneapolis: University of Minnesota Press, 1993). See also Terry Alford, *Prince among Slaves: The True Story of an African Prince Sold into Slavery in the American South* (1977; New York: Oxford University Press, 1986), and Douglas Grant, *The Fortunate Slave: An Illustration of African Slavery in the Early Eighteenth Century* (New York: Oxford University Press, 1968). There are also documents of interest on this subject in *Slave Testimony: Two Centuries of Letters, Speeches, Interviews, and Autobiographies*, ed. John W. Blassingame (1977; Baton Rouge: Louisiana State University Press, 1997).

A compressed or distilled version of the general position of converts or captives who had grown old during their enslavement can be seen in the reported response of an elderly Jamaican woman to the question of "whether she considered having been brought from Guinea (for she was by birth a Coromantee) as a misfortune?" To which, according to the newspaper report of her death at the age of 110, "she gave a decided preference to the lot which had befallen her, being sensible that she enjoyed much greater happiness by coming to this country, and that she thought this last was a lucky circumstance for all Africans, even those whom, in her long experience, she had known treated the worst." Under the dateline Kingston, (Jamaica), April 6, the obituary ran in the *Maryland Gazette*, September 29, 1791, p.1, col. 3.

5. *Virginia Gazette*, July 10, 1752, p. 3, col. 1. See Rhys Isaac, "On Explanation, Text, and Terrifying Power in Ethnographic History," *The Yale Journal of Criticism* 6 (1993), 217, for a reference to this report and a description of the lasting impact it had on him. Less dramatic than the brief report appearing in the *Gazette* and no doubt more typical of those captives who committed suicide are references contained in court or legislative records such as the claim for public compensation that reports that Quamee, identified as an African, had run away and was subsequently "outlawed and drowned himself in his escape." *The State Records of North Carolina*, ed. Walter Clark (Raleigh, N.C.: P. M. Hale, 1886–1907), 22:859.

6. *Francis Porteus Corbin Papers*, Perkins Library, Duke University, microfilm at Colonial Williamsburgh research library, List of Negroes at Silfoon Quarter, December 16, 1712. Bertram Wyatt-Brown opens his essay "The Mask of Obedience: Male Slave Psychology in the Old South," *American Historical Review* 93 (December 1988):1228–29, with a description of how Abd-al-Rahman Ibrahima, "son of Sori, the alimami, or theocratic ruler, of the Fulani tribal group," was forced into submission by "Thomas Foster, a dirt farmer of Spanish Natchez," after Foster bought him in 1788, shaming him by, among other indignities, cutting off "Ibrahima's long plaits of hair," which in his culture reduced him, "a Fulani warrior . . . to the level of a tribal youngster" (1228–29). For a more extended description of Ibrahima's remarkable experience as a slave in Mississippi see Terry Alford, *Prince Among Slaves: The True Story of an African Prince Sold into Slavery in the American South* (New York: Oxford University Press, 1986).

7. Robert Carter Diary, 1722–27, MS, Alderman Library, microfilm M-113, Colonial Williamsburg Foundation Library.

8. *Charleston Gazette*, June 25, 1788, p. 3, col. 1. For a sampling of other similar ads see *Virginia Gazette*, 1768; *Augusta Chronicle and Gazette of the State*, September 30, 1797, p. 3, col. 4; *South Carolina Gazette*, December 1–8, 1758, p. 4, col. 3. Most of the sources cited in note 4, chap. 1, discuss the efforts of captive Africans to return to their homes and/or offer an analysis of the ads for escaped "new Negroes." For additional examples see P. Morgan, *Slave Counterpoint*, 446, and Gomez, *Exchanging Our Country Marks*, 217. More typical than the notice quoted in the text is the following ad announcing the capture of "Three Negro

Fellows . . . all *Africans*, [who] speak very broken *English*." The three, according to the ad, were "taken up at Pope's Creek" in a boat. *Maryland Gazette*, September 24, 1772, p. 3, col. 1.

9. *South Carolina Journal and Country Journal*, November 21, 1769, p. 3, col. 3; *Charleston Gazette*, June 25, 1788, p. 3, col. 1.

10. *Slavery in the United States: A Narrative of the Life and Adventures of Charles Ball, A Black Man* (1836; New York, 1837), 219. Isaac Fisher, an editor-amanuensis, wrote the narrative based, according to Fisher, on Ball's recollections. Fisher assures readers that all descriptions of Ball's personal experiences are based entirely on Ball's description of them, and reported as accurately as was humanly possible, but also indicates that some other material came from other "reliable" sources. In the case of the quote cited in the text, the narrator is introducing a story involving Ball, but the opinions offered in the introduction, which serve as a rationalization for the behavior that Ball describes later, could easily be a combination of the editor's own views, to the extent that he found them compatible with Ball's. Ball does not give his birth date but estimates that he was around fifty at the time of publication, which would have placed his birth in 1780. He also notes that he was separated from his mother and siblings by sale in 1785, remaining in Maryland with his father and grandfather, who, he says, was brought from Africa to Maryland in 1730.

On the historical credibility of the Ball narrative, see John W. Blassingame, "Using the Testimony of Ex-Slaves: Approaches and Problems," in *The Slave's Narratives*, ed. Charles T. Davis and Henry Louis Gates Jr. (New York: Oxford University Press, 1985), in which he notes that it was "the only narrative included in U. B. Phillips's justly acclaimed *Plantation and Frontier Documents*," (81–82) Phillips having early in this century, as the leading authority at that time on "American Negro Slavery," questioned the authenticity of virtually all slave narratives. Phillips's endorsement would have been similar to Blassingame's, who explains, "A comparison of the narrative with antebellum gazetteers, travel accounts, manuscript census returns, and histories of South Carolina shows that Ball accurately described people, places, rivers, flora and fauna, and agricultural practices in the state" (81). A native Georgian and a Southern apologist, Phillips obviously believed the narrative had the ring of authenticity.

11. The following is one of a handful of ads using the term "outlandish" that can be found in newspapers published in the low country: "Taken up and confined in the Gaol of Washington District, an outlandish NEGRO FELLOW . . . named FRIDAY." *City Gazette and Daily Advertiser* (Charleston, S.C.), August 3, 1798, p. 3, col. 3.

12. G. Mullin, *Flight and Rebellion*, 17.

13. *Postscript to the Virginia Gazette* (Purdie and Dixon), May 19, 1774, p. 1, col. 1.

14. Morgan District [North Carolina] Superior Court, *Slave Records*, 1790–97, April 1793, September 25, 1795. North Carolina Archives.

15. *Virginia Gazette* (Dixon and Hunter), December 19, 1777, p. 4, col. 1.

16. *Virginia Gazette*, September 14, 1769, p. 4, col. 1.

17. *Maryland Gazette*, August 20, 1761, p. 3, col. 1.

18. *Diary of Landon Carter*, I:295.

19. *Virginia Gazette* (Rind), March 10, 1768, p. 4, col. 2. Nor is his response to Nassau atypical. In a runaway ad for his slave Phil, he expresses the same underlying sentiments: "Had he been near a vessel," Carter sneers, "I should have thought he was gone to increase the black regiment forming in Norfolk harbor; but really he is too weakly and idle to be desirous of going where he must work for his freedom, as it is called." In another instance, Carter informs his readers that, although his slave, General, has a strong body, he is "remarkable as a runaway having lost both his legs, cut off near the knees, which being defended by leather, serve him instead of feet." He "speaks readily," Carter adds, "without restraint, seeming to aim at a stile above that used generally by slaves, though something corrupt." Carter then places a stipulation on the five-dollar reward he offers for General's capture; it would be paid only "provided the taker up do chastise him before he brings him home; and his ingratitude, and want of pretense to leave me, forces me to

enjoin severity in the chastisement." Ibid. (Purdie), April 5, 1776, and *Virginia Gazette or American Advertiser* (Hayes), December 18, 1784.

20. *Maryland Gazette*, August 27, 1761, p. 3, col. 1.

21. *Virginia Gazette* (Rind), May 31, 1770, p. 4, col. 2; *Georgia State and Savannah Chronicle*, August 29 [or 25], 1779, p. 4, col. 2; *South-Carolina Advertiser and General Gazette*, August 27, 1778, p. 2, col. 3; ibid., October 28, 1780, p. 1, col. 2. Note also the following: "Run-AWAY, or STOLEN . . . a short, likely, yellowish **Negro Woman**, about 26 years of age, named BECKEY, of the Ebo country, but looks more like a country born, and speaks tolerable good English." *South-Carolina Gazette and Country Journal*, December 5, 1769, p. 3, col. 2.

22. *Royal South Carolina Gazette*, June 20, 1780, p. 2, col. 2; *South-Carolina Advertiser and General Gazette*, August 19, 1784, p. 3, col. 1. Note also in this connection the following: "Ran away . . . a NEGRO fellow named Sampson . . . He is remarkable by having a blemish in one of his eyes, is designing, cunning rogue, though would often appear silly, or a fool, by which means he disguises himself." *Maryland Gazette*, September 18, 1777, p. 2, col. 2.

Chapter 6: Being Hailed

1. A notable recent exception is Gomez, *Exchanging Our Country Marks*, 166.

2. *The Interesting Narrative of the Life of Olaudah Equiano, or Gustavus Vassa, the African. Written by Himself* (1789), reprinted in *I Was Born a Slave: An Anthology of Classic Slave Narratives*, ed. Yuval Taylor, (Chicago: Lawrence Hill Books, 1999), 89.

3. Occasional exceptions to this impression serve, ironically, to accentuate it: "*A Caution to Slave Drivers*. Altho' there is no danger of a mans being hurt by the law for killing a negro, it might be well for some people to know how to punish without killing them. I saw a man tried at Tarborough Court the other day for whipping a negro to death. A Physician who dissected the negro at the time of the inquest was held over him, gave the following account: 'There was no sign of stripes on the back—he counted about 70 on the belly, which cut through the skin—he made an incision with a knife through the cavity of the belly, and he found that there was one continued bruise from the breast to the waistband, which was full of bruised blood from the external to the internal surface.' This extensive bruise appeared more than commensurate to the stripes that were counted, which was easily accounted for by the evidence which stated that the negro had actually received between 2 and 300 stripes; many of which were not so hard as to cut the skin, but from their repetition in the same places were sufficient to produce such deep bruise; and consequent death." *The Star* [Raleigh, N.C.], April 19, 1810, p. 4, col. 3. On the "Law and the Abuse of Slaves" see Thomas D. Morris, *Southern Slavery and the Law*, chap. 8.

4. *South Carolina Gazette*, June 22–29, 1765, p. 1, col. 1; and *South-Carolina Gazette and Country Journal*, October 12, 1773, p. 3, col. 3. For a recent discussion of branding during the Middle Passage, see Gomez, *Exchanging Our Country Marks*, 156–59.

5. Ibid., 156–59.

6. *South Carolina Gazette* (Timothy), May 18–25, 1734; ibid., March 15, 1735; and ibid., August 9–16, 1735.

7. *South Carolina Gazette*, November 10, 1759, p. 3, col. 3; *Maryland Gazette*, August 6, 1767, p. 2, col. 2.

8. Ads for "new Negroes" were tied to the economics of the trade that were both local and international, as well as to the seasonally defined importation cycle and colonial or imperial legislation regulating it. For surveys of the transatlantic slave trade, drawing on the most recent research on the subject, see Gomez, *Exchanging Our Country Marks*, and Philip Morgan, "The Cultural Implications of the Atlantic Slave Trade: African Regional Origins, American Destinations and New World Developments," *Slavery and Abolition* 18 (April 1997):122–45.

9. *Documents Illustrative of the History of the Slave Trade to America*, ed. Elizabeth Donnan (Washington, D.C.: Carnegie Institution of Washington, 1930–35), 2:464, 290.

10. Quobna Ottobah Cugoano, *Thoughts and Sentiments on the Evil and Wicked Traffic of the Slavery and Commerce of the Human Species, Humbly Submitted to the Inhabitants of Great Britain, by Ottobah Cugoano, a Native of Africa* (London, 1787), in *Unchained Voices: An Anthology of Black Authors in the English-Speaking World of the 18ᵗʰ Century,* ed. Vincent Carretta (Lexington: University Press of Kentucky, 1996), 149–50.

11. Equiano, *Interesting Narrative,* 61–63.

12. In that sense, naming also served owners as a means of "hailing" captive Africans into subjection, as a means by which the responsive subject "comes into being as a consequence of language, yet always remains within its terms." See Judith Butler, *The Psychic Life of Power: Theories in Subjection* (Stanford, Calif.: Stanford University Press, 1997), 106–11, for a discussion and analysis of Louis Althusser's theory of interpellation or "hailing," which Althusser developed in his influential essay "Ideology and Ideological State Apparatuses (Notes towards an Investigation)," *Lenin and Philosophy and Other Essays* (London: NLB, 1971), 162–70.

13. Butler frames the issue of response with a series of questions: "where and when does the calling of the name solicit the turning around, the anticipatory move toward identity? How and why does the subject turn, anticipating the conferral of identity through the self-ascription of guilt? What kind of relation already binds these two such that the subject knows to turn, knows that something is to be gained from such a turn? How might we think of this 'turn' as prior to subject formation, a prior complicity with the law without which no subject emerges?" *Psychic Life of Power,* 107.

14. *Georgia Gazette,* November 10, 1796, p. 2, col. 1.

15. In Virginia newspapers virtually all statements either implicitly or explicitly link a fugitive's inability to give his or her name or that of an owner, to the time the fugitive had been in the colony. And where equivocal phrasing such as "perhaps cannot" or "probably cannot" is not used, "can't" and "cannot" were the words used to express greater certainty. In no case is "will not" used.

More typical than estimations of a fugitive's ability (and in some cases willingness) to give his or her name or that of an owner on request are characterizations of the fugitive's ability to speak English, ranging from "not at all" or "not a word" to "exceedingly well." In the former case the implied expectation, relative to the question of responsiveness, is equivalent to that of "cannot" or "probably cannot." The general sense of the ads is that until a fugitive had demonstrated an ability to speak or understand English it was more reasonable to operate under the premise that he or she could not respond than that they would not. The issue of willingness to respond is rarely raised in runaway ads, because, it appears, there was no need to do so given the uncertainty regarding all aspects of the behavior of recently arrived captives.

16. By contrast, because the issue could not be avoided by captors who were required by law to give notice of a fugitive's capture, "taken up" notices often state that fugitives "cannot, or will not" give the information requested of them.

17. *Maryland Gazette,* October 26, 1769, p. 2, col. 3.

18. *Georgia Gazette,* June 22, 1768, p. 2, col. 2.

19. *Virginia Gazette* (Purdie and Dixon), October 7, 1773, p. 2, col. 3.

20. *Georgia Gazette,* November 10, 1796, p. 2, col. 1 (emphasis added).

21. *Virginia Gazette* (Purdie and Dixon), November 4, 1773, p. 3, col., 1.

22. *South-Carolina Gazette and Country Journal,* February 25, 1772, p. 3, col. 2.

23. *South Carolina Gazette,* September 3, 1753, p. 4, col. 1.

24. *South Carolina Gazette,* May 4–11, 1765, p. 2, col. 2.

25. Schwarz, *Twice Condemned,* 80–81. See also Edward Ball, *Slaves in the Family* (New York: Farrar, Straus and Giroux, 1998), 187. For related references to amputations in colonial laws that sanctioned them see Morgan, *Slave Counterpoint,* 263–65. In the same source (394) there is also a numerical itemization of marks of physical oppression appearing in the runaway ads.

26. Equiano, *Interesting Narrative,* 93–94.

27. *Virginia Gazette or American Advertiser* (Hayes), August 27, 1785. The following offers a more extended and equally explicit description, but not by way of admission: "*Notice to whom this may concern,* That on Saturday, the 21st inst. A negro fellow named WILL, was taken on the plantation of Daniel Wallicon, sen. Near to Augusta, by his negroes, whom they delivered to their master; and as he was bringing him with an intention of delivering the fellow, as he said, up to justice, he died the same day, and from the creditable witnesses who came before me, it appears this was occasioned from the cruel usage he received from said Wallicon. This fellow was of the Angola country, about 5 feet 5 inches high, about eighteen or twenty years of age, had the ball and part of the nail of his thumb on the right hand, cut away; remarkable small feet and hands, had a hole bored through each ear, and had some of his country marks on his breast, and from his manner of talking, seemed to be but a little time in this country. He was asked his master's name, but refused telling it." The notice is signed "D. Hunter, J. P. [Justice of the Peace]" His explanation for publicly posting the notice was that "this unfortunate circumstance has come within my knowledge, I therefore think it necessary to make it public, that from this description, the owner may ground his proof for a restitution." *Georgia State Gazette and Independent Register,* August 25, 1787, p. 3, col. 3.

28. For instance, the following brief ad: "RUN-AWAY, FROM the subscriber on the 12th instant, a negro wench named JUDE, about 25 years of age, dark complexion, she has lost three toes off one of her feet." *Augusta Chronice and Gazette of the State,* November 23, 1799, p. 3, col. 3. A sampling of a large number of additional examples includes Lucy, "about 25 years of age, American born, . . . having one joint of her big toe and the toe next off at the Joint of one foot" *Augusta Chronicle and Gazette of the State,* November 22, 1800, p. 3, col. 4; Rose, "very remarkable, by having the great toe of her right foot cut off" *Royal South Carolina Gazette,* September 10, 1782, p. 3, col. 2; Toby, "remarkable for having one of his great Toes cut off." (*South-Carolina and American General Gazette,* November 24–December 8, 1775, p. 3, col. 3); and Samson, "a new Negro Fellow . . . has lost one of his little Toes" (*Maryland Gazette,* October 3, 1771, p. 4, col. 2).

29. Acknowledging them, meanwhile, had the added, though clearly unintended, effect of casting doubt on the source of other markings. Frankness in one made silence relative to others seem innocent, or less suspicious. In colonial society, as indicated, many whites were whipped publicly, albeit not as often or as severely as were blacks, and some whites had their ears cropped, although again not as often as did blacks (or in as many different ways), whereas missing toes and fingers, or parts of them, seem to have been unique to blacks as marks of correction. In the course of researching this book I did not collect or systematically read ads for runaway white indentured servants, but I gathered a sampling and read many more as part of my overall approach to the newspapers I have cited. The statement in the text reflects impressions based on that survey. See also the article by Prude cited earlier (chap. 3, n. 18). See also Morgan, *Slave Counterpoint,* 270–71.

30. Kay and Cary, *Slavery in North Carolina,* 83–89, and their article "'The Planters Suffer Little or Nothing': North Carolina Compensations for Executed Slaves, 1748–1772," *Science and Society* 40 (fall 1976):288–306. According to Jordan, *White over Black,* 154: "castration was dignified by specific legislative sanction as a lawful punishment in Antigua, the Carolinas, Bermuda, Virginia, Pennsylvania, and New Jersey."

31. For a further discussion of castration, see chap. 7 below.

32. Equiano notes in this regard: "I have seen a negro beaten till some of his bones were broken, for only letting a pot boil over. It is not uncommon, after a flogging, to make slaves go on their knees and thank their owners, and pray, or rather say, 'God bless you." Immediately following this reflection, he makes the related observation, "I have often asked many of the men slaves (who used to go several miles to their wives, and late in the night, after having been wearied with a hard day's labour) why they went so far for wives, and did not take them of their own master's negro-women, and particularly those who lived together as household slaves. Their answers have ever been: 'Because when the master or mistress choose to punish the women, they make the husbands flog their own wives, and

that we could not bear to do.'" Equiano, *Interesting Narrative*, 224 (1794 edition reprinted in Caretta, ed., *Unchained Voices*); the passage does not appear in the early edition reprinted in Taylor, ed., *I Was Born a Slave*].

33. Typical are ads that point out that a fugitive "has the Ends of three of his Fingers cut off his left Hand" and that "he is well known in Charles-Town from his saucy and impudent Tongue"; or an ad that notes that the runaway had a brand and then describes the slave as being "very crafty," and later in the same ad that he has whip marks; or in another ad that the fugitive has a brand, and then later notes that "when closely examined has a very bad look." Or in a notice describing a captured fugitive the comment that, in addition to his country marks, he had been marked on the right buttock and has lost a joint of one of his toes. *South Carolina Gazette*, November 28, 1775, p.3, col. 3; *Virginia Argus*, January 5, 1803, p. 1, col. 5; ibid., September 2, 1800, p. 4, col., 2; and *South Carolina American General Gazette*, April 30, 1779, p. 4, col. 2,

34. One ad for "Two NEW NEGROES" notes, "They went away with five or six Wenches, of the same Country, . . . who had most of them one of their fore Teeth out." Of the two fugitives advertised for, one was a man and the other a woman, both from "the Grain Coast." Only the woman, however, was reported to be missing "one of her fore Teeth." *South Carolina Gazette*, December 12, 1774, p. 4, col. 3. Kate, according to another ad, was "A New Negro Wench . . . Of the Congo country," who could "not tell her master's name, nor where she lives" and had "lost three or four of her front teeth." *Charleston Gazette*, December 6, 1787, p. 3, col. 1. In a similar vein is the reference to an unnamed "New Negro" man who had "a scare on his nose, and one of his fore teeth gone." *South Carolina Country Journal*, June 20, 1769, p. 3, col. 3. Or Tom, who was taken up with Dick ("both *Africans*"), and is described as having "lost two of his upper fore teeth." *Virginia Gazette*, December 5, 1777, p. 3, col. 1. It is also important to note that unlike ads in which missing appendages are mentioned ads noting missing foreteeth nearly always make reference to "new Negroes." See also the example offered by Gomez, *Exchanging Our Country Marks*, 192.

Chapter 7: Impudence

1. Most studies of slavery in one or more of the southern colonies survey the laws of relevance to the institution. P. Morgan, *Slave Counterpoint*, as on most other subjects on slavery in the eighteenth century South, is an especially valuable source. Even more so is the comprehensive survey and analysis provided by Thomas D. Morris, *Southern Slavery and the Law, 1619–1860* (Chapel Hill: University of North Carolina Press, 1996). Although limited to a single colony Schwarz's *Twice Condemned* is relevant to any discussion of slavery and the law in the American South before the Civil War. See also his *Slave Laws in Virginia* (Athens: University of Georgia Press, 1996), and Donna J. Spindel, *Crime and Society in North Carolina, 1663–1776* (Baton Rouge: Louisiana State University Press, 1989).

2. Charles Ball, who finally escaped from slavery in the 1830s, some fifty years after his birth in Maryland, encountered a number of African-born slaves during the course of his captivity in various parts of the American South, the first of whom was his grandfather, "old Ben," who had been captured and brought to Calvert County, Maryland, in 1730. Ball describes in some detail his experiences with three of those he met, including his grandfather, but indicates that he knew and worked with many others. At one point in his narrative, written for him by Isaac Fisher, he offers a series of observations identifying what he takes to be characteristics that distinguish African-born slaves from those born in America. "The native Africans are revengeful," he observes, "and unforgiving in their tempers, easily provoked, and cruel in their designs. . . . They feel indignant at the servitude that is imposed upon them, and only want power to inflict the most cruel retribution upon their oppressors; . . . they desire only the means of subsistence, and temporary gratification in this country, during their abode here." By contrast, he continues, "The slaves who are natives of the country . . . like all other people, who suffer wrong in this world, are exceed-

ingly prone to console themselves with the delights of a future state . . . , believ[ing] that those who have tormented them here, will most surely be tormented in their turn hereafter." In this view, "discontent" for Creole blacks worked "out for itself other schemes," and when they converted to Christianity their latent or repressed bitterness and anger toward whites and what had been done to them could be incorporated, silently, into their new faith. *Slavery in the United States: A Narrative of the Life and Adventures of Charles Ball, A Black Man* (1836), reprinted in *I Was Born a Slave: An Anthology of Classic Slave Narratives*, ed. Yuval Taylor (Chicago: Lawrence Hill Books, 1999), 268–69, 355.

3. Though Ball's views in this regard (see the previous note) harbor a number of demeaning and disparaging characterizations of both "native Africans" and "American slaves," the discussion itself mirrors the behavioral patterns that historians have long recognized as having distinguished between "new Negroes" and acculturated and country-born slaves.

4. *Maryland Gazette*, January 14–21, 1729, p. 2, col. 2.

5. Ibid.

6. Warren M. Billings, "The Law of Servants and Slaves in Seventeenth-Century Virginia," *Virginia Magazine of History and Biography* 99, no. 1 (January 1991):45–62.

7. In addition to the sources cited in note 2, chap. 3, see Russell Menard, "From Servants to Slaves: The Transformation of the Chesapeake Labor System," *Southern Studies* (winter 1977):355–89, "The Maryland Slave Population, 1658 to 1730. A Demographic Profile of Blacks in Four Counties," *William and Mary Quarterly* 32 (January 1975) 29–54, and his "The Africanization of the Lowcountry Labor Force, 1670–1730," in *Race and Family in the Colonial South*, ed. Winthrop Jordan and Sheila L. Skemp (Jackson: University Press of Mississippi, 1987), 81–161; and Allan Kulikoff, "The Colonial Chesapeake: Seedbed of Antebellum Southern Culture?" *Journal of Southern History* 45 (November 1979):513–40.

8. *Maryland Gazette*, December 24–31, 1728, p. 2, col. 2.

9. Note, for instance, this quote from Schwarz, *Twice Condemned*: "As is well known, masters possessed nearly unlimited legal authority to punish their slaves for misdemeanors and lesser offenses" (80).

10. *Virginia Gazette* (Purdie and Dixon), July 30, 1772, p. 2, col. 2.

11. *The Star* (a weekly newspaper published in Raleigh, N.C.), April 19, 1810, p. 4, col. 3.

12. Typical of the shaming tactics used to discipline whites were instances in which a husband who suspected his wife of infidelity tarred his wife's backside. Similarly, justices of the peace ordered women to be "ducked" for the crime of "outspokenness." In another reported instance, "Yesterday a man was paraded through the streets, covered with feathers, stuck in a coat of tar, as a spectacle for the execration of others more honest than himself. This *worthy* went on board of a vessel, where he saw some goods so bewitching as to induce him to break, at least one of the commandments, which says, 'Thou shalt not steal.'" *Charleston Gazette*, January 2, 1788, p. 2, col. 3.

13. Captive Africans could be shamed, as Ibrahima's case illustrates. More typical was the practice of stripping captives of their clothes and shaving their heads. Although rationalized for health purposes, Gomez, *Exchanging Our Country Marks*, says "the psychological implications of denuding are both clear and clearly intended—profound humiliation and disintegration of identity" (159). In the ads for runaway "new Negroes" it is not unusual to read that a fugitive's head had been recently shaved (see, for example, *Georgia Gazette*, April 19, 1775, p. 1, col. 1, or the *Augusta Chronicle and Gazette of the State*, September 15, 1792, p. 4, col. 2). In most cases it is not indicated who was responsible for the shaving. However, in a few instances it is attributed to the fugitive: e.g., "commonly shaves the fore part of his head," *Georgia State Gazette or Independent Register*, December 23, 1786, p. 3, col.2. In ads that identified "country born" slaves with recently shaved heads it is clearer more often that they had shaved their own heads. There are occasional references stating that a fugitive's hair had been cut or that his or her head shaved as a punishment, inferring that this would have, or was intended to have, a shaming effect. But most of these references explain that the hair was cut in an irregular way to make it more difficult for the slave to

run away: *Baltimore American and Daily Advertiser,* August 8, 1801, p.3, col. 4; *Virginia Gazette* (Dixon and Hunter), October 17, 1777, p. 2, col. 1; *Maryland Gazette,* October 19, 1786, p. 4, col. 1. For a fascinating study of the slaves' hair as an expressive medium see Shane White and Graham White, "Slave Hair and African American Culture in the Eighteenth and Nineteenth Centuries," *Journal of Southern History* 41 (February 1995):45–76, and also by the same two authors, *Stylin': African American Expressive Culture from Its Beginnings to the Zoot Suit* (Ithaca, N.Y.: Cornell University Press, 1998), 37–62.

14. Robert Olwell makes a related point when he suggests that black market women in Charleston were tolerated as unruly women rather than impudent blacks: "the resistance of the market women largely took the form of verbal aggression and 'impudence.'" Female slave marketeers, he indicates, may have chosen to express resistance through "[r]idicule, bluster, and wit" precisely because "they felt confident that such verbal insolence from 'disorderly' women was unlikely to provoke a violent response." Olwell, *Masters, Slaves, and Subjects,* 176.

15. The most extensive discussion of this issue is found in Marvin L. Michael Kay and Lorin Lee Cary, "'The Planters Suffer Little or Nothing,': North Carolina Compensations for Executed Slaves, 1748–1772," *Science and Society* 40 (Fall 1976):288–306, and Kay and Cary, *Slavery in North Carolina,* chap. 3. See also Diane Miller Somerville, "Rape, Race, and Castration in Slave Law in the Colonial and Early South," in *The Devil's Lane: Sex and Race in the Early South,* ed. Catherine Clinton and Michele Gillespie (New York: Oxford University Press, 1997), 74–89.

16. *Maryland Gazette,* January 14–21, 1729, p. 2, col. 2.

17. Ibid.

18. *Maryland Gazette,* April 8–15, 1729, p. 4, col. 2; *Virginia Gazette,* February 18–25, p. 4, col. 1; *Maryland Gazette,* December 19, 1750, p. 3, col. 1.

19. *Columbian Museum,* April 14, 1797, p. 3, col. 3.

20. On this topic see Schwarz, *Twice Condemned,* 18, 22, 135, 140, 143, 188, 195.

21. *Virginia Gazette* (Rind), February 4, 1768, p. 4, col. 2.

22. *Hall's Wilmington Gazette,* April 20, 1797, p. 4, col. 4.

23. See for instance *North Carolina Gazette* (Newbern, N. C.), May 5, 1775, p. 4, col. 1; ibid., May 22, 1775, p. 4, col. 1; ibid., March 24, 1775, p. 4, col. 2; ibid., July [day unclear], 1755, p. 4, col. 1. Or in the case of Isaac and Sally both were outlawed by the New Hanover, N. C., County Court for "lurking in swamps and woods and obscure places and committing injuries to the inhabitants of the state." See *Wilmington Gazette,* April 3, 1800, p. 3, col. 5.

24. *Wilmington Gazette,* May 5, 1803, p. 3, col. 5. In the same vein is this ad from the *Virginia Gazette,* May 4, 1769, p. 3, col. 3. Peter, according to the ad had been born Charles City County, Virginia, and was in his forties. He was very fond of liquor; a sly, artful rogue if not watched; took with him numerous clothes including "sundry other of his wife's clothes"; also took a gun and a fiddle, "which he likes to play when drunk or drinking; when drunk he becomes very talkative and impudent." "I suspect he is gone to Amelia county, to Mr. Tanner's, as Mrs. Tanner, alias Mrs. Johnson sold him to Mr. Richard Hayles, and by him sold to the subscriber, as he often told the other Negroes that if ever I used him ill he would go to his old mistress, as she never sold him to Mr. Hayles, but only lent him during pleasure, and that he would go to her and be protected." For these reasons, "The said Negro is outlawed; and I will give £10 to any person or persons that will kill him and bring me his head, separate from his body."

25. William L. Andrews, *To Tell a Free Story: The First Century of Afro-American Autobiography, 1760–1865* (Urbana: University of Illinois Press, 1986), 206.

26. *South Carolina Gazette,* April 5–12, 1739, p. 2, col. 2.

27. *Extra-South-Carolina Gazette,* August 1, 1769, p. 2, col. 2; *Charleston Gazette,* July 10, 1798, p. 3, col. 2.

28. And of course those who helped in thwarting attempted murders, like those who betrayed slave conspiracies, were recognized for their assistance, but it was difficult to

reward such behavior when the only equivalent gesture by slave owners would have been to free them. The dilemma this posed could be perplexing, as in the case in which a mistress's life was "saved . . . only, by interposition of a fellow and wench, who had long lived with them." "What species of reward ought to be bestowed on the faithful negro," the writer of this report asks, "who at the risk of his own, saved his mistress's life, and gave the alarm to the neighbouring families." Perhaps freedom did not occur to the writer, or perhaps he or she thought about it but felt constrained not to mention it. *South-Carolina Weekly Museum*, March 4, 1797, 285–86.

29. *South Carolina Gazette*, August 6–15, 1741, p. 2, col. 2.

30. *Virginia Argus*, September 5, 1800, p. 3, cols., 2 and 3. The crime and execution, according to the preface to the "confession," occurred in Diuguidsville in Buckingham County, Virginia.

31. *The Times; and District of Columbia Daily Advertiser*, August 1, 1801, p. 2, cols., 2 and 3. Originally published in the *Lancaster Journal* (Pa.). Illustrative of shorter "confessions" that appeared more frequently in newspapers is the following report from the *Maryland Gazette*, April 27, 1797, quoted in Eric Robert Papenfuse, "From Redcompense to Revolution: Mahoney v. Ashton and the Transfiguration of Maryland Culture, 1791–1802," *Slavery and Abolition* 15 (December 1994): "Her motive for this most horrid act [poisoning her master's children] appears to have been an expectation of being free, if all the members of a particular family (the Bowers') from whom she was possessed, were dead. She had been informed that a clause in the will of the late Mr. Bowers, of the same county [Kent], had destined his slaves to be free, if all his family should die!" (48–49)

32. The report on the trial itself appears in the *Virginia Gazette and Alexandria Advertiser*, January 27, 1791, p. 3, col. 1; subsequent responses are in the February 10 and 17 issues.

33. See chap. 45, "Farmer Washington," in Flexner, *George Washington*, 449–55, on Washington's frustrations in trying to make his plantation more profitable, and "Black Mount Vernon" for the many frustrations and problems he encountered as a plantation manager.

34. *Virginia Gazette and Alexandria Advertiser*, February 10, 1791, p. 2, cols. 1–3.

35. *Virginia Gazette and Alexandria Advertiser*, February 17, 1791, p. 2, cols. 1–4.

Chapter 8: The Divided Self

1. The biographies are in part 2 of Douglas Deal's invaluable *Race and Class in Colonial Virginia*. See also T. H. Breen and Stephen Innes, *"Myne Owne Groun": Race and Freedom on Virginia's Eastern Shore, 1640–1676* (New York: Oxford University Press, 1980), and more recently Berlin, *Many Thousands Gone*. For a brief but extraordinarily rich summary of slavery in the colonial South during the seventeenth century, see Philip D. Morgan, *Slave Counterpoint*. On the challenge to any effort to create the sort of biographies Deal attempted see the preface to Lorena S. Walsh, *From Calabar to Carter's Grove: The History of a Virginia Slave Community* (Charlottesville: University Press of Virginia, 1997).

2. On the black image in art by Dutch painters, see Blakely, *Blacks in the Dutch World*.

3. Walsh, "Charles County, Maryland, 1658–1705," 192–94.

4. In addition to Berlin, *Many Thousands Gone*, see his "From Creole to African: Atlantic Creoles and the Origins of African-American Society in Mainland North America," *William and Mary Quarterly* 53 (April 1996):251–88. Also essential on this subject is John Thornton, *Africa and African in the Making of the Atlantic World, 1400–1800* (1992; Cambridge: Cambridge University Press, 1998); and Peter Linebaugh and Marcus Rediker, "The Many-Headed Hydra: Sailors, Slaves, and the Atlantic Working Class in the Eighteenth Century," *Journal of Historical Sociology* 3 (1990):225–52.

5. Berlin, "From Creole to African," 254, and Berlin, *Many Thousands Gone*, chap. 1.

6. Berlin, "From Creole to African," 253, 268.

7. Ibid., 286–88. On the fate of the charter generation, in addition to Berlin, see J. Dou-

glas Deal, "A Constricted World: Free Blacks on Virginia's Eastern Shore, 1680–1750," in *Colonial Chesapeake Society*.

8. Berlin, "From Creole to African," 288.

9. Ibid., and Berlin, *Many Thousands Gone*, chaps. 10 and 11.

10. *South Carolina Gazette*, December 3, 1772, p. 1, col. 3.

11. Berlin's explanation of his use of the term "creole" is relevant and applicable here and throughout the book. It was not used, he says, only to denote nativity but also "to capture cultural transformation." Berlin, "From Creole to African," 254, n8.

12. *South Carolina Gazette*, March 15–March 22, 1734–5, p. 1, cols., 1 and 2. For background and context see Marc L. Harris, "What Politeness Demanded: Ethnic Omissions in Franklin's *Autobiography*," *Pennsylvania History* 61 (July 1994), 288–317. Harris's article is also relevant to part one of this book. It begins: "One of the most surprising aspects of Benjamin Franklin's *Autobiography* is one of its least noted: readers cannot possibly carry away from it the least inkling of Philadelphia's multi-ethnic nature."

13. Roughly coincident with the beginning of the institutionalization of slavery in the colonial South, and at the height of that process throughout the British West Indies, the "noble negro" made his and her appearance in Western literature. See Davis, *The Problem of Slavery*, 371–74, 472–80, and Gates, "The History and Theory of Afro-American Literary Criticism," chap. 5, for analysis that helps frame the discussion that follows.

14. Wylie Sypher, *Guinea's Captive Kings: British Anti-Slavery Literature of the XVIIIth Century* (Chapel Hill: University of North Carolina Press, 1942), 110, 131. The sentence that follows the one quoted in the text marvels, "Poetry is indeed more marvelous than history—or ethnology."

15. See Davis, *Problem of Slavery in Western Culture*, 477, for a discussion of "some significant points of authenticity" contained in Behn's novel.

16. Sypher, *Guinea's Captive Kings*, 103–104.

17. Ibid., 103.

18. The phrase is from Ralph Ellison: "It is not culture which binds the peoples who are of partially African origin now scattered throughout the world, but an identity of passions. We share a hatred for the alienation forced upon us by Europeans during the process of colonization and empire and we are bound by our common suffering more than by our pigmentation. But even this identification is shared by most non-white peoples, and while it has political value of great potency, its cultural value is almost nil." The quote is from a 1958 interview with Ellison, "Some Questions and Some Answers," reprinted in *The Collected Essays of Ralph Ellison*, ed. John F. Callahan (New York: Modern Library Edition, 1995), 293.

19. Sypher, *Guinea's Captive Kings*, 103–4.

20. *Maryland Gazette*, November 7, 1750, p. 3, col. 2.

21. Ibid.

22. P. Morgan, "Three Planters and Their Slaves," 57.

23. Ibid., 57–58.

24. See Morgan, *Slave Counterpoint*, 382–83.

25. Society for the Preservation of Spirituals, *The Carolina Low-Country* (New York: Macmillan, 1931), 94. Quoted in Dena J. Epstein, *Sinful Tunes and Spirituals Black Folk Music to the Civil War* (Urbana: University of Illinois Press, 1977), 41.

26. Morgan, "Three Planters and Their Slaves," 57–58. For other greetings see Morgan, *Slave Counterpoint*, 383. See also Olwell, "'Reckoning of Accounts,'" 43, where he remarks on a letter Laurens sent to one of his overseers regarding Stepney, a letter that notes that Laurens sent "old Stepney to s[t]ay three or four Weeks to assist in turning and watching the new Indigo. He is very honest & if you will speak to him he will not allow anybody within his sight to rob you. . . . [G]ive him a dram & a Little Toddy every day but not too much." Olwell then remarks: "Apparently, even the obedience of an 'honest' slave could not be secured without 'speak[ing] to him' to create a personal tie, and some appeal to self-interest by offering a material reward." More generally, Olwell observes, regarding "the

receipt of provisions" by slaves that "[i]n the public ritual at least, slaves bought their sustenance not with their labor, but with their 'gratitude.' In 1759, for instance, one plantation agent wrote his employer 'that your Negroes were all well pleased to receive their cloathes & desired me to thank you for the same.'"

See also Eric Foner's account in his *Nothing but Freedom: Emancipation and Its Legacy* (Baton Rouge: Louisiana State University Press, 1983), 80–81. See Richard D. E. Burton, *Afro-Creole: Power, Opposition, and Play in the Caribbean* (Ithaca, N.Y.: Cornell University Press, 1997), for a full account of Monk Lewis's experiences.

27. *Maryland Gazette*, October 25, 1787, p. 2, col. 3;

28. *Edenton Gazette*, March 23, 1810, p. 3, col. 4; *The Times, and District of Columbia Daily Advertiser*, July 24, 1800, p. 3, col. 4; *Baltimore American and Daily Advertiser*, January 1, 1800, p. 1, col. 1; *Georgia Gazette*, June 26, 1794, p. 4, col. 4.

29. *Lynchburg Press And Public Advertiser*, November 16, 1819, p. 4, col. 4; *Maryland Gazette*, August 26, 1762, p. 3, col. 2.

30. *Virginia Journal*, March 31, 1785, p. 3, col. 3.

31. *Virginia Gazette* (Dixon and Hunter), December 19, 1777, p. 4, col. 1.

32. *Virginia Gazette* (Dixon and Hunter), November 13, 1778, p. 3, col. 1.

33. *Virginia Journal*, March 31, 1785, p. 3, col. 3; *South Carolina Gazette*, October 13, 1757, p. 4, col. 1; *City Gazette* (Charleston), July 6, 1798, p. 1, col. 4; *American Gazette* (Norfolk), November 7, 1797, p. 4, col. 3; *Edenton Gazette*, March 23, 1810, p. 3, col. 4; *Virginia Argus*, January 5, 1803, p. 1, col. 5; *Edenton Gazette And North Carolina General Advertiser*, January 11, 1820, p. 3, col. 4.

34. *South Carolina Gazette*, May 22–29, 1755, p. 4, col. 1; and the *Norfolk Herald*, November 10, 1803, p. 1, col. 3.

Chapter 9: Being and Becoming Creole

1. James Hugo Johnston, *Race Relations in Virginia and Miscegenation in the South, 1776–1860* (Amherst: University Massachusetts Press, 1970 [completed as Johnston's dissertation, 1937]), 52–54.

2. Ibid., 52.

3. Sidbury, *Ploughshares into Swords*, 215–16.

4. Ira Berlin, *Slaves without Masters: The Free Negro in the Antebellum South* (New York: Random House, 1974), 76–78.

5. Edmund Berkeley Jr., "Prophet without Honor: Christopher McPherson, Free Person of Color," *Virginia Magazine of History and Biography* 77 (April 1969):180.

6. Ibid., 187–89.

7. Ibid., 180.

8. Ibid., 182–83.

9. Ibid., 183.

10. Ibid., 187.

11. The following discussion of Chavis draws primarily on Edgar W. Knight, "Notes on John Chavis," *North Carolina Historical Review* 7 (January–October 1930):326–45. See also Stephen B. Weeks, "John Chavis: Antebellum Negro Preacher and Teacher," *Sourthern Workman* (February 1914):101–6.

12. Knight, Notes on John Chavis," 331.

13. Ibid., 331.

14. Reginal D. Butler, "Evolution of a Rural Free Black Community: Goochland County, Virginia, 1728–1832," (Ph.D. diss., Johns Hopkins University, 1989), 85.

15. *Virginia Gazette* (Dixon & Hunter), December 19, 1777, p. 4, col. 1.

16. Philip D. Morgan, for instance, notes in his study of runaways in colonial South Carolina, "Sixty per cent of the 1,525 runaways whose ages were listed were in their late teens

or early twenties." Morgan, "Colonial South Carolina Runaways: Their Significance for Slave Culture," *Slavery and Abolition* 6 (December 1985):72–73. Shane White notes of South Carolina runaways, "Of the adult runaways 87.*% are male and 12.2% female." White, "Black Fugitives in Colonial South Carolina," *Australasian Journal of American Studies* 1 (July 1980):26. Note also his discussion of the "literature on the role of black women in slavery (in particular eighteeth-century slavery)."

17. In addition to the studies by White and Morgan, see also Morgan's broader analysis of ads from throughout the colonial South in his *Slave Counterpoint*.

18. *Edenton Gazette, and North-Carolina Advertiser*, April 27, 1808, p. 3, col. 4.

19. *South-Carolina Gazette and Country Journal*, July 18, 1775, p. 3, col., 2.

20. *Virginia Gazette* (Purdie), August 21, 1778, p. 4, col. 2; *South Carolina Gazette*, March 6–13, 1749, p. 2, col. 2; *Charleston Gazette*, September 22, 1798, p. 1, col. 3; *Augusta Chronicle and Georgia State Gazette*, August 6, 1791, p. 4, col. 2. This ad concludes as follows: "As I am acting as attorney for said hairs, I do hereby forewarn all persons not to meddle with said negroes, as they will answer the contrary at law."

21. The slave was Joe Fossett, a member of the Hemings family who ran away from Monticello unexpectedly in the summer of 1806, and whom Jefferson freed, along with John Hemings, in his will. Born in 1780, Fossett was the son of Mary Hemings, and thus a member of the most privileged black family Jefferson owned. Indeed, "All the slaves freed by Jefferson in his lifetime or in his will were members of this family." In 1807, the year after Fossett had run away to be with his future wife and to protest their separation, Fossett, whom Jefferson described as "strong and determined," was made head blacksmith at Monticello. It is not certain that he knew how to read and write, but other members of the Hemings family could and Joseph Fossett, like his mother, could sign his name and therefore was probably more literate than most other slaves at Monticello. Lucia Stanton, "'Those Who Labor for My Happiness' Thomas Jefferson and His Slaves," in Onuf, ed., *Jeffersonian Legacies*, 168.

22. *Virginia Gazette* (Rind), February 15, 1770, p. 3, col. 3; ibid. (Purdie and Dixon), December 5, 1771, p. 3, col. 2; *State Gazette of North-Carolina* (Edenton), May 14, 1795, p. 11, col. 1; and *North Carolina Gazette* (New Bern), July 18, 1777, p.3, col. 2.

23. *Virginia Gazette* (Dixon & Nixon), February 26, 1779, p. 3, col. 2; *South Carolina Gazette*, October 10–17, 1761, p. 1. Col. 2; and the *South-Carolina State Gazette, and Timothy & Mason's Daily Advertiser*, December, 1797, p. 1, col. 3.

24. *Virginia Gazette* (Purdie and Dixon), August 4, 1774, p. 3, col. 2.

25. *Diary of Colonel Landon Carter*, 1:286–92. See Isaac, *Transformation of Virginia*, 321–57, for a now classic analysis of this incident.

26. *Virginia Gazette*, May 14, 1767, p. 3, col. 2.

27. A case in point involved "a yellow Negro Woman, named *Celia*" wearing "an Osnabrigs Petticoat and Waistcoat, and a blue and white Cotton Handkerchief; she is entertained by Negroes, and has been conveyed by them through most of the Counties on the Western Shore [Maryland]; she at times dresses in Mens Cloaths, and changes her own and Master's Name, when it suits her; and at other times pretends to be free." Or Jenny, who had been "seen lately in Williamsburg in the habit of a man." Margaret Grant took with her "sundry womens apparel, but has since disguised herself in a suit of mens blue cloth clothes, attending as waiting boy" for a white convict servant, John Chambers, who had also run away from the same advertisers. Molly, according to her owner, would "not scruple to disguise herself as a man, in order to get on board some vessel." The intent to board ship usually indicated an intention to flee beyond the reach of local authorities and by so doing to become permanently free. Men are less often described as being likely to dress as women, but a few are. A "Mustee Man named Ben," for instance, was "lately seen dressed in women's cloaths, and we are informed, frequently goes out in that disguise in the evenings." *Maryland Gazette*, August 14, 1751, p. 3, col. 2; *Virginia Gazette* (Rind), August 8, 1776, p. 3, col. 1; ibid. (Purdie and Dixon), March 22, 1770, p. 3, col. 2; *South Car-*

olina Gazette, January 7–14, 1764, p. 3, col. 2; ibid., December 24–31, 1763, p. 1, col. 3; *South-Carolina and American General Gazette,* February 20–27, 1769, p. 3, col. 4.

28. *Raleigh Minerva,* February 26, 1819, p. 3, col. 4.

29. *Maryland Gazette,* April 17, 1760, p. 3, col. 2.

30. *Virginia Gazette* [Purdie & Dixon], June 6, 1771, p. 3, col 2).

31. *Lynchburg Press And Public Advertiser,* May 10, 1819, p. 3, col. 3. Harry's owner, who was eclipsed in this telling by Harry's more distant roots in the area and in his participation in its settlement, was "Mrs. Wiley Jones, residing in the 'neighborhood' of this town, who, our readers will recollect is the Revolutionary Lady, that made the elegant reply to Coil. Tarleton, the 'brave but ungenerous man,' who disliked to bear the name of his gallant antagonist Col. Washington extolled."

Immediately following this notice was another, reporting that Robin, who was "a little older" than Harry, had died. He too, according to the brief account of his death, had spent a great portion of his life "near this place." The item concluded by noting that, "These instances, though rare in a southern climate, satisfactorily prove, that by a temperate and uniform course of life, we may enjoy a full share, and not to be called from this world, till we arrive at a good old age."

32. See Cheryll Ann Cody, "Slave Demography and Family Formation A Community Study of the Ball Family Plantation, 1720–1896," (Ph.D. diss., University of Minnesota, 1982) for a discussion of these issues, especially chapter 6. Also her chapter in *Working toward Freedom,* 119–42, "Sale and Separation Four Crises for Enslaved Women on the Ball Plantations, 1764–1854."

33. On the Butlers see Jean B. Lee, *The Price of Nationhood: The American Revolution in Charles County* (New York: W. W. Norton, 1994), 211–13.

34. Ibid., 213–15.

35. Key's case is described by Warren Billings in "The Cases of Fernando and Elizabeth Key: A Note on the Status of Blacks in Seventeenth-Century Virginia," *William and Mary Quarterly* 30 (1973), 465–74. It can be followed in surviving records that have been conveniently collected by Billings in his *The Old Dominion in the Seventeenth Century: A Documentary History of Virginia, 1608–1689* (Chapel Hill: University of North Carolina Press for the Institute of Early American History and Culture at Williamsburg, Va, 1975), 165–69. For another case later in the same century involving a suit by a mixed race black for his freedom dues, which were due him by law as the son of an African father and free woman after serving as a servant for 31 years, see Kathleen Brown, *Good Wives Nasty Wenches,* 212–13

36. See Herbert Gutmann, *The Black Family in Slavery and Freedom, 1750–1925* (Vintage Books, 1976), chapter 2. Also, Cheryl Cody, "Kin and Community Among the Good Hope People After Emancipation," *Enthnohistory* 41 (Winter 1994), 25–72. Good Hope and other similar plantations, however, were atypical of many others where less effort was made to preserve family units: Cody, "Sale and Separation," 121.

37. Most of the earliest wills were collected by John Bryan Grimes, *North Carolina Wills and Inventories* (Raleigh: Edwards & Broughton, 1912). The quoted fragment is from Susan H. Brinn, "Blacks in Colonial North Carolina" (Master's thesis, University of North Carolina at Chapel Hill, 1978), 16. See also chapter 4.

38. *Charleston Courier,* June 17, 1803, p. 3, col. 1.

39. All of this varied of course from area to area within each colony and between them, especially when you consider the different nature of the topography, climate, and economic base that distinguished each colony from others, even neighboring ones, but especially between those clustered around the Chesapeake Bay and the ones further south in the low country. Characteristic of those differences were the different rates and composition of population and economic growth characterizing each colony. You see this in the ads in a number of ways: in the terminology used, as we discussed regarding "outlandish" and "sensible" in part 2, and in the greater number of captive Africans found in lowcountry newspapers relative to those in Chesapeake ones.

40. The rest of this quote reads as follows: "Certain it was that a slave so considered himself, for no matter how hard he had labored during the day as his master's property, he shed his chattel state as he left the field behind, and he entered his own cabin as a person. This life which he led with his own people, apart from the ever watchful eye of his master, was the life that made slavery endurable." Guion Griffis Johnson, *Ante-Bellum North Carolina: A Social History* (Chapel Hill: University of North Carolina Press, 1937), 522.

INDEX